3

HEADS OR TAILS

To Penny & Gerry
firm friends of Jane & myself

HEADS OR TAILS

A LIFE OF RANDOM LUCK AND RISKY CHOICES

A Memoir
Arthur T. Hadley

Arthur T. Hadley

Glitterati
INCORPORATED

New York

First published in the United States of America in 2007 by
Glitterati Incorporated
225 Central Park West
New York, New York 10024
www.Glitteratiincorporated.com

FIRST EDITION 2007

Design by Susan Hayes

ISBN-13: 978-0-9777531-5-4
ISBN-10: 0-9777531-5-8

Printed and bound in the United States of America
by Edwards Brothers Incorporated

9 8 7 6 5 4 3 2 1

A diamond is a brilliant stone
To catch the world's desire
An opal holds a fiery spark
But a flint holds fire.

— Christina Rossetti,
"Jewels" From *Sing-Song* (1893)

For Jane
Who held all these stones, and more,
in the palm of her life.

HEADS OR TAILS

ONE

FATE, LUCK, CHANCE, AND FEW CHOICES

Nineteen forty-eight; I turn my new red Ford convertible into the curving bluestone driveway of my family's house in Glen Cove, Long Island, the house where I grew up. Six years before, just eighteen, on graduation from Groton, I left here to enlist in the Army as a private in the Armored Force (Tanks). The time then was June 1942, six months after Pearl Harbor. My classmates moved on to Ivy League collages: Harvard, Yale, Princeton, or for the few less-qualified, non-Ivy choices. Three years later, I am back, a wounded, decorated, tank captain who has spent a year and one day in Army hospitals. I enter Yale as a freshman. There I am told to get my mother's permission to have a car while at college.

This afternoon I am totally happy as I pass between the seven-foot-high rhododendron bushes that line the curving drive. I have completed four college years in three, made Phi Beta Kappa, and in a few months will graduate magna cum laude. I am safely divorced from my first wife, whom I married while in the Army. Beside me sits Mary Hill, age twenty-five. I know my family like and admire her. Like my mother, she is a Vassar graduate. She works for *Vogue*, is attractive, and has money. Three weeks ago Mary agreed to become my wife. I will wait till after dinner, then announce our engagement. I expect well-deserved, joyous congratulations and praise.

For dinner, my nineteen-year-old, youngest sister, Barbara, now at Vassar, joins Mary, myself, Father, and Mother. The family dining room is paneled in dark wood relieved by several Dutch flower paintings. You enter from the marbled front hall through double doors. At the far end French doors open onto a small stone porch with steps leading to the back lawn. A splendid rosewood table seems to almost float down the room's twenty-seven-foot length. My father, fifty-six, sits at one end, my mother, fifty-four, at the other. They are trim and erect, my mother still slim. Father wears a tuxedo, mother a long evening dress. Until their eighties they will most always change for dinner. The dinner is served by the family waitress; she is assisted in the pantry by the downstairs maid who doubles as assistant waitress. Unseen in the large kitchen work cook and a cook's helper. The length of the table plus the enormous, pink Venetian glass candelabra with candles lit at the table's middle permits back-and-forth talk, but makes serious conversation difficult. I easily manage to wait with my news till after dinner.

By then, we all have moved into the high-ceilinged library painted dark green. It too opens off the entrance hall through an open arch; another arch leads into the living room. The main wall of the library, twenty-six feet long with a fireplace in its center, is filled with books, close to several thousand, the majority of which have probably been at least glanced through by one of us, and many read. The end wall contains two French doors, and the wall opposite the books, three. These open on either the covered front porch or to small iron balconies. Between these doors stand chest-high antique bookcases. Some hold family photographs, mementos, small statues, or favorite books. Strategically placed table and standing lamps brighten the room for serious reading.

The fire does what fires skillfully laid by maids do: blazes. My mother and Barbara read on the couch opposite the fire, recently slip-covered for summer. My wife-to-be tries to relax in a chair a bit behind the couch, waiting. Father takes down a book and settles in his favorite easy chair, stage right of the fire and couch. I am slightly to the right of him toward the entrance arch. When standing Father is still six-foot-two and in fine physical shape. Though not athletic, he rowed for Yale. When he returns from work in the "City," he walks the half mile down to the beach, a bathrobe over his bathing suit. There he swims for fifteen minutes followed by a life guard in a rowboat. The life guard, an ancient Norwegian sailor, cannot swim. Father then walks uphill back home.

He graduated from Groton and Yale summa cum laude. He was first in his Harvard Law School class, editor of the *Law Review*. He practices corporate law in a famous New York firm. His name recently became part of the firm's title: Milbank, Tweed, Hope and Hadley. His personal clients include the Rockefeller brothers and the New York Stock Exchange. He is serious, reserved, and strong-minded. These traits are fortunately leavened by an ability to tell appropriate stories, a superior memory, and generous pro bono work.

Now with book in hand, he smokes one of his favorite cigars, a Ramon Allones, and enjoys his brandy.

It's time. I stand and announce, "I have good news. Mary Hill has agreed to become my wife."

Silence.

My father closes his book, lays his book on the chair's arm, and places his cigar carefully in the ashtray by his brandy glass. He rises and walks over to where my wife-to-be sits. He kneels on one knee before her, reaches out and takes one of her hands in both of his.

"Mary, Mary," he says, "do not marry my son, Arthur, he is absolutely no good and will bring you nothing but unhappiness." Then he rises from his knees, walks back to his chair, sits, takes up his cigar, and continues to read. My sister bursts into tears and runs from the room. My mother gasps, "Morris." Mary gapes. I am paralyzed. Where did this come from? What to do? I rise and walking toward Mary say, "Darling, I think we had better go back to New York."

What is going on here? The ancient Greek philosophers Aristotle, Plato, and Socrates and their followers would have known the answer: Fate. Fate, caused this outburst. No Choice either by myself or my father could alter this moment. Fate, *Moerae*, determined before birth, completely controlled life. Chance, Luck, and free Choice were illusions. Oedipus was destined to kill his father, bed and marry his mother, end howling blind to scream: "Thy portion esteem I highest, who was not ever begot." No Chance or Choice, whether inflicted on him by others, leaving him exposed to die at birth, or his own Choice, to live in another country, could alter that Fate. So also Medea will murder her children and Creon condemn his daughter, Antigone, to death and destroy his own city. No way out. No Exit. Later, philosophers of the Middle Ages, Thomas Aquinas, Saint Augustine, and John Calvin followed the Greeks' belief. Fate, now seen as God's will, ruled all.

Most recently particle physics plus the realization that the rules of probability, like the law of gravity, apply universally, and Heisenberg's uncertainty principle, all challenge the omnipotence of Fate. Heisenberg holds that the description of anything, from an atomic particle, through life, to the stars, should be seen as a "function of probability." As these discoveries weaken the dominance of Fate, they raise the important of Chance, Luck, and free Choice, at the other end of a seesaw.

To explore the power of Fate, Chance, Luck, and free Choice on our lives — yours and mine — we need working definitions of these words. In today's fractured and combative world, they have been given many meanings by different beliefs. I have culled definitions that I find both accurate and helpful. Since the meanings I have given the words are my choices I have *italicized* them. When *Fate, Chance, Luck,* and *Choice* appear *in italics* in this book they have the following meanings.

Fate is more limited in power than before, but still remains a major force. Fate governs the time and place into which we are born, the parents we have, and our unique mix of genes, plus most of our early upbringing. Practically all of what our Fate dictates to us happens before we are born. We have no Choice. We arrive with much of who or where we are already set. Einstein or Eisenhower, born black in eighteenth-century Virginia, are going to pick cotton. Joan of Arc born in a time of peace will, one hopes, live happily, avoid fire. No athlete without genes for perfect hand-eye coordination will win at Wimbleton.

Chance and Luck. Here I deviate most from common usage. Chance and Luck are usually used interchangeably, both meaning almost the same thing. Not here. The italicized word Chance denotes a major event, something that affects a wide area, even the whole world. A war, a Depression, a hurricane, nuclear weapons, a terrorist attack, or a tidal wave: these are Chance. Chance's little brother, Luck, is powerful but restricted. Luck is what happens to you or to another few individuals at the same time. With the power of Fate over our lives lessened by the new physics, the importance of Luck rises. Many find it difficult to accept Luck's power. Luck, like free Choice, has become controversial. I hope this book will make it easier for you to understand and accept your Luck, both good and bad.

I once heard one of the great men of the times just passed, Dean Acheson, say, "I've often heard it said that a man cannot succeed without luck. That is nonsense. A man cannot succeed without a great deal of luck."

Choice is where the ancient battles of belief began and where war still rages. Can I or anyone make a free Choice? If so, how free? How do we know? Duns Scotus in the late thirteenth century was perhaps the first to argue that some free choice might be possible. Wisely, he was not sure; men were being burned alive for less. Modern philosophers, like Descartes and Hobbes, allowed some limited form of uncontrolled Choice. Reason's partial ability to contain passion was used as an example. Bergson, chief among the more recent combatants, argued for Choice's almost total freedom. Heisenberg regards Choice as another probability function. Others still firmly hold the more ancient view. These modern determinists: Marxists, extreme behaviorists, one school of economists, and many among the strongly pious believe that the human brain structure, or environment, or God, or economic necessity governs practically all human Choice. While I do not believe this, I do not slight the strength of this belief.

In Kipling's famous "M'Andrew's Hymn," M'Andrew, a chief ship's engineer, glories in the subjugation of himself, and all things, to divine will.

> From coupler-flange To spindle-guide I see thy Hand, O God —
> Predestination in the stride o' yon connectin'-rod.

But even M'Andrew admits his Choice to stray once.

Choice, as used here, is largely free, though it can be limited by Fate, Chance, and Luck. Where you live and how you live affects Choice. If, as a boy, you are brought up to believe all blonds are dangerous, the probabilities are that, as a man, you will either run from them or toward them. But the probabilities are low that you will see them clearly. If, as a girl, you are brought up to believe all football players are stupid studs, your Choice, as a woman, will face equally skewed probabilities

Luck can obviously affect Choice. You and I would not normally jump out of a second- story window onto the street. But if our hotel room and corridor were on fire we might well make that Choice.

"To flip the dime" or "flip the coin" are phrases that express complete, sometimes even heroic, freedom of Choice. Two friends of mine talked about and practiced coin flipping. General James M. Gavin, parachute leader at Sicily, D-day, and Arnheim, told me that looking back at his Normandy battles, he realized he often took too long to make a decision. He took time to solve problems that had no best answer. When he commanded the 82nd Airborne at Arnheim, their next jump, he carried a coin in his pocket. When he felt he had too little time or information to truly consider a decision, he flipped his coin. Soon after we met in Washington, he lent me a book on the strategy of coin flipping.

Lester Zwick, the *Herald Tribune*'s tough, professional, cigar-chewing, chief of circulation, used to complain when decisions at the paper were avoided or slow, as they too often were: "We got to flip the dime and see what happens." Lester described himself as "a poor Jew, trying to explain to well-brought-up WASPs how to put out a newspaper that sells. It's a tough job! These WASPs are dignified! They wear hats!" In reality he was a well-read and thoughtful man, hiding behind his largely inaccurate description of himself. We often found ourselves a lonely and unpopular twosome who saw the *Tribune*'s problems that others avoided. "Were did you learn to flip the dime?" he asked.

With these definitions in hand I can start to explore my life. What is my *Fate* at birth? What strengths and burdens does my *Fate* provide on which *Chance, Luck,* and *Choice* could work effects far greater than my father's outburst. I am now far from where my parents wished and for which they programmed me. How like the White Rabbit did I grow?

As in *Tristram Shandy*, my early life starts not just before I'm born, but before I am conceived. Thirty years before my birth, two formidable and tenacious women roomed together at Vassar. One was Millie Cummnock, daughter of Arthur Cummnock, a master mechanic from Jedburgh on the Scottish border. He had landed as a young man in Boston with nothing but a quick mind, strong body, and his bag of tools. From there, Arthur Commnock rose to own a cotton mill in Lowell, Massachusetts. Millie's roommate, Helen Morris, daughter of the governor of Connecticut, was a distant descendent of a signer of the Declaration of Independence. Millie and Helen got on famously. They decided that when they found husbands and had children, their children would marry. So, when their children, Kay Cummnock Blodget and Morris Hadley, met, the idea powerfully took with my father, not with my mother. She was having a lively time at Vassar, was a debutante, and thought my father — as she would later report — "something of a goopus." She turned him down twenty-three times by her count, twenty-one by his.

Then Chance, in the form of WW I, intervenes

My father-to-be had taken artillery ROTC at Yale. He graduated first in his Officer Training Class at Plattsburg, New York, in 1917. As such he became a major, and after some time as an instructor, took command of an artillery battalion ordered overseas. Before leaving he bought himself a new pair of riding boots. Dressed in these, he proposed once more. My mother, K, always said the boots made the difference. My father, never disputed this. Mars strikes again. On his return home, K and Morris got married. Their wedding took place in Prides Crossing, Massachusetts, July 12, 1919, on the grounds of a mansion my mother's father had rented. Millie Cummnock had married John Wood Blodgett, the first non-Indian born in north Michigan. He was once treed by a bear on his way to school. By his and his father's efforts, John, who left high school to help his father in the woods, had become a wealthy and respected lumberman. Helen Morris had married Arthur Twining Hadley, son of a Yale professor of Greek and Latin. At their marriage, Hadley was a young economics instructor. By the time of my parent's wedding he had become president of Yale University, the first not to be a minister.

Photographs and newspaper clippings reveal the wedding to have been an event. President Woodrow Wilson and former President Taft were both invited, as was the entire Cabinet. My grandparents did not know the entire Cabinet, but agreed it would be bad form to leave out the few they did not know. The president did not show up. Taft and several Cabinet members did.

I do not know where I was begot. My parents never volunteered. They would have been horrified had I asked them. I am born in the New York City's Doctors Hospital in the East Eighties, in a room overlooking the East River. As well as my father, my grandmother Hadley is present. Immediately it is determined I am a boy, to be named Arthur Twining Hadley II. She leaves the room and goes to one of the newly invented pay telephones in the building to call Groton School long-distance, a difficult process in those days. After some time, she reaches the Reverend Endicott Peabody, headmaster of Groton, who had married my mother and father. Legend records their conversation.

"Cotty, I have good news. Morris's child is a boy, Arthur Twining the second."

"Helen, that is indeed good news."

"Would you be good enough to enroll him in the class of 1942?"

"With pleasure, Helen. He shall have a place."

Before you say, "Oh lucky boy," a correct and justifiable comment, remember the words of President John Adams to his son, John Quincy Adams: "You came into life with advantages which will disgrace you if your success is mediocre.... If you do not rise to the head not only of your profession but of your country, it will be owing to your own laziness, slovenliness, and obstinacy."

Such *Fate* carries unique burdens. Besides such burdens, *Fate* slips a joker into my gene pool. I am wildly dyslexic in the days before both the ravages and advantages of that genetic cross are known. In my family, orderliness and brains mattered above all. I show neither. I learn early and often that I am "a profound disgrace." Till I am fifty-three and my wife, Jane, stops the nonsense, when I make a mistake I would grimace and cry: "Stupid idiot." As Keith Douglas wrote shortly before his death two weeks after D-day, "Do not envy me, I have a beast on my back."

Fate also doses me excessively with energy, most times an advantage, at others definitely not. My prep-school classmates call me "the energy hound." I remember one of my finest sergeants, Jerry Speier, saying to me in Holland: "Now, Lieutenant Hadley, stop trying to energize me." In war, later as a reporter or as an editor and now-and-then a political press secretary, this unusual energy most always works for me. At other times it makes me impatient with the normal pace of life, and I take some disastrous leaps partially blind.

When I am fifteen months old, my father's legal work takes my parents to Japan for eight months. I am left behind (I later think of it as abandoned) in the family's apartment at 955 Park Avenue. This happens again when I am two; this time for ten months. During both absences I am left in the charge of two nurses. One, Miss Carruthers, I vaguely recall as very old and frail. The other was a trained RN, Nurse Nelly Martin. She would enter and reenter my life many times when my parents were away. Responsible for my care, she also oversaw the house and staff. She was a short, pleasant, rotund woman, all efficiency and bustle. Now and then during the absences, an "aunt and uncle," Dr. and Mrs. Norman Ditman, would arrive. The aunt, named Grace, was a distant relation of my maternal grandmother. The only memory I have of them is that Uncle Norman bought one of the first radios and several times let me fiddle with the dials. In my teens I picked up hints there had been some sort of problem with money.

Now an instant moment of Luck, with a resonance out of proportion

My father and mother return from their ten months in Japan three months before my third birthday. On that day Miss Carruthers brings me early to Pennsylvania Station, where the trains from the west arrive. Positioning me strategically, she tells me once again that when she sees my father coming, she will point me at him and give me a little push. Then I am to preform as trained. I will run to him, throw my arms about his legs and, looking up — important to look up — deliver my well-rehearsed line. A clutch of grown ups head toward me. Aimed and discreetly shoved, I take off running, somewhat handicapped by the long underwear and the leggings I am forced to wear. I throw my arms around the legs of one of the black "red cap" porters carrying my parents' luggage. I look up and say with feeling: "Daddy, Daddy, it's nice to have you home."

The importance to me of this luck is how it affects my father. Several years later, when I was six or seven, he confronts me with a list of sins. Included in these: "The time you deliberately embarrassed me before your mother by embracing the porter's leg and calling him your father." I did not argue with him. I knew by then it was no use to argue. Nor could I tell Mother. She would tell him and his anger increase.

Several months after the wrong-daddy incident, I and Miss Martin get shipped to Aiken, South Carolina. Grandmother and Grandfather Blodgett rent a house there each winter. They ship their favorite horses down from Grand Rapids. At three, I have little memory of Aiken. I recall the general warmth of Grandfather and Grandmother. Grandmother in particular lets me climb on her and sit in her lap. I don't do that with either Mother or Father. In photographs, I am playing on the lawn incredibly over-dressed in an overcoat with collar and leggings. Most of the time I spend crushing chalk, putting the chalk in my watering can, and filling the cracks in the stone walkways about the house with chalk dust.

On my return from Aiken, Father says there is a surprise for me in, "our room." I realize he means "my mother's room" at the end of the corridor — a room I have never entered before. I go into my mother's room. She is in bed. Beside her, couched in her left arm, is a strange-looking package with a face. I am told that this is my new sister, Katherine Morris Hadley, later known as "Winks." This is indeed a surprise, of which I have received no warning.

Now again *Luck*, extreme good *Luck*, strikes for myself, for Winks just born, for John still to come three years later, and for Barbara six after that. When I first see my sister in my mother's arms, beside the bed stands a new nurse: Mabel, another surprise, about which I have received no warning.

I look at the new ruler of my universe. She is thin, about five-foot-six and is wearing a trim, white uniform. She remains with the family for almost twenty years, until Barbara goes off to Vassar. She presides over our lives with insight, patience, and justice tempered by compassion. The only action she takes with me I do not understand is to insist that in the bathtub I dry my eyes not on a towel but with a washcloth. The towel was dry, the washcloth wet and often soapy. My eyes stung but I used the washcloth. One does not argue with Authority.

I dread each Wednesday and every other Sunday, her days off. Then either my parents or some other stranger will be put in charge of us. They mess it up. We get wet feet, overtired, forget to go to the bathroom, successfully commit crimes, and miss our favorite radio programs. I know by now I can fool my father all the time, my mother part of the time, and Mabel never. Still, I hope she will be back tomorrow when we wake up. Sometimes, on her days off, I see Mabel dressed up. I'm surprised at how she looks. She hardly looks like Mabel. She has on a dress and lipstick and is pretty. When I think of the other witches posing as nurses I have met, I realize how fortunate we were.

Some years after the war Mabel retired and went to live in an apartment in Garden City, a close-in suburb of New York. I would go to visit her there. She is always so glad to see me, while I am shy and embarrassed by the infrequency of my visits. What gift could I conceivebly bring her in return for the love and kind thought she brought us.

Poor Winks, or Kathy, as she later preferred to be called. Her birth *Fate* breeds tragedy. She was a roly-poly, kindhearted, easygoing person who loved horses. Her nature made her trusting and malleable, easy to impose upon. Siblings fight; I still cringe at some of the tricks I played on her. For a time we talked a private language, which I mistranslated for my parents to get her into trouble. She grows into a nice, ordinary girl in a home where ordinariness is a disease to be eradicated. My parents try to mold her into their high-powered image. She is given painting and piano lessons. When she wanted a dog, she was given a canary to take care of first to prove she was responsible. She hates the bird. It died. No dog.

She is sent off to board at Ethel Walker, an academically rigorous and socially stratified girls school, which she dislikes, and does not do well. Then when she wants to go to a Western college where she can handle the work load and ride horses, she is instead placed in Vassar, through the influence of our father, then chairman of its board.

Kathy is not alone here. Other girls were treated so by parents with rigid standards. Bea Hand, wife of John Gunther, and daughter of the famed Judge Learned Hand, told me: "I could have come home pregnant and been forgiven by Father. But a grade of B was an everlasting disgrace." A wealthy date of mine remarked: "Every time I asked a difficult question, I was bought a new car."

Kathy makes two unhappy marriages, and converts to Judaism, giving the finger to her parents — perhaps unconsciously, but with sufficient reason — all the while trying to escape her programmed life. Then at the age of thirty-seven she is murdered, with the youngest of her three sons, by the terrorist group the Black September. They placed a bomb on her flight to New York from Israel, where she had attended a fund-raiser. She had not merely a beast on her back, but a herd of dragons.

The summer after Winks was born, I am sent off to Vassar Nursery School. I board there from June 27, three days after my fourth birthday, to July 27. I still have the school's records of that time. They detail how I appear to outsiders. I do not recognize that person. They find an activist. I remember a spectator, a stranger at the feast.

One report states that I am very nervous at first and given to tantrums. However, I get better as I "grow more accustomed to my surroundings." I calm down. In their final report on me, the staff wonders "where I learned such a sense of responsibility and to be so respectful of other people's property, as if I came from a poor family." They had never met Mabel.

They record my IQ as 153. They also grade me on the Smiley Blanton M.D. Behavior Chart. On *"Aggressiveness"* I have "Faulty Ego Adjustment. Has his own way at all costs. Never considers the rights of others." On *"Self Confidence"* I again have "Faulty Ego Adjustment. Absolutely confident and sure of his own decisions. Takes everything as his due."

This last comment raises the basic issue of *Fate* and *Free Choice*. Did my genes predestine me to always try to go my own way? Did I have the help of *Fate* in some of the choices I made, as the Choice to enter the Army directly after Groton rather than start Yale. At that time the world I knew and came from, my family, Groton School, Yale itself, insisted I was wrong. I believed I chose against my upbringing to move outside of *Fate*'s boundaries. Certainly *Fate* had set me in place and time, given me my IQ, and caused my dyslexia. Had *Fate* also dictated I would flip the coin?

In another eleven categories such as : *"Demonstrativeness"* or *"Mood Stability"* I manage to hit close to Doctor Smiley's *"Ideal Average."* *"Social Adequacy,"* however, trips me up again. "Autocratic. Never left alone. Leader of his gang." I do not trust this Doctor Smiley. The person I remember did not have that worldview.

Is this another example of Burns's trenchant observation:
One thing the Good Lord hanna' gee us
To see ourselves as others see us.
Or did I develop a veneer?

The chief lesson I carry from nursery school is that power can be unjust, evil go unpunished, good unrewarded. Behind the school is a large yard about the size of half a football field. In the yard stand wooden blocks of various sizes. We students love to play on them. The smaller blocks can be piled together so we can climb up on them to reach the top of four huge blocks that each hold about eight children

As our class is playing on the high blocks, a boy deliberately pushes one girl off. She is not a particularly nice girl and often has bad breath. But we all know a crime has been done. We turn on the boy who pushed, and beating him with our fists, shove him off the box. The teachers miss the first crime, see only our retribution. They assume we have all been fighting, including the poor victim, and should all be punished. We protest and try to explain. They do not listen. We are forced to sit on the ground for the rest of the play period. Only a boy called George is praised. He leapt off the box and hid at the beginning of our fair, if crude, justice. While we sit in punishment, he plays happily on the blocks in the bright sun.

After my return from nursery school that summer, my parents take off again four five months. The home is left to Mabel and, once again, Nelly Martin. This time when my parents return I recognize them. After all a maid is calling them Mr. and Mrs. Hadley and they are coming through the front door of our apartment.

The winter I am three, *Fate, Chance,* and *Luck* all combine to shift my future.

Chance: that in the early twenties the philosopher, John Dewey, beginning with his book, *The School and Society,* creates a new system of education. His method, generally called "progressive education" has begun here and there to flourish, and be recognized as an interesting, if radical, program. Progressive education abandons rote learning to stress creativity, individual responsibility, and the joy of knowledge both for itself and as a tool for life.

Fate: that I was born into a family that knew and valued such people as Arichbald MacLeish, who later became poet laureate of America. MacLeish had been a friend of my father's both at Yale and Harvard Law.

Luck: that they invited Archi to dinner at 955 Park Avenue. My parents had already enrolled me in Buckley, the leading WASP preparatory school in New York City. A school that emphasizes Christian virtues, discipline, rote learning, and Latin. MacLeish, one of my two godfathers, urged them not to force me into that mold so young. Progressive education, he argued, of which a New York school called Dalton is probably the leading example, worked to strengthen individual initiative, courage, character, and original thought. He was sending his own daughter, Mimi, to Dalton, with excellent results. Later I could go to the inevitable Groton to be finished off. He persuaded my parents to change their minds. I still wonder who switched first; I suspect my mother. From the age of four through eleven I attend Dalton.

Only two other interventions will so fundamentally effect my life. The first, *Chance:* America enters World War II in 1941. The second, *Luck*: In 1965, I meet Jane Byington Danish, then just becoming a psychoanalyst of note. A former Miss Chesterfield, she possesses Dalton's outlook and values fused with the Army's sense of disciplined effort, which led her to graduate summa cum laude from college.

Dalton School, just starting out, occupies an ornate tree-shaded brownstone on West 72nd Street with a large backyard. The atmosphere is much more like a home than a school. The school's unstructured world, with its emphasis on individual work and thought, turns lessons into fun. I start to realize that art and poetry and life are not separate but together. And that originality, even stretched to oddness, can bring praise. Equally important, the religious and ethnic mix at school quietly and invisibly inoculates me against that dreaded WASP disease, anti-Semitism. At eleven years old I am on the Dalton football team. The boys' school stopped at seventh grade. In the backfield were Ziegler, Chapel, Hyman, and myself. We were undefeated. How can one be anti-Semitic in that backfield with a championship record?

I have a ball at Dalton. Most days I am at the school door early, anxious to get in. Marks are not used; supposedly one studies for the thrill of learning. I guess some fortunates do practically all the time; I do part of the time. I belong to a great gang, act in plays, and am on both the football and basket ball teams. Then there are all the girls. Other private schools in New York have either boys or girls. Dalton is coed. From the time I am eight or nine, I am usually in love with one or another of the girls: Gail, Ann, Nancy, Betty, Joan. They are so different, so bright, so exciting, and make such good friends. When I was nine, I save enough of my nickel-a-week allowance to buy Nancy Underwood a string of blue beads from the five-and-ten. I slip them into her hand on her birthday, then flee from her home-room covered with embarrassment. Of course, now and again, girls become nothing than more good targets for a clandestine, elastic-propelled paperclip.

The winter I am five, chicken pox breaks out at Dalton. As we students walk through the school door we must pull back our collars while the school nurse checks the back of our necks for spots. For several weeks I walk through the inspection safely and on into school with no spots. Today I and about ten others are pulled from line and sent to a separate room. We all have chicken pox spots. We wait in the room, some like me for a long time, while mothers and nurses are rounded up to take us home.

Chance created the chicken pox epidemic that infected many students all over New York. *Luck* made me one of them, providing another clue to Father's actions. As he had told me that hugging the porter was a deliberate act, now he also tells he believes I acquired chicken pox deliberately. I wished to infect my mother and thus injure John, with whom she was pregnant. The "profound disgrace" is not merely a disgrace, but evil.

• • •

When I am six, we move from 955 Park Avenue to 1095. We live in a much larger space on the floor underneath the penthouse. Father had figured out how to put the two apartments together to make one large one. Mother always felt Father had sold her a "bill of goods" while she was in the hospital having John. He said, she would report shaking her head, "We'll put a door here and another through there and it will be just fine. It isn't. It's a rabbit warren."

The move certainly isolates me even more from my parents. I grow up at 1095 for six years from six to twelve. I can perfectly recall my room (also the playroom), Winks' room, and less perfectly, John and Mabel's. I have no memory of my parents' room, its location or furnishings. I cannot be certain that I am ever in their room. Unknown territory. As they say on medieval maps, "There be Dragons."

The servants — four of them by now — and the kitchen are totally out of sight. We only traipse through long corridors to eat in the main dining room every Sunday for lunch. Then we get roast beef with roast potatoes and vanilla ice cream. Sometimes the ice cream is served with chocolate sauce, sometimes with maple syrup, sometimes with butterscotch sauce that freezes into a hard crisp film as it hits the cold ice cream. The rest of the time we eat with Mabel in a tiny children's dining room on our side of the apartment. Mabel does not eat with us on Sundays.

At 1095 I first see another part of my mother. Home from Dalton one day, probably because I am sick — I am sick a lot at that time — I find Mother and a man standing by a wall. In her hand she holds up a stick. Later I learn he is a painter and the stick holds a paint sample. It's 1931, deep into the Depression. He is pleading:

"I swear to God Mrs. Hadley it's the same color."

"Your God may tell you it's the same color. But my God tells me it's different. And my God is paying for this job. Not a nickel until it's repainted."

Luck: The year I am ten, *Luck* deals me a wonderful sixth-grade homeroom teacher, Mrs. Denny Underwood Warren. A woman I believed then is the most beautiful woman I will ever see. One time, she tells us everyone must learn a poem.

Mrs. Warren reads to us about ten poems, asking each of us to pick out the one we like best and memorize it. Everyone chooses a poem except me. There are none I like. Mrs. Warren says if I'll stay after school she'll read some more poems just for me. Staying after school is no big deal at Dalton. Many of us are so engrossed in our work that at times we all do stay. After quite a few poems she reads one:

> I'm a rough dog, a tough dog, hunting on my own
> Not for me the fireside and well filled plate
> but the cold outside, hunger, cuff, kick and hate.

Now why do I pick that poem? I am a sickly, overly cosseted boy. When the gang goes exploring in the forbidden basements of apartment buildings near school, I am the one who hangs back. I see horrible consequences lurking in every shadow. I mean my nurse called the police once to take me away just because I am digging a hole in the park. I am then still in leggings, meaning I'm four or five. Do I want to be that dog? Evidently.

Mrs. Warren later finds me two other poems by Edna St. Vincent Millay that still cause me to choke up when I read them. "Does the Road Wind Up Hill All the Way?" and "Clothes for a King's Son." In the latter an impoverished mother dies knitting wondrous, magic garments for her son. Like the "rough dog" neither of them appear to bear any resemblance to my external circumstances. But they all spoke to me. Now I know why.

With Mrs. Warren's encouragement, I write my first poem, a hymn to Athena, and it wins a school prize. So begins my lifetime love affair with writing and poetry. I live surrounded by poetry and mighty lines of prose as others live surrounded by their faith. Poetry sees me through horrible hours, helps teach me tears, or at least to show courage. As Jane lies unconscious in her hospital bed, bags of morphine dripping into her right arm, her heartbeats increase as her body fights her end. The words of Kent to dying Lear burst into my head: "Break, heart. I prithee, break," At Groton I learned the parts of a sentence. At Dalton they handed out tools for life.

• • •

Unfortunately, in the midst of all Dalton's excitement and tooling up for life, I read only poorly, spell hardly at all, nor do any math. My dyslexia, a condition then practically unknown, goes unrecognized. The kindly faculty, anxious to inform rather than examine, never twigs that I am learning nothing but acting, ancient Chinese history, and English. That is English, apart from grammar, punctuation, and spelling. I once ask about punctuation. The teacher explains it's very simple. If you want to pause for a long time, you put in a period; for a shorter time a comma; and for a betwixt and between time a semi-colon. For a totally new idea use a paragraph. (She was absolutely right. For everything except English examinations!) At school my originality and an unusually fine memory, the flip side of my dyslexia, plus bluff, carry me through. At home my parents are too distant to see the symptoms of my total lack of orthodox learning.

Fate: Like a gangster's feet when about to meet the fishes, each summer my *Fate* works to set me in concrete boots of class. In June, we move from the city to the country, Glen Cove Village on the north shore of Long Island. Glen Cove, though starting to change, is still rural with fields and farms — my father is once chased by a cow while walking to the railroad station. Each May a moving van takes the family's favorite furniture to Glen Cove. In the fall, the furniture moves back to New York. Not everything moves. The player piano stays in the country. The city did without for about eight years, then gets its own piano. The large dining room tapestry of lords, ladies, and unicorns stays in the city, as did the dining room table. But several couches, lamps, my parents' beds, cartons of books, some of the kitchen utensils, the guest room furniture, linens, parents' clothes, children's and servants' clothes, and some carpets all make the outbound and return voyages.

The Glen Cove house is set on slightly under two acres of lawn and trees three-quarters of a mile from Long Island Sound. In front, a vast lawn around seventy yards in length, slopes gently toward the property next door, which lies between us and the Sound. All that can be seen of that large property are some of its treetops. The trees on that property worry to my father. He believes they will grow to where they will block his view of the water from our front porch. They never do.

To the left as you face the Sound, a gentle hill slopes down from the lawn to the front flower gardens, framed by two giant weeping willows. Beyond them, hidden by trees and bushes, is the back drive, first gravel, later concrete. That drive leads to a well-hidden, four-car garage, with chauffeur's apartment above and a gardener's cottage for a gardener and family. Out back of the gardener's cottage are more flower and vegetable plantings, some with cold frames.

The east, or right side our land as you face the Sound, is bordered by the road to the public beach on which stands the Pratt Garage. There's a high, green wooden fence along that side and also a stand of pine trees. My first bedroom at Glen Cove faces that road and garage. The shouts and music from the garage scare me and keep me awake at night. I sometimes wake in the dark, hearing what sound to me like gigantic trucks hurtling up and down the beach road. My father tells me not to worry about that. "They are only bootleggers. It's best not to talk about them." I never talk. They frighten me also. Our front drive of bluestone gravel is also on the east side of the house. It curves gracefully from road to front door inside a large stand of rhododendrons. A stone statue of a seated Pan playing his pipes stands opposite the front door. Cars draw up before the statue at the base of five large stone steps that lead up to the door.

At the rear of our property, the kitchen side, the nonsound side, lies a cool and shaded area with tall trees, elm and oak plus a line of cherry trees along the road. There is also room for a back garden for vegetables, including a large tilled bed for corn. At nine, three years before I leave for Groton, I move to an isolated room over the kitchen and back door. About five in the morning I wake up to talk clandestinely to the milkman. He drives a truck with a standup steering wheel. We whisper quietly together in the dark while he leaves bottles by the back door. I never get caught.

In the evening before I fall asleep I can hear the train whistles on the Glen Cove Oyster Bay Line. To me the whistles hoot: "Out. Out. Out." Years later Jane, who knew hard times as she grew up on the upper west side of New York, tells me she lay in bed and listened to the whistles on the Hudson River boats and the honking taxis. They said to her: "Out. Out. Out." Totally different, we fit in every way.

Our house is in the North Shore Colony, a group of estates that were legally bound together in the twenties. Newcomers must be voted in to join. There are about twenty members. The Colony's purpose is to close off certain interior roads between the houses to further increase privacy. The Colony maintains a private beach, with two bathhouses, male and female, and a long pier that juts into the water. At its end a gangplank leads down to a float with steps and a diving board. The far side from the steps and diving board has bumpers draped over it to aid in landing small boats or sea planes. (The brother of one of the colony's members has invented the first commercial amphibian plane.) A second float with low and high diving boards and a water slide is anchored farther out. All this is presided over by Martin, an elderly, retired Norwegian sailor who has the first foreign accent that I have heard.

North Shore Colony beach is about one hundred yards long. On the far side of our pier, to the left as you face the Sound, is the even longer beach of the Red Spring Colony, an organization like North Shore. On the right of our beach, a stone wall stretches from the end of our beach road out into the sand to stop several yards above high tide. A small brook flows out from behind the wall into the Sound. This stream, in dry weather scarcely a trickle, and even after a heavy rain less than two feet wide and ankle deep, divides our Colony beach from the public beach, with its much smaller strip of sand. On weekends the public beach is quite crowded. It lies at the end of a narrow public road quite far from the Glen Cove Village itself. I occasionally spot our maids there. Yet no one, not even teenagers, ever taunts us from the public beach or crosses over, or to plague Martin, even pretends to cross. The invisible barrier of class separates the two beaches as earth from moon.

The farther side of the public beach, away from the brook, backs up against the Pratt breakwater that juts fifty or more yards out into the Sound. Beyond the breakwater lies Pratt land with several miles of private beach and two docks. Each of their docks boast little houses at their pier ends with awnings. The Pratts I am told are very wealthy, old money, Standard Oil, good people. The land they own by themselves is ten times larger than our whole North Shore Colony.

Guarded by Mabel, Winks and I play on our beach all summer. Usually I have on shorts, an undershirt, shirt, socks, and sneakers. Sneakers worn without socks are known to "draw the feet." Sand always gets into the socks and itches. Winks and I both wear floppy white hats to protect us from the sun, as we play shoveling sand into a bucket, or work a toy steam shovel. When it is two hours after lunch, Mabel allows us into the Sound to wade or swim with a ring, cold water being bad for the young digestion.

When I am six, a pilot in a tiny light plane — some precursor of the Piper Cub — is circling some thirty feet over the public beach. On one turn he banks too steeply and crashes into the wet sand just above the water edge, nose first, tail high into the air, fuselage crumpled. A woman, whom I now assume he was circling the beach to impress, cries, "Scotty, Scotty," runs toward the plane, but at the last moment hangs back. So do all the rest.

On our beach, a young lifeguard assists Martin that summer. He jumps from our pier, sinks down in the sand with the shock of his leap, then races toward the plane shouting: "Get him out before it burns! Get him out." Though he is over eighty sandy yards away, and has to cross the brook, he is the first to reach the plane, yank open the door, pull out the pilot.

Luck: The lifeguard's action gives my six-year-old self a life-long insight. Not the importance of action, but of knowledge: "He knew what to do." Knowledge promises safety. In my midteens I will come across Houseman's:

> My thoughts were of trouble
> And mine were steady.
> So I was ready.
> When trouble came.

I knew that already. I'd used it. What you know when there is no time to think can save your life.

• • •

I stay distant from both the public beach and stream. Partly this is from obedience to commands from my parents and, more importantly, Mabel. But the overriding reason is fear. In the spring and fall when the weather is cold, we go to play by the low breakwater, which breaks the cold wind. Enormous crows scuff the sand on the breakwater's far side. I know these crows to be gigantic. Their caw terrifies; their silence is worse. When they are quiet, their talons make high, squeaky, squinchy sounds in the sand. I am certain more giant crows hide behind other walls that border parts of the beach and beach road. They also lurk in the woods. Most days I know I have done something dreadfully wrong, though I do not know what; or if I knew what, I could then stop. The crows have found me out. They know. They will gang up to eat me.

I am often filled with fear. Back in the city, until we moved to 1095, I have been afraid of the noisy toilet next to my bedroom. When I flush, I know all the waters of the world will rush out of its bowl, flood the apartment, and I will drown. Maybe the dinosaurs will return. But if I don't flush, I am punished by shame and made to go back and flush. One time I crap on the floor, but that brings worse shame. So I flush and race to hide my head under the pillow, waiting for the deluge, trying not to hear the noise. With my parents away, there is no one to whom I can tell my fear.

In the new apartment, my parents now home, I become afraid the building will burn down... the sound of fire engines in the night terrifies me. I keep repeating: "fireproof house, fireproof house," over and over, a magic mantra Father has given me to ward off fright. It does not work. The night of Roosevelt's election, I am frightened by the loud sounds, horns honking, and explosions all night. I have not been warned of the noise. Father explains the election, and how glad he is that Roosevelt won. If he had lost, we might have had a revolution and he was ready to move to Canada. Another fear to deal with. In the summer I am afraid of thunderclaps and lightning.

Then a serious new fear is given me, the dread of being kidnaped. Charles Lindberg, a revered national hero, the first man to fly the Atlantic, has a baby who is kidnapped and killed. In our family, and others like ours, the deed breeds terror. Guards are hired, schedules changed. We do not go that far, but stern warnings are issued to us children, new instructions given to Mabel and nursemaid hired to assist her. The dont's placed on me multiply. Don't talk to strangers. Don't stand near the edge of our property. Don't ever, ever go near a parked car. Don't play with the children from the Pratt Garage. Don't answer the phone. Don't go near the road. Don't ever talk to strangers.

This last two are particularly difficult to obey. A gas line is being laid down the side of the road on which we live. Soon we, the houses down the public beach road, and the Pratts beyond will no longer have to cook with coal, though coal will still heat our houses. A platoon of men wielding picks and shovels dig ditches and lay pipe. They come right across our vegetable garden to our house and down the back drive to the gardener's. They seem glad to see me in white shorts and hat standing by the road to watch them work. I ask them questions to which they give answers in a language I don't understand. After a while, Mabel or the nursemaid comes to whisk me away.

On our property along the road grow cherry trees. When the cherries are ripe, people, mostly young boys, climb the trees to pick the cherries. When my father is at home and sees or hears them doing this, he chases them away with threats to call the police. I ask why he does this? He patiently explains there is a law called "the law of attractive nuisances." If they fall and hurt themselves while picking cherries on our property, they can sue us and take our money.

"Even if they shouldn't be there?"

"Even if they are trespassing. Should not be there."

A new fear. Sued and our money taken even when the other person is wrong. This world I live in is a very dangerous place. We are fortunate and blessed, as Mother and Mabel say. But the place is dangerous. Constant thought and care are required of me.

Years later I discover part of the "why" behind the constant fears. "The profound disgrace" didn't deserve all that we had. He, I, didn't deserve anything . Anything at all. I was a fraud. Someone about to be found out. Destroyed.

"Oh, Arthur," Jane with her arms around me. "Oh, Arthur, how did you ever escape?"

The grounds about the house are run by Mr. Harris, the head gardener. He lives in the gardener's cottage on what he calls "down the back of the estate." He is a wise, laconic, and humorous Highlander from Drumnadrocket, north of Inverness. He possesses not merely a green thumb, but green fingers, eyes, nose, and probably toes. He also shovels the coal into the hot-water furnace for the house. In the fall before we return to New York, he fires up and shovels coal into our furnace. In steam railroad slang, he "throws the coal to the mole." Until recently, old-time pilots sometimes used it. "If we don't see ground at 100 feet, throw the coal to the mole and climb."

His assistant, Tony, is Polish with limited English. Tony bicycles to work and back from Glen Cove Village each day. He also does this on Sunday when he comes to crank the ice-cream freezer by hand. A veteran of the First World War, he receives the "veteran's bonus" in the thirties and, bicycle put aside, buys an ancient car. Now you can hear him coming for miles. The day before I volunteer into the Army, I have my final conversation with Tony. He is on his knees weeding around the base of the bushes at the end of the lawn.

"Tony, I've come to say good-bye. I'm going into the Army tomorrow,"

"The Army, Mr. Arthur?"

"Yes, Tony."

"Wacha da feet, Mr. Arthur, wacha da feet."

"Thank you, Tony, good-bye." Excellent advice, both as soldier and in Vietnam as a reporter.

Harris, his wife, their eldest daughter, Chris, and the twins, Alice and May, who are my age, live in the gardener's cottage. Harris, kind, forbearing and understanding, becomes my first grown-up friend. The twins and I play together constantly. No other children our age live close. From four, when I arrive at Glen Cove, until I go away to boarding school at twelve, Alice and May are my close friends. At least I hope they felt that way about me; I certainly did about them. Over the years as we grow up together, we throw a tennis ball back and forth, kick a soccer ball, play running bases, and hide-and-seek, and watch the back drive being transformed from gravel to concrete, making it much better for bike riding and roller-skating.

Later, we would just sit on the concrete side walls at the base of the new back drive and talk about life. I remember in particular how proud they are when their mother finally lets them peel the potatoes. Before that she had said they were too careless and left too much potato on the peeled skins. Since I was not allowed to eat Eskimo Pies (not healthy), on the rare visits of the Good Humor truck to our road, I give them my part of my saved allowance money — I got a dime a week — to buy us all Eskimo Pies.

Still, in retrospect, we have a curious friendship. We never go farther into each other's homes than the kitchens. I go into the Harris's kitchen for cake and milk. Mrs. Harris is a marvelous baker. They go into ours, which they call "the big house kitchen," for cake and milk or ginger ale, but neither I nor they go any farther. As we play, we are always playing "out back" as they call that portion of our grounds, which is screened by trees and bushes from the big house. We never play on the vast front lawn or even in the side gardens. I do not invite them to play on the Colony Club Beach, nor they me on the public. I do not meet their other friends, nor they mine. They are not invited to my birthday parties, nor I to theirs. I do not think I said more than five sentences to their attractive, older sister, Chris. That same invisible barrier that separates the public beach from the Colony Club beach exists here.

Mr. Harris — I did not learn that his first name is Edward till after the war — soon morphs from friend to hero. In the dark hours of extreme danger, he allies himself with me against the enemy, my parents. Hiding nearby after some unfortunate indiscretion, I will hear my father or mother tersely ask Mr. Harris if he has seen me? "No, Mr. Hadley" or "No, Madam," he invariably replies. Seconds before, he has smiled at me as I bolt into the bushes, or burrow beneath a pile of raked leaves.

Then, when I am eight, we work the great crabgrass scam together. The lawns about our place have become perforated with crabgrass. Harris and Tony are on their knees for long hours digging out the tenacious clumps. I manage to convince my parents that I should help them, and be payed two cents a clump. After some discussion, my kind offer is accepted. Some time later, my parents vanish for a few days into one of those mysterious black holes into which parents disappear. I suggest to Mr. Harris that he give me several of his bushel baskets full of crabgrass to show my parents on their return, and that we split the profits. We are able to do this twice before I sense suspicion in the air, and announce that I am tired of pulling up crabgrass, and am going back to just playing. I am congratulated on my helping. Mr. Harris and I split eight dollars.

Harris teaches me many things. How to kick a soccer ball, the importance of Scotland and of Robert the Bruce. (As they grow older, all the male friends of Chris and the twins seemed to be called "Brucie.") I learned to plant a garden from him, beginning with radishes, and many years later, under the influence of Keats, going on to "a wealth of golden peonies." I also learn some measure of patience and interior discipline. I am not to water so fast, I must soak the ground. I cannot play with the hose. He, more than my father, becomes my image of how a man should behave. Perhaps from him seeped in my love of Robert Burns, of salmon fishing, a good dram, and of Jane, who was half Scots.

Luck: fine Luck that he "came with the place" and could bestow such gifts.

At my eighth birthday party there is a treasure hunt in which everyone races to be first to find clues. Taking a shortcut across the boards that cover our compost pit, my friend, Henry Morgan, then slightly tubby for his age, crashes through them.

"That's a large friend of yours," Harris says to me later.

"That's Henry Morgan," I reply.

His face crinkles into smile.

"A Morgan in my compost pit. Ha, ha, ha."

I am sure that the moment Harris learned it was a Morgan in his dump, he realized that the promise of America was true. The wrench of leaving his Highland home in Drumnadroukit became somewhat lighter.

When mother discovers that there are no three-, four-, or five-year-olds in the North Shore or Red Spring Colonies for me to play with, she organizes a playgroup. She will do the same for my eldest sister three years later. I have no idea how or where she finds and chooses the group's members. She gathers about ten children who arrive, delivered by chauffeur, nurse, or mother at our house once a week. Two of these selectees, Lawrence "Larry" Hughes, who became a thoughtful and respected publisher, and Eileen Bowdoin, who married Russell Train, the environmentalist, remain my oldest constant friends. Two others from then died in World War II: a bomber pilot and a submariner.

In addition to conceiving the project, my mother hires a supervisor, and buys the play equipment: a sandbox, a croquet set, a playhouse, and jungle gym with three swings and a climbing rope. The children always come to our house to play. If it rains there is no playgroup. Several times a year, a bird lady walks us about the Colony so we can listen to birds. This is not a success. We are more fascinated by her ability to whistle different birdcalls than by the birds themselves.

My birthday parties from five to ten years of age are largely composed of boys and girls from the playgroup. My seventh birthday party, while a great success from my point of view, is not viewed with the same enthusiasm by my parents. For them it occupies more the category of hiding in the coal bins and triumphantly emerging to leave black coal smudges on walls and furniture.

In mother-to-mother communication, or mother-to-nurse or nurse-to-nurse, my guests are instructed that they are to be dropped off at three in the afternoon and picked up at five-thirty. This seems to me too short a time play with friends. On the appointed day, I stand at the top stone step of those leading to the front door in my white shirt, shorts, and a tie tied by Mabel.

As my friends are dropped off by chauffeurs or nurses, sometimes both, I say to whomever delivers them: "There has been a change in plans. We are eating later. Come back at seven."

"Right, seven," the chauffeurs and nurses reply. I wisely do not try this subterfuge on the few mothers who drive up to the front steps. After cake and ice cream, that extra hour plus provides a grand and exciting time. We hide in the gardens, we swing on the willow branches, we crawl through the coal bins, then chase across the lawns throwing coal at one another. We climb on the jungle gym, try to climb the pine trees, and with croquet mallets, see who can hit the croquet balls farthest into the bushes. The girls enjoy the borrowed freedom as much as the boys. Cynthia Loyd-Smith throws coal with speed and accuracy. My mother and Mabel chase frantically after us trying to corral one here and another there. "I don't know what has happened," my mother keeps saying frantically.

My father arrives home from the office, expecting to find my guests gone and to enjoy a peaceful martini on the porch. My mother presses him into her two-woman posse. Where could the absent nurses and chauffeurs possibly be? However, when the first few of the picker-uppers arrive, the guilty party is soon revealed. "The young master told us." The net closes. I have had a great many birthday parties since then. Not until Jane begins arranging them are any so chockful with fun.

TWO

CHANCE AND THE
FIRST GREAT COIN FLIP

I have six glorious years at Dalton. My friends are many, close and fun, the teachers helpful, the learning exciting. I write my first poem that wins a school prize. I have major parts in plays and Christmas-Hanukkah pageants. I produce a finger painting that wins a citywide second prize: "Men Fishing about to Drown" Dressed all in black, two men are fishing while an extremely phallic fountain spurts water toward the heavens above them.

Unfortunately in the midst of this Arcadia, I read extremely poorly, spell hardly at all, and cannot do such simple math as addition, much less fractions. My dyslexia, a condition then scarcely understood, goes without recognition. The kindly faculty, anxious to inform and nourish rather than examine, never uncover my lacks. The only problem that surfaces at Dalton is that I am sick a great deal. The problem, later diagnosed as tensions at home, is treated with chest rubs and steam.

Choice: Choice on my part without any consideration or understanding of the consequences. At school I use my fine memory, the flip side of my dyslexia, along with my originality, plus bluff, and Dalton's self-grading system to create the illusion of doing well. At home my parents are too distant to discover my basic inability to read, write, or do math.

At age eleven the roof falls in. On my entrance exams for Groton I get, with 100 being the best, a 10 in math and a 14 in English. My parents stare at me in horrified amazement. What have they spawned? What will their friends think? A Hadley, grandson of a Yale president, who cannot make Groton. "The profound disgrace" plays center stage. I hear Mother and Father wondering: Should they have chosen Buckley? Would I have turned out all right there?

To answer that question with prejudiced hindsight: the *Luck* of entering Dalton and not following my *Fate* to a school like Buckley to me remains the greatest *Luck* of my early life. How would I have been formed at the vulnerable age of five years surrounded by lifestyles I would later meet. What sort of children would I have? Where would the man come from that Jane would marry? What work would I do? As the Völuspà hisses to Odin from her ice-bound cave, which is called in the Eddas colder than a mother-drowned child, "To ask that question is to know the answer."

Chance: Dyslexia has recently been recognized, studied, and understood. The genetic link to ambidextrousness has been uncovered. Dr. Samuel Orton, an expert on this condition, has opened an office on East 79th Street.

Dr. Orton gives me a series of tests. They are fun. I sit strapped in a huge electric chair that is plugged in and full of machinery. Sensors are attached to my wrists. The room is darkened and small lights flash at various parts of the room. I have been told to clench my hands into fists when I see a light flash. The chair can detect intervals of less than a second, and so determine which fist squeezes first. I also draw shapes with the right hand, then the left, and throw darts at a target, first with one hand, then the other, next with one eye covered, then the other. I read and repeat out loud meaningless words.

There are also picture puzzles where different events must be matched. In one a boy with his schoolbooks is going out the front door. I put in the picture a clock with the wrong time showing.

"He is going to school at five in the morning?" asks Dr. Orton.

"He likes to get to Dalton early," I answer. There is a wiseass in every crowd.

Fate: Orton's test results confirm my genetic *Fate.* I am dyslexic in spades, my two hands and eyes nearly equal. However, my right hand and eye are slightly stronger than my left; they react a fraction of a second faster. I must immediately be stopped from using the left hand in play or work. Several afternoons a week and on weekends, I must study under an Orton-trained tutor.

I will never get over my dyslexia, Dr. Orton prophesies. While I can be trained to function in many professions, I will have trouble with spelling and mathematics all my life. I will continue to mispronounce and reverse letters: "saw" for "was," "on" for "no." Orton foresees correctly. That genetic *Fate* remains with me. Until the advent of the spell-checker in the computer, I need a secretary to do my mail or else I have to use only the simplest words. A small, red book called *The Misspeller's Dictionary* becomes my bible. I work for magazines, where I have time to check words, rather than newspapers.

Dr. Orton also gives pluses. My work will be original. I will approach and solve problems in new ways. My memory, aside from spelling and numbers, should be excellent. The pluses too come true. I easily memorize poems, although if I write them down, their words are misspelled. My books have explored fresh ideas, uncovered new trends, and (I hope) added insights. Much to the delight of my children I once quickly solved Rubik's Cube. They take my solution back to their campuses. One does not often earn respect from critics as tough as these. On the other hand the math of foreign-exchange rates remains impossible. Paying a bill anywhere, I will almost get punched out or thanked so profusely I realize I have inadvertently made another instant millionaire. Years later I find a far different benefit. When I see a schizophrenic, sympathy wells. There but for one different genetic cross go I.

Orton's findings produce immediate horrible effects. I am forbidden to act in Dalton's plays. I must drop afternoon sports to study. The boarding camp, Menaga Lodge in the Adirondacks, where for several summers I have had a good time, will be switched to a tutoring camp, Merriweather in Maine. I will be tutored twice a week there. I needed no expensive gyro compass to locate trouble, my dime-store model finds darkness everywhere.

The troubles begin with tutors and explode exponentially at Camp Merriweather. I have spent months in several places where I cannot remember a single bright day. For example, the fields and farming dorfs that thread the Siegfried Line between Übach and Aachen, I would swear these towns and fields are always cold, wet, and dark. When I visit them twenty-five years after the war, the sun shines and the fields blaze with color. I even hear birds and am amazed.

Camp Merriweather is another such place. Pines march down upon it from three sides. The lake on the Fourth of July is still icy. We sleep and live in cabins that contain a long corridor with cots on each side. The whole camp is done in 3D: dank, damp, and dismal. Its twelve-hole outhouse casts a smell over the area several times a week. I cannot remember any food but cornmeal mush and lumpy oatmeal. The rain is constant. We never go camping in the woods, learn no skills, and cannot take canoes out alone. Everyone is from Boston. They know each other. They think differently. I know no one and am alone with few friends.

Menaga Lodge was sunny. We slept in two-story cabins with screened porches and on actual beds. We learned to camp, light no-paper fires with one match, make cocoa or coffee over the fire, and practice first aid. Several times a season we actually went camping in the woods for several days. After you pass your canoe test — jumping out of a canoe wearing clothes and shoes with a bathing suit underneath, then getting shoes and clothes off, and yourself back in the canoe — you can paddle a canoe around the lake alone. There I was a leader and had friends.

I have been told by Father that at Merriweather I will be tutored several times a week as at home. Instead, I am in class all morning every morning but Sunday. And it is not just for my spelling and English grammar. I am starting French and Latin, two subjects I have never studied. When I write home about this small discrepancy between fact and fiction, my father replies that he and Mother had not fully understood how the camp works. But since Merriweather works this particular way and cannot change; a good start in Latin and French should be helpful. He also points out that fiction (my fix-sun) is not spelled with an "x."

Luck and Choice

Some time in the last two weeks at Merriweather, the camp holds its traditional war-canoe race. We campers are divided into three large canoes, each containing twenty-one of us, ten paddling on each side and a captain in the stern to command and steer. Supposedly the boat crews are created equal. But, like many "supposedlies," the results this year bear no relation to the stated purpose. Two canoes are full of the largest, strongest boys. The third contains the light, the weak, and the small. I smell a fix by our counselors and suspect bets have been laid. My boat, the third, is so weak that I, generally a dropout loner, end up elected captain. The other two canoes laugh at us as we paddle out. They go off by themselves to splash water on one another and boast about by how much each one will win. I take my boat off by ourselves to practice.

I have read enough boys' books by Ralph Henry Barber to know that teamwork is the key to rowing. I believe paddling must be the same. I exhort my crew that size gives no advantage; teamwork matters. If some paddles go into the water too early or come out too late, the boat's speed will be checked. I will shout a beat so that all paddles go in and out of the water together, and we will win. Campers have sat down randomly in the canoe. I get the lefties and the righties shifted to their strongest sides. We take a few moments to practice.

The race is close. The stronger boats almost catch us in the end. We win. Today I can still hear myself shouting a phrase from a Barber novel, my body braced into each word, "We've got the race, now keep it! We've got the race, now keep it!" I learn a deep, emotional lesson that afternoon. At certain moments I can lead men. Only at some moments, not at others. Much later, I discover how to distinguish such times. I learn to avoid fights I can't win. I don't rush in and fall on my face as often. I learn that, while I can occasionally move mountains, I am the world's worst ditchdigger. When moved, the mountain may land in the wrong place, but the ditch goes round in circles. The war-canoe victory gives me a wee dram of confidence, a small, well-needed dram.

Fall comes. As a parting gift for Groton I am given the mandatory Bible. I hear Mother say to Father: "You write his name in it. His handwriting is impossible." Mother, Father, and I spend the night in the Hadley family home in New Haven, the house where my father grew up and where Grandmother Hadley lives. I sleep in my father's boyhood room, where I listen to the streetcars rumble by and smell the ozone created when their brushes make uncertain contact with the overhead wires. From there they drive me to Groton School, a place my father loved and where he succeeded.

Color everything at Groton brown. Indoors and outdoors, all brown for six years. Not the alive browns of polished pear wood, shined shoes, or fresh trout, but of week-old mud and winter's dead leaves. The school is another place I have trouble to recall a fine day. In May of 1946, four years after graduation, I come back to visit. I sit on the mowed lawn, called the "Circle," around which the school buildings, two dormitories, a gymnasium, the chapel, classrooms, and headmaster's house cluster. The grass is bright green, above, the apple trees hold sweet white blossoms. The sun is pleasantly hot, causing the red brick buildings to shine. In my school memories, these do not appear. I walk, head down around a colorless, frozen circle, half old dirty snow, half mud. Global warming can cause extraordinary changes.

I am the only Daltonian Groton has ever seen. An endangered

species. Of the twenty-three boys in my class, called a form — we are first formers — all the New Yorkers come either from Buckley, four of them, or from similar schools. Of the Bostonians, six are from Dexter, a feeder school for Groton and its rival St. Marks. Twenty-three percent of my classmates are, like myself, sons of graduates. Their fathers, like mine, attended the school under the same head-maste, as I will — the rector, the legendary Reverend Doctor Endicott Peabody, one of the three founders of the school, now in his late seventies.

The Groton of 1936 has changed little from my father's day in 1906. The rector no longer plays football on the varsity as he had at the school's founding in 1884. Before that he had been the minister in Tombstone, Arizona, at the time of Marshal Wyatt Earp, hero of the gunfight at the O.K. Corral. In my second year at Groton (second form), curiosity gives me courage to ask the rector about Earp. The rector answered kindly that he had held Earp's coat during a gunfight. Once after dinner at the Peabody home, Earp was about to leave. "Hold my coat would you, Reverend? I see a man outside wants to kill me." Earp walked out the Peabodys' front door. There was a sound of gunfire. Earp came back inside. "I can put my coat on now, Reverend."

Peabody's massive presence and control envelopes all. Tradition rules everywhere. We are wakened at seven, as my father was, by the tolling of the great schoolhouse bell, "the outside." We race to the bathroom, take the compulsory cold shower, brush our teeth, and wash our faces in individual tin bowls that hang on hooks below the shelf with our tooth brush, face towel, and soap. We roughhouse a bit, then dress in jackets and ties in time to make the last roll-call bell before breakfast. After breakfast electric bells summon us to morning chapel in the school church. The church was built by William A. Gardener, another of the school's three founders and one of the richest men of his day. His oceangoing yacht was second only to J. P. Morgan's in size. Morning classes are divided into six periods that begin at eight-thirty and end at one. Each period is in a different classroom and about a different subject. We are moved from class to class by bells. The first long bell marks the end of the last period; two short bells the beginning of the next. You had best be in your seat by the last ting of the two short rings or you may get a black mark. Get caught running in the halls to make the last ring, two black marks. Finally, bells deliver us to supper, another set to evening study hall. A final set of bells for evening prayers that come before further study for the older boys and bed for the younger.

The rector usually says "good night" to each young boy in the first two forms as we troop upstairs. Often Mrs. Peabody stands beside him to also say good night. This is no mere gesture. She keeps a mother's eye upon us new kids. In the middle of the winter term of my first year, she tells my dorm master, A. Gurnee Gallien, that I look "peaked" and should take an afternoon nap several times a week. She writes my mother she has done this. I nap. Sundays there are no classes and we go to church twice, at eleven A.M. and five P.M. You could go to church three times on Sunday, if you take early Holy Communion. A wise move if you believed you were in some kind of trouble.

Several nights a term, parlor nights, evening study ends early for the first two forms and Mrs. Peabody, usually along with one of her grown daughters, Betsy or Marjorie, play games with the boys in one of the two forms. The most exciting game is "Parson Parson Lost His Hat." To begin, each boy around the Peabodys' big dinning table chooses a color for the chair in which he then sits, say pink, or green, or purple. If his color is called, "Green" and you did not immediately give the correct answer, "Who sir? Me sir?" you had to go to the last place at the table. This meant that everybody then moved up, and you now have to remember the color of the new chair into which you now move. After about five moves, with a color change each time. the game gets difficult. You also go down to the bottom, if you answer "Who sir? Me sir?" when you are not in the chair of the color just called. For the impatient like myself Parson's Hat requires intense concentration. Fortunately the game ends with milk and cookies.

Sports, not studies, hold the highest rank. They are compulsory and played or practiced every day but Sunday, from the end of afternoon study hall until five. Then the great outside bell tolls and all race for the gym to shower, put on stiff collars, white shirts, ties, and patent leather shoes for supper. Since the bigger boys play and practice closer to the gym than us little boys, and can run faster, they get to the showers first. This means that often small guys race to our dormitories to change into supper clothes unable to shower and covered with dirt and sweat. Still, we look clean, though our stiff colors might be a bit limp. There are no sports on Sunday; the Bible demands a day of rest. So strict was this rule that students could throw a ball back and forth among themselves, but another student could not run bases between them. These anti-sport rules left the bigger boys free, if they so wanted, to haze the little boys on Sunday. Some did.

In studies, English, sacred studies, French, and Latin hold pride of place. Since the founding of the school, they have been required courses for all six years. However, a year before I arrive, history is made an elective for the upper school, forms four, five, and six. The only Ph.D. on the faculty is hired to teach this novel subject. Before such liberalism strikes, only dummies who flunk Latin are allowed to take history instead. Learning is still by rote.

Marks are usually given daily. Two years before I am to graduate comes more change, wonderful for me. Seniors who show an aptitude and special interest in some subject are allowed to take tutorials. These are seminars, once-a-week meetings one-on-one with a master, to explore the chosen subject. No marks, the only requirement a well-crafted final essay. There are no courses in art; though a music teacher who plays the organ and leads the choir gives a few students piano lessons, but not for academic credit.

Doctor Peabody loves to tell the story of how he hired the school music teacher. He went up to Harvard, where he had heard of a senior who was an excellent piano player and gifted in music. The rector's interview with the candidate went satisfactorily, but the young man seemed unduly nervous.

"Why are you in such a fidget?" Peabody asks the student.

"Well you see, sir, this interview has lasted longer than I expected. I'm on the swimming team and we are swimming against Yale this afternoon. I am afraid I may miss the meet."

"Oh you're an athlete. Why didn't you tell me? I'll double that salary I just offered you."

In fairness to Groton I must report that the teaching in English and history were excellent. When, after four years in the army, I enter Yale, I am able to enter senior honor courses in both subjects, and even courses in the graduate school. Only a few masters at Groton actively mocked and distrusted the progressive system from which I came and let me know it. On the other side, several history and English masters are kind, helpful, try to understand my problems and later place me in charge of school programs and encourage me to write.

The school is still isolated, a kingdom unto itself. The roads from Boston are narrow and twisting. Parents visit the school at most twice a year, staying in Parents House, a school-maintained inn, across the road. With permission, provided you had no black marks against you, you could lunch there with your parents after church on Sunday. We all sleep in cubicles, small horse stall-like spaces that no self-respecting horse would tolerate. The cubicle entrance is at the end away from its window and opens on the long corridor of the dormitory. The dormitories are segregated by forms, and are basically long corridors each of which contains roughly twenty-five cubicles, and has a master's bedroom and study at one end. A hanging curtain can be pulled across a cubicle entrance for some privacy. Inside the cubicle stands one school-supplied bureau, all of them the same. Only pictures of the family and a mirror can grace the bureau. Nothing goes on the walls.

In the dormitories, and everywhere about school except in an actual class, prefects control our lives. All sixth-formers are prefects. They have the same power to punish and give boys black marks as do the masters. Several prefects have cubicles in each dormitory to help keep order. Two are assigned to a dining room table to take charge in the absence of a master. Black marks are serious trouble. To expunge just one black mark requires two hours' work on the weekend, either helping a master with his house or garden or just walking around the circle or down to the river and back. Black marks can be cumulative. Suppose a prefect in the gym hears you take the Lord's name in vain when you can't find your baseball glove, that is a four-black-mark offense. That's eight hours' work. More than you can do on Saturday and Sunday. Some punishment time will carry over to the next weekend. Fear of punishment and some street smarts enables me to avoid most black marks, though being a wiseacre occasionally does me in.

In some ways life is luxurious. All meals are formal. We sit down by forms at long tables, while maids wait on us. Maids also do the laundry, make the beds, and clean the dormitories several times a day. Janitors maintain the buildings and scrub the latrines. Outside, the lawns are mowed, trees trimmed, repairs done, boilers fired and boardwalks laid in winter by a group of men known to all boys and most masters as "the sons of rest." The food, planned and supervised by a dietician, is as good as at many hotels. The rector loves his meals. He eats lunch most days at the raised head table with his wife, two unmarried daughters, selected sixth-formers, and guests. Sundays we have Dr. Peabody's favorite: roast beef, browned potatoes, Yorkshire pudding, and ice cream. Daily at breakfast there are hard-boiled and soft-boiled eggs, hot and cold cereal, milk, juice, cocoa, coffee for the older boys, and bread and toast with butter and jams.

Students are divided by their abilities in each subject into A and B divisions, sometimes even into upper A, B, and C divisions. There is no need to guess where I am. I am at the bottom with the dumbest of the dumb in all subjects. I manage to keep my head above water there, maintaining most of my grades above sixty, but few above seventy. I am in shock. I try to cope with my new life without fully understanding why or how. I realize I am no longer one of the show dogs but one of the mutts at the bottom. And a noisy, messy mutt at that.

In English, originality brings no rewards. What counts is understanding the parts of a sentence. How these parts further divide into even smaller parts, that can take on confusing multiple personalities: transitive and intransitive, regular and irregular, or suddenly become participals. We must learn all these and the punctuation that goes with them. In Latin, since I have never been taught grammar and cannot spell, I have real difficulty. In addition the teacher, a kindly man in his last year at the school, had taught my father. I sense his embarrassment, not for me, but for my father who has such a son. In French my spelling and my lack of grammar cause the same problems, though not as severe. In math, always my weakest subject, I manage fairly well in the B division. At the bottom of the bimonthly reports sent home, dyslexia goes unmentioned. Instead, the rector writes, "Considering his ability, his marks are not good." Or in another report, "His marks are erratic and he should do much better. His cooperation in class has not been what it should be." Such phrases become a mantra.

I wish someone had explained to me how different Groton would be from Dalton, and not just in the schoolroom. When the first freeze comes and there is skating on Lake Romain, all the other 175 boys break out hockey sticks and hockey skates. I break out the figure skates given me by my mother. Forty years later, I will set a speaker by our pond on Martha's Vineyard, so Jane and I can waltz round and round on the ice. But back then no unseen future "a wonderful when" gave any balm to the teasing in the "painful now."

The opening week of school in our first sacred studies class the Reverend Peabody expounds on Groton. "Of course," he says, "Groton is not a progressive school. But then I doubt any of you know what that sort of school is."

A hand goes up in the third row. "I do sir, I come from Dalton."

"Oh yes, Hadley. And how do you like it here?"

"So far I like Dalton better, sir."

Many year later classmates still shake their heads and remind me of the episode.

We new boys are in the dormitory of Arthur Gurnee Gallien, who becomes one of the few Groton masters with whom I grow friendly. He even encourages my writing and though a new kid helps me get articles in the third-form (middle school) newspaper. My second year at Groton, second form year, Mr. Gallien becomes my English teacher in division C, the lowest section. I flunked the final examination in lower C English the year before because of spelling and punctuation mistakes. We study essays. I find the year fascinating, however, my marks in English remain much the same; I flunk or barely pass. Grammar and spelling remain beyond me. The next to the last day of school I take my English examination. I am afraid I have failed it and must do school work for another summer. That evening I look up from my study hall desk to see Mr. Gallien coming toward me. The worst is not yet to come; it is here.

"Arthur," he says. This is already an extraordinary event. Masters always use students' last names. We students mostly do the same amongst each other. I am not certain to this day of the first names of some classmates.

"Arthur," he repeats, "I have to give you homework for this summer. You failed the examination. But I have had you moved up to A division next year. We can't keep you in C any longer." This is perhaps the largest gift I will receive at Groton, a double jump, from C past B to A. No longer down with those for whom the closing bell is the best part of their English class. In A, thinking counts as much as spelling. Next fall my English marks begin their slow rise from sixty, or worse fifty-five, to the eighties, the nineties, and two years later, even ninety-five. And there is spillover. The history department also moves me to A. My marks rise there. The math department then decides I can move to A. That is their mistake. I get moved back. In Latin, French, and later German the miserable sixties and fifty-fives continue

How do I get through Groton? By activities. I write. I end as editor of the *Grotonian*, the school literary magazine. I also win the Poetry Prize twice. I debate. I and MacGeorge Bundy, who later became President Kennedy's national security adviser, are the only two Grotonians to twice win the President Franklin D. Roosevelt Debating Prize. I act. Senior year I am president of the Dramatic Society. I also captained the basketball team. This is the only position to which I am elected by my classmates rather than installed by the faculty. Captaincy obviously works for me before the Officer Candidate School (OCS) selection board.

Mr. Gallien moves behind the scenes to help me in other ways. In addition to teaching English and being master of the first-form dormitory, he runs Hundred House, one of the school's two dormitory buildings. Fourth-form year (corresponding to freshman year in high school) students move from their desks in the large study halls into studies, small rooms off a school corridor, each with a window and a door. Most studies are doubles, even triples. I have a coveted single study down Library Corridor, the quietest hall in the school. The next year, fifth form, the European war has crowded the school with refugee students. Rather than sleeping in a dormitory cubicle like everyone else, I have an unheard of luxury — a sleeping study with a bed. Only the senior prefect has the same luxury. Sixth form, my final year, I have another single study again off Library Hall, and a single room off Mr. Gallein's first-form dorm. All this gives me privacy and peace in which to read and write.

Luck

Shortly before the end of my third-form year I get whooping cough. I cannot seem to shake it and remain confined to the infirmary for just under a month. One day I look out my infirmary window to see the unbelievable, the family station wagon and Al Hanson, our chauffeur. I have been told nothing about this. He is here to take me home. The school's maids have my trunk already packed. This means that I will take all my final examinations at home, including Latin. This could be my last Latin examination. I have received the seldom-given permission to drop the subject next year. But so far I have flunked every term-end Latin examination at Groton and several make-up examinations. This examination I will take at my desk in my Glen Cove bedroom. I use an illegal trot and open Latin dictionary. I pass with a complimentary sixty. All I have left from Latin is a recurrent nightmare, fortunately ended some thirty years ago, that I have flunked Latin and must remain imprisoned in Groton while the rest of mankind enjoys the world.

Finally I get through Groton as I have gotten through life, with the help of poetry. Not poetry in the abstract, but the direct connection between specific poems or lines of poetry and my life. A connection first shown me by Mrs. Warren at Dalton. (When he discovered my dyslexia, Dr. Orion had predicted an ability to memorize might well become a flip side benefit of my condition.) Poetry helps me understand choices in life and their different rewards. I visit places, imagined or real, strikingly unlike those where I live. Emotionally and mentally, I escape Groton by poetry. And through that escape comes the hope, and even a belief, that real escape may be possible. I live surrounded by poetry as some live surrounded by faith.

In my last three years at Groton, both in the library and in English classes, and with the outside help of friendly English masters, A. Gurnee Gallien, Malcolm Strachen, and James B. Satterthwait, I begin to read and study the ancient and modern giants. I memorize large parts of them so I can carry them with me for help. Sections of T. S. Elliot's *Four Quartets* for example:

> The ragged rock in the restless waters
> waves wash over it
> storms disshelve it
> On a halcyon day it is merely a sea mark
> But in the somber season or the sudden furry is what it always was.

From speeches and lines from Shakespeare's plays and sonnets to Sandburg, e.e. cummings, and Archibald MacLeish's "Face down beneath the sun, feel the always coming on." And "Try it in South Chicago on Memorial day."

I also memorize a lot of Swinburne. Not much of what he wrote has stayed with me. Probably I swallowed his poetry as an antidote to Groton. With chapel twice a day, no girls, and sins everywhere, who could resist:

> Change in a trice
> The lilies and languors of virtue
> For the raptures and roses of vice.

Now, there was something I could see myself doing. I should start watching for chances as soon as possible. And how about:

> Will you yet take all oh Gallien? But these thou shall not take
> The laurel, the palms and the paean,
> The breast of the nymphs in the brake.

That's good stuff to keep a boy awake during a long sermon on evil.

Houseman leaped off the page:

> I to their perils of cheat and charmer
> Came clad in armor
> By stars benign.
> Hope lies to mortals and most believe her
> But man's deceiver was never mine.

Arnold's "Dover Beach," Wilfred Owen's accurate pictures of war, both Rosettis, and even translations of the *Eddas*. I gobbled them all. I write an Eddic poem with rhymes on the first syllables about Tyr, who staved off Ragnarock, the end of the world, for thousands of years by permitting the World Wolf, Fenrir, to bite off his sword hand.

Jane also loved and used poetry. Poetry, other literature, plus her psychoanalytic training wove together to form the empathy, sympathy, and knowledge with which she reached out to patients, friends, and family. Whatever was going on, Jane "got it" fast. Chiseled on her side of our tombstone are lines she selected herself that Robert Burns wrote for his father, with a sex change of course:

> If there's another world she lives in bliss.
> If there be none she made the best of this.

I will be beside her with e.e. cummings:

> one's not half of two.
> it's two are halves one."

Bored stiff by my classes except for English and history (and later under an extraordinary master, German), I read and read and memorize. Meanwhile I grow bigger and stronger. As early as my first year away at school, Mother writes in the log she keeps about me, "I don't understand how Arthur has stayed so healthy. He was always sickly at home." Sometimes in the Army, when the war heated up, someone would remark, "God this is [expletive deleted] awful." I would reply, "This is nothing compared to my family dinner table." They would smile, thinking the lieutenant was joking to ease the tension. I was, sort of.

As I bounce my way through the brown-gray sameness of Groton days, the important moments of life happen on vacation. However, definitely not on my first summer vacation from Groton, after my first-form year, when I am thirteen. I have a tutor, with the Dickensian name of Benjamin Brain, to help with my Latin, English, and French. Mother and Father are absent again, and life is kept firmly on the track under the returned RN, Miss Nellie Martin, and Mabel. I have two pleasant memories of that summer. I am allowed to give up horseback riding, which I do not particularly enjoy, and take up sailing. From the instant I step in a boat I'm enchanted. I have kept up sailing most of my life. Five times Jane and I will charter a forty-foot sailboat with a captain and crew of two and sail down the Turkish coast and neighboring Greek isles, with a couple who are close friends, for ten of the most exotically entrancing weeks of our lives. And without the mortar fire experienced while exploring temples along the Thai-Cambodian border.

The other pleasant memory concerns my triumph over Benjamin Brain. Brain and I become sworn enemies. I don't know why. We just do. He tries to make me spell, write, and read faster. But Brain has committed a strategic error. Not a mere tactical mistake; a strategic error, comparable to Jeb Stuart's leaving Lee blind at Gettysburg. He has made an enemy out of my friend the chauffeur, Al Hanson. Once when I have done something unspeakable to Brain — at least I hope it was unspeakable — he runs after me intent on physical punishment. He is a little portly and I have a temporary lead. But I know it is only temporary. I scoot through the side door of the garage hoping to find a hiding place. My friend Al Hanson is standing by one of our cars with an oil can.

"Brain's after me," I gasp. I see Hanson take the can and throw oil in front of the door I have just run through

"Keep going," he orders. I get the message. By the time I hear

Brain's surprised cry of terror and Hanson shout, "Careful, Mr. Brain. Floor's slippery. Are you hurt bad?" I am halfway to my super-secret hiding place beneath the bushes at the lawn's foot.

The summer after my second-form year is better. I am fourteen and take a European trip with Mother and Father. Unfortunately Father and I squabble a bit. The original battle begins in the middle of the winter term before the trip. Father offers me a choice. I can go to Europe with him and Mother or, since I like sailing so well, he will buy me a sailboat. One or the other. This is a hard choice. I incline toward the sailboat. By now I know not to trust my father. He can be unfair and tricky with words. I write back thanking him, and that his choice is difficult. What sort of sailboat does he have in mind?

He replies that Seawanaka Yacht Club, of which he is a member and I a junior member, is introducing a newly designed racing class of sailboats, and he will buy me one of these. He has sent for plans. He will look at them and send them on to me. When the plans arrive I am horrified. These are big boats for grown men to race. They sleep two. They have a toilet. I won't have the strength to raise the sails. None of my friends will be in boats so large. Who will clean the toilet? I will never be able to find a crew. I reply that the boat is too big. He writes a nasty letter implying that I am a coward, ducking true competition. I decide to go to Europe. I enjoy the trip, the ocean liners, the food, the battlefields, the mountains, and glaciers. One moment has a lifelong effect.

Mother often takes me to museums, and since we like different parts of them — she is not keen on knights in armor and battle scenes, nor I on Impressionism — we devise a fine working system. When we enter the museum, we synchronize our watches, pick a time to meet near the front door, then wander off on our own.

Fate and Luck

Today, after roaming the Tate in London, Blake's "Soul of the Flea" fascinates me. I walk back toward the entrance to meet Mother and Father. In a long gallery, my eyes glance at a carved stone head. Suddenly I am terrified, physically scared, as if I were attacked by a gang of men in masks. That head is the head of a man who wants to kill me. Me. Right now. Right now and forever. My terror is such — I am reporting this accurately — that I do not go straight toward the head to discover what it is and by whom created, but circle round to the statue's back to read the base without the eyes resting on me. The head is "The Bomb Thrower" by Jacob Epstein.

The effect is instantaneous. Dalton and my genes combine to open me to the statue. From then on I walk through museums differently. I try to feel the emotion of art as I do of poetry. I had listened enough and read enough to realize I have felt the much-revered artistic experience. Art expands for me, though I continue to like story pictures. My favorite small museum, the Alte Pinakothek in Munich, abounds in both.

Some forty years later, I stand before El Greco's "View of Toledo" in New York's Metropolitan Museum, a painting whose appeal for me has worn somewhat thin. A seven- or eight-year-old boy pauses before the picture. "Mummy, Mummy, they are murdering people to death in that picture." His exact, unforgettable words. Right before me, a lucky kid is having my "Bomb Thrower" experience. Mummy takes him by the hand and pulls him on. "It's a landscape by a man called El Greco. He had eye trouble." A slow and painful death is too good for that woman.

In addition to the "Bomb Thrower," I see another disturbing image in England. As a key lawyer for the International Aluminum Company, Father, Mother, and I get to visit an aircraft factory building Spitfires. In the last part of the process, the propellers are fabricated. A solid block of aluminum is placed in a gigantic press. A switch is thrown. Slowly, slowly, the press closes. In the course of over an hour, an aluminum propeller is squeezed out.

I point out to my father that the signs on the two giant, complex squeezers say "Krup Essen." Father questions our escort. He replies that England does not produce any presses with enough power to produce the propellers, so the machines have been purchased from Germany. A good lesson for a future reporter.

I see the sunrise from Zermatt turn the Matterhorn pink. Our large American car has to be pushed up the last hundred yards of the pass between Austria and Germany. The pass is so steep the carburetor float jams. In Munich, I see soldiers everywhere: in the beer halls, at the music festivals, standing guard in front of Nazi monuments and the fabulous art and science museums. In the latter Mother gets too close to a powerful magnet and her watch is ruined. Then back to Paris for the boat train and home on the French ocean liner, *Normandy*.

Chance and Luck

The next winter, that of my third-form year when I'm still fourteen, a moment of such force hits me that I still call that moment my "Paul on the road to Damascus moment." Or more specifically, my "*Hellzapoppin* Moment." The two are both involved because the experience begins as an outgrowth of Dalton. Among the good friends I made there is Robert Lichtenstein. Bobby now calls me up to say he has tickets for *Hellzapoppin,* a risque vaudeville show on Broadway — and on my family taboo list. He invites me to have dinner first. I accept, keeping quiet about the *Hellzapoppin* part when I tell Mother I am dining with Bobby. At dinner, we are joined by two girls our age from Dalton. After dinner we all go to the show. We have great tickets in the third row. *Hellsapoppin* is wild and naked, full of jokes I don't understand, and great fun. I remember the intermission because it begins with two clowns yelling at each other from the aisles across the audience. The one closest to me holds balloons. The one far away yells, "What has Mae West got that I haven't got?" The one nearest me yells, "Balloons! balloons! for sale." Even I get that joke.

At intermission the four of us stand up to stretch. I look around the theater and think, "Wow, I'm glad I don't see any of my Groton friends here; I'd never live it down at school being seen with these people." I'm stunned. I realize I have just become a Groton snob. Everything I feared has happened. These are my true friends here. Right here. Right now. With me. Not those at Groton. As Paul on the road to Damascus, my world changed. I cannot claim the change as my choice. The experience came. Just flooded in. From then on, I am inoculated against the anti-Semitic flu and the equally deadly "I am born superior" virus. (The Army provided a booster shot against both diseases to watch those die who had received so little.) I know I've slipped at times, but they were slips, not falls. I also become aware that the alembics around the Groton Circle brew potent visions that poison drip by drip. Nothing that happens during the time I spend at Groton so effects my life until Pearl Harbor, December 7 my senior year.

The summer of my third-form year, when I have just turned fifteen and have passed Latin with the aid of whooping cough, the whole family returns to France. Mother, Winks, John, Barbara, and Mabel leave in early June. Father and I remain behind so I can finish exams and stop most whooping. Mother has rented a large house, with a trout pond, in the hills outside of Annecy, in northern France, near the Swiss border. Father and I cross on the *Normandy* together, one of her last crossing before the war. As you descend the stairs into the dining room before dinner, a carved statue of a somewhat naked beauty holds out a bucket of caviar from which you may scoop as often as you wish. The bucket is continually replenished.

Before the trip, Father and I sit on deck with the ship still docked. My father leans over to me and whispers, quoting Hamlet "Speak not of what you have heard," by pronouncing of some doubtful phrase, "'we could an if we would' or 'well, well we know,'" tells me I must not indicate in any way that I recognize the father of one of my friends, Mr. Winthrop Aldrich, the president of Chase Bank. He is traveling under an assumed name on a secret mission to Europe, to prevent another world war. I recognize this as important news. The father of a girlfriend stopping a war. I vow to keep quiet. We sit in silence. After a few moments the *Normandy*'s loudspeakers announce to all on board and dock side: "Will Mr. Winthrop Aldrich, whose passport is not in order, report immediately to the captain's cabin. Will Mr. Winthrop Aldrich, whose passport is not in order, report immediately to the captain's cabin." I am old enough to realize that secretly stopping wars gets complicated.

Several nights later, out at sea, Mr. Aldrich and a wealthy friend, over dinner, offer Father the presidency of a well-known railroad. In our cabin Father explains to me the two men were feeling "a bit expansive" and what happened doesn't mean a thing. I have a great time on the *Normandy*, but I am not too enthusiastic about the Annecy deal. What am I going to do there in the hills above a lake in France with no friends? My enthusiasm does not increase when informed on the car trip from the boat to Annecy that I will have a tutor. There will also be an English-speaking French woman to help Mabel look after Barbara, John, and Katherine.

The villa my mother has rented lies at the edge of the woods at the base of a hill, about a twenty-minute bike ride north of the town of Annecy. The trees embrace it and the trout pond at its rear. Inside are the usual: living room, dining room, kitchen, six bedrooms — one for Mother and Father, one each for myself, Katherine, and John. Barbara, then five with long blond curls, and Mabel sleep together. The extra bedroom stores our baggage. There is also one bathroom, plus a washbasin in Mother and Father's room. There is quite a jam-up for the one bathroom in the morning. The villa no longer exists. In the eighties when I try to find it on a trip with Jane, vacation homes have overrun the villa's location, the surrounding farms, and most of the wooded hill.

About my tutor, luck steps in. Not enough luck to be placed in italics and capitalized because it changes my life, but enough luck to give me a memorable summer. My tutor, Theo Stump, is a junior master at a school outside Geneva, and on the Swiss national ski team. An alive, handsome, slow-tempered, humorous man, he makes a fine companion. He takes me down to the beach at Lake Annecy and introduces me to his French friends. There is a club there, just out of town and alongside the lake, where Theo, his friends, and I all hang out. We play Ping-Pong together, swim, rent sailboats, drink panaches (half lemonade, half beer), and have a ball. "Arthur, Arthur," they beg me in French, "please use your American accent. When you try your French accent it kills us."

In England the year before, I went bicycling by myself on several afternoons, and I had watched bicyclists on previous trips to Europe. I greatly wanted to take a bicycle trip in France. However, the whole question of my bicycle is contentious. After seeing that British bicycles are light and have three speeds, attributes common to

U.S. cycles today, but then unknown outside of Europe, I ask for such a European cycle for my birthday or Christmas, or a combined gift for both if the foreign bikes are very expensive. My father refuses, saying American bicycles are built better. When my father goes away for a week in the spring, I persuade my mother to buy me a three-speed English Raleigh for my birthday. This causes a bit of tension between Father and myself. The word "sneak" is vigorously employed.

Mother has brought my three-speed cycle over to Annecy. In August, when Father has returned from France to the States, I suggest to Mother that Theo and I take a bicycle trip down the Rhone Valley to Marseilles. Theo, who has a three-speed bike like mine, takes up the idea and pushes for it. Mother agrees. Theo and I outfit our bicycles with saddlebags that hang from a rear rack down over both sides of the back wheel. We purchase extra inner tubes, the necessary maps and guides, and take off down the Rhone Valley to the Mediterranean. The weather cooperates: mostly dry and hot but not scalding. We cycle on main roads only occasionally. Usually we stick to rural roads marked on our Michelin maps with green lines and symbols such as eyelashes that indicate good views and pleasant scenery.

Each morning we get up around seven, when the country inn or small hotel we have chosen the afternoon before wakes up. We have a system about where we spend the night. We see a place we both like. Theo checks the rooms and negotiates a price. I check the toilets. Then we put our heads together and decide. We eat the local food: chicken, a fish from the Rhone or a nearby stream, and drink the local wine and sleep soundly. We must have sometimes chosen with skill. When Jane and I retrace some of my route in the early eighties, one of our small country inns has metamorphosed to three Michelin stars with a helipad.

On waking, Theo and I first stand in line for whatever sort of bathroom there may be. We breakfast on fresh bread, cheese, jam or honey, coffee for Theo, hot chocolate for me. We strap our bags on our bikes and take off while the day is still cool. Several mornings the backs of our shirts are pleasantly soaked by the dew on the weeping willow branches that hang above the narrow farm trails and brush us as we peddle. Soon our thoughts begin to move in the rhythms of our pumping legs.

There are few cars on even the main roads in those pre-war days, and even fewer trucks that spray the air with diesel fumes. We have the smaller roads mostly to ourselves as we move through the mixed smell of dust and grapes. Our wheels echo back from crumbling, chalk-white cliffs or the narrow streets of farming towns where children look up from their play to wave at us. Now and then we glimpse the Rhone, a streak of brown through the green fields of grapes and wheat. The road can change suddenly from asphalt to dirt, where we must pay more attention to cycling, to prevent a puncture or crash from a concealed rock. Often the roadside is baked brown and dry, its desolation heightened by the carefully farmed fields before and after.

We spend a day in Orange with its famous Greco-Roman theater. I am captivated by the giant statue of Caesar that dominates not just the open theater but the whole countryside. For the first time, I physically come to understand how people came to believe him a god. We spend several days in Avignon, staying at a small hotel at the town's center on the Place de Horlogue, both to do our laundry in the bedroom sink and to see the sights in town and surroundings.

One day it rains and the awnings over the hotel's sidewalk cafe start to bulge downward with water. I take a broom and push up at the straining bellies to spill out the water. I succeed, but most of the water drenches me. I am so happy, all I can do is laugh. Theo starts to laugh also. So do the other patrons. At that moment Theo and I bond, no longer tutor and ward, but friends. The fun and great times actually increase. On we peddle, the Pont du Gar, Nîmes, Arles with its arena, deserted back then. We begin to hear rumors of coming war. At the restaurant in Arles where we eat one evening I say to Theo, "The proprietor doesn't look to happy."

"That is because," Theo replies, "you have just eaten all his Roquefort for the week."

Several days later signs are posted on trees and walls. "Order de Mobilization General." France moves toward war. I must get to Annecy, Theo to his Swiss Army unit. We load our bicycles on crowded trains and rattle slowly back.

These three weeks of bicycling through France are my boyhood's happiest time. I will have other happy times, ecstatic times when the world spins with energy and love, when life completes itself in Jane and me. But they are grownup times. These three weeks, just as World War II breaks out, mark the end of my boyhood. Even back at Groton, I feel the change. School and I are on more even terms. I still make mistakes, I don't work any harder, except in English and history, but I more understand the school. I haven't grown up. I am a long way from there. Even after the war, I won't grow up completely until I marry Jane, and that is another chapter.

Back in Annecy, mother presciently decides that we must not return as planned on an Italian Line steamship. If we were in Italy when it entered the war on the German side, we could be imprisoned for years as enemy aliens. She and I motor to Geneva to turn in the Italian Line tickets at the line office there, and get our money back. The Italian chief of the office weeps as he takes the family tickets and hands mother Swiss francs.

"Tous le monde finis, Madam. Tous le monde finis."

Mother knows the U.S. consul in Geneva, who tells her to drive to Le Havre as that is where the United States will send ships to evacuate Americans, but not to wait in Le Havre itself as that city may be bombed. Mother is at her best in times like this. She tells us not to worry. She, her brother, Mother, and her father, John Blodget, were caught in France at the outbreak of World War I, and Grandfather Blodget chartered a yacht to get themselves and several other American families stranded in Europe back to America. We will find a way.

We do. We all pile into the car and in two days Mother drives us across France to L'Etrat twenty miles north of Le Havre. L'Etrat is a seaside retreat on the English Channel famous for its oddly shaped cliffs. I unstrap my bicycle from the back of the car to explore the coast. Two weeks later the U.S. liner, *Washington*, arrives from the United State at Le Havre to pick up those stranded like us. Mother, Mabel, and the two girls have two cabins, John and I cots 23 and 24 in the empty swimming pool. Donald Budge, the tennis champion, has a cot about four down from us. His feet hang way out over its end. After several days Budge and a sensuous Hollywood dancer with a cabin reach some sort of agreement. Budge no longer uses his swimming pool cot. I resolve to work harder on my backhand.

Fourth-form year, except for the pleasure of having, thanks to Mr. Gallien, a single study rather than a desk in the school room, passes like the first three. I work hard at English, history, and math and scrape by in the rest, while I spend my time reading and writing. I now take both French and German, the latter language that for some reason I find easier to learn, though I can't spell in German any better than in French, or English for that matter. My marks remain low. I wait for summer like the rest.

That summer, the end of my of my fourth-form year, I spend most of my time at the Seawanica Yacht Club, a good hour's drive away. Since at sixteen I am not able to drive, to relieve the pressure on Al Hansen, my mother buys me a speed boat, a small Cris-Craft, which I name the *Flit*. The name "Flirt" having already been appropriate by a senior member of the yacht club. Hansen gives me a quick lesson on motor maintenance, oil changing, bearingcup grease, bilge pump cleaning, and I'm off in a world on my own. I am severely told by both Mother and Father that the *Flit* is strictly for going back and forth to the yacht club only. Nothing else.

"Right," in the words of an Army phrase already becoming popular on the radio, "I am on message, sir." Am I on message. Way on message, the message planted firmly on the *Flit*'s floor with my foot upon its neck. When a breathtaking girl from the Beaver Brook Summer Dances waves to me from a club or private dock, I am to speed right by? Particularly after I've finagled the purchase of a surf board with my allowance? My allowance is now seventy-five dollars a month, with which I am to purchase clothes and everything else I need, except school supplies. Other than the *Flit* I have an average summer. My diary turns largely internal to record a list of girls with whom I fall in and out of love and a few mild escapades. The Seawanica junior crew, of which I am the jib man, wins the South Shore of Long Island Sound Championship on its way to the Nationals.

However we are defeated in the next round by the team from the Connecticut side.

Fifth-form year is easier and different from the first four. To begin: thanks to Mr. Gallien, I have the privilege of a sleeping study. If I am careful not to bend the rules too far I can live the life of a senior, a sixth-former, while still in the fifth form. My friend George Myers, later killed as a B-24 pilot over the Ruhr, shares the other sleeping study next to mine.

A third sleeping study, which also boasts a parlor, is occupied by Frederick W. Whitridge, the senior prefect, one form ahead of myself, and the head boy in the school. Though we are in different forms, because we both have sleeping studies he and I hold long talks and become firm friends. This is unusual between boys in different forms. Fred is six-foot-two, a quiet, thoughtful, good man without being obsequious; the son of a Yale house master and professor of English. He plays on the football and baseball teams and is liked by all; moreover, he can laugh at himself. He is known familiarly to his face, with respect not mockery, as "Trumpet Trunk," because of his fine New England nose.

One spring day as we stand by his parlor window looking out on the Circle at some unfolding scene, he says, "Arthur, Arthur, will we ever get over what Groton has done to us?" If the senior prefect, the head boy of the school, feels so, what is this confused rebel to think? Though he moves to the West Coast shortly after college, we continue to write back and forth and remain friends. In the end Fred breaks most of the way out. His battle is harder than mine. He fit the mold better.

Chance and Luck

Then *Chance*, in the rise of German anti-Semitism, and *Luck*, that Groton needed a new master to teach Latin and German, combine to bring to Groton from Hamburg Dr. Ernest L. Lowenberg. In Hamburg Dr. Lowenberg had run his own progressive school until forced by the Nazis to flee. In the cold, Protestant, ritual-soaked, learning-by-rote world of Groton, the school and this Jewish, progressive educator somehow managed to bond — a marriage that says much about the excellence of the new headmaster, Dr. John Crocker. There are difficulties, or perhaps harmonious tensions. Dr. Lowenberg, with his head cocked slightly to one side, his European-cut double-breasted blue suit, and a cigarette pointing upward from his lips, certainly is different from most of what Groton then was. For me he is not just a master; he becomes a role model. Everything in his life has been destroyed or greatly changed. He does not give up. He does not get mad. He looks about, reads books, thinks, and lives. He takes the world as it exists, accepts, and inwardly smiles. He believes totally in progress, but tests all change against his thoughtful values.

With Lowenberg I have a new ally on the faculty. He knows all about dyslexia. In German classes we change from learning verb tenses to struggling with Rilke, Mann, Falada — even Goethe. Memorizing German poetry raises your mark no matter how you spell the words. He and his wife become lifelong friends. Later they will visit Jane and me on Martha's Vineyard. "I always hoped, Arthur, you would survive. How did you two meet? You both must tell me."

Outside class you ask Lowenberg a question, and he puffs a few times on his cigarette, then holds it in the European fashion, between thumb and index finger, the burning tip inward, and begins his answer: "When you are asking me that, I am first asking you this." Next a bomb explodes in your mind. I now have an intellectual stimulus and an emotional refuge. A small part of Groton has become like Dalton. I enjoy visits to his house near the school just to listen. His house smells more like Europe than New England. It is warm in February. His wife's cakes are delicious, his coffee strong. My last year at Groton I have a tutorial with him on educational psychology and philosophy. These sessions are pure pleasure.

Some typical Lowenberg dicta still instruct me with pleasure and a smile. "The question is not can you trust your children. The question is when."

"That student will be able to find himself a center of life so small that no one will be able to tell if he is a success or not."

"A perfect system of education merely assures that children will more perfectly repeat the errors of their fathers. But is that not what most fathers want?"

And then his two last sentences to me as I said good-bye on leaving Groton for the Army. "The condition of your shoes will have more to do with your Army life than the condition of your mind." And then what must have been for him difficult words: "Remember that when you kill a German, you will be killing one of the people that produced Goethe."

Lowenberg works a miracle around the Groton circle. He remains there to leaven its education for twenty-two years. "Sometimes I find a student I can get to before Groton gets inside him."

Extra curricula activities become both more intense and interesting. I want very much to be editor in chief of the *Grotonian*. This prize usually goes to the boy who gets the most articles into the *Grotonian* his junior year. I spend a great deal of time writing. For the first time this year Groton has a basketball team. That is a sport I can play reasonably well. I practice a great deal, fouls and jump shots, and eventually become captain. I am on the debating team, which means traveling to other schools.

Then there are letters to and from girls. Important dates to be made for winter vacations events, dances, track meets, and just plain meetings. And lots of thought about girls. Which ones do I like best? What is love? Am I in love with her or her? How would I know? Should I accept this invitation on the twentieth for a pretty good dance, when I might get an invitation for a better one held on the same night. I once solved this problem by attending two dinner dances on the same night. The taxis back and forth are expensive. But the fact that I am the only fifth-former present at the second dance, while most of the men are not just sixth-formers but in college, made the challenge worthwhile. Also, at the second dance, my date is one of the most beautiful girls on the floor. I meant to go back to the first dance. I never made it.

Mother always chastises me for my emphasis on pulchritude. "Remember, they are all going to look the same in middle age, and some of the less pretty ones now will have more money then." Her exhortation to "Marry a rich woman and put the money to work" becomes a mantra I can repeat in my sleep. Father would sometimes weigh in on the same subject. Any time I mention a new girl they find something wrong with her or her family. Finally, I fight back. One summer night at dinner I make up a girl who I say I have just met at a dance. She is extraordinarily lovely and thoughtful. I supply a suitable North Shore Long Island name for her. Mother thinks her family may have been in the trash-hauling business. Father believes they have been involved in "unfortunate litigation." When I say the girl is entirely made up, he calls me a liar, and with anger orders me from the dinner table.

Love, particularly physical love, has little welcome at Groton or in my family. A wonderful English master, Malcolm Strachen, lashes out at his class one morning when they show no understanding of why Romeo and Juliet took such risks. "Remember," he tells his class, "Romeo and Juliet lived and loved more in their short lives than most of you will in your longer ones." I pass members of his class as it ends and the boys come out still laughing at the absurdity of the lovers' course and Strachen's words. I think, "Not me. Not me. I will be as happy as they."

In the winter term I have a large part in the school play, *RUR* (Rossum's Universal Robots) by Karel Capek. That means lines to learn and many rehearsals; all work I enjoy. Finally Groton establishes a British War Relief Society. My diary does not reveal how I became the head of this outfit, but I did.(Perhaps my mantra has become, "I will do anything to neglect my school work.") We join with Windsor, a girl's school, to successfully raise money for an ambulance. I have a picture of the ambulance pasted into my diary with "Groton School, The Windsor School" boldly displayed on its side, "Young America Wants to Help" painted above.

Members of the British War Relief Society at Groton also knit socks. This creates a good deal of press interest, as boys in other private preparatory schools are drilling with dummy rifles. Reporters arrive to visit the school, take pictures, do stories. As the leader of the knitting episode, I am often interviewed. Guy Richards of the *New York Daily News* does a detailed article on the war work at

St. Paul's, St. Mark's, and Groton, with the focus and pictures on Groton's knitting. He describes me as "the spark plug of the effort, a rangy, whimsical bundle of energy." A nice praise; I am not sure how accurate.

Three years later, just three years, in a time of change everywhere, my head protrudes above the turret of the special tank I command. A loudspeaker is attached spewing words to convince Germans to surrender. We are maneuvering along a German forest road. I see Guy Richards standing at the roadside. I order the tank to pull into the trees and stop. I climb down to greet Richards. Not surprisingly, he does not recognize the nineteen-year-old helmeted first lieutenant as the sixteen-year-old sparkplug Groton knitter. But he has heard of the famous talking tank, and when he learns how we met in the past, gives it a big story. This publicity helps me and others in our efforts to get loudspeakers more widely used, and so saves lives.

In spring term, the hours of drill spent with the Groton School firefighting team pay off. The weather has been exceptional dry and forest fires break out everywhere. At two-thirty on Monday, April 28, the great outside bell begins to toll. I know it cannot be anything but a call to the fire-fighting team. I race to the back of the gymnasium, where equipment is stored and where there are meant to be cars to take us to the fire. I grab an Indian pump, and with the boy who is second to arrive, jump into a car driven buy a master's wife. She takes us to the fire. We are the first there and help a couple of town and state fire trucks lay out hose. The fire begins to get out of hand. I remember my friend Whitridge looking at the fire in amazement and saying in awe, "It's spreading. It's spreading like wildfire," before he realizes what he has said.

   More trucks arrive and I take my Indian pump to try to contain an edge of the fire. I fail. I get separated from my Groton team. To get out of danger, I jump on a state fire truck, with a driver known as Red. Red turns out to be a skilled, senior firefighter, and we race along back roads with fire all around us, heading for a fire line where his radio reports houses are in danger.

"Where are we going?" I ask one of the riders on the truck.

"New Hampshire." New Hampshire, that could be a problem. I've no money to even make a phone call. When we get to whereever it is we are going, women from the houses along the road are doling out coffee, doughnuts, and cake and saying "Thank God you're here."

My diary records I am in heaven: "I am doing real work, with real men, for a real purpose." We lay out hose and take up hose, grab Indian pumps and put down Indian pumps. Finally we get relieved. I hitch a ride to Ayer, the nearest big town in Massachusetts close to school. There is a master in a car by the train station looking for stragglers. I am the last straggler. The team goes out again the next day under the stricter supervision of several masters.

Telling Mr. Lowenberg about the fire I realize how clearly he sees me. He says he had been talking to Jack Crocker, the new headmaster about the firefighting.

"I hope all the boys get back safely," Crocker had said.

"You won't know that, Jack, until the last boy comes back."

"Who will that be I wonder?" muses Crocker.

"Why, Hadley of course," Lowenberg told him.

The war begins to effect America more and more. It even reaches into Groton where we make our own beds on Sundays. I burn to do something. Father makes it clear that if I run off to Canada to join its Army, since I am under eighteen, he can and will extradite me home. He says he can also stop me from signing on as a deckhand on a freighter joining a convoy to Britain. Then he gets wily. If he can find me a job as exciting as any I have suggested, will I take it instead? That sounds fair; I will still have a choice.

He wins. He has a friend who owns gold and copper mines in the mountains and jungles of Ecuador. He will pay for my trip to Ecuador, and once there, I can work in a mine if I so want. I meet his friend, Mr. Sewall Tynge. We get on well together and my summer is set. On May 5, I go to Ayer to get a passport photo. My cheap white suits for the tropics arrive on May 15, and I get my first typhoid shot. School ends. I pass the last French examination I will ever have to take. I have two weeks of dancing and parties on Long Island. I pass my junior driver's license test on the first try. I borrow a family car to take a girl to the World's Fair, breaking the rule about no driving in New York on a junior licence. Two days later I board a boat for Ecuador, along with Mr. Tyng; John Marquand, the writer, and his son John Jr.; and Mr. Tyng's stepson, Henry Luce III.

I spend most of the boat trip south fighting off a cold I pick up by making the mistake of swimming in the freighter's small swimming pool. I realize that Mr. Tyng's mines must be important because we are all seated at the captain's table. I pal up with Jimmie, an Ecuadorian going home after his fifth-form year at Andover, and Frank, a junior at the University of Southern California, who is on that university's tennis team. We play a lot of Ping-Pong. The three of us take in sights as the ship loads and unloads cargo at both ends of the Panama Canal. This is the first time I see the poverty of Latin America. Naturally I do not understand the why. My diary merely records, "Some of the people live in a disgusting way with naked unwashed babies crawling in the street."

Three days later when we steam up the Guayas River to the port of Guayaquil, I find things much better. The city streets are clean and tree shaded, the smells less intense. When the ship anchors in the river, Mr. Tyng's staff come out in a private launch to meet us. They take care of the paperwork and our bags, and we speed ashore in the launch, past the rafts selling bananas and plantains. We remain in Guayaquil three days in a newly completed grand hotel, wonderful light fixtures but no lightbulbs. At night, everything is still done by kerosene lamp and candlelight. We dine at the consulate for two nights, where Mr. Tyng and the consul, an old friend, discuss business conditions in Ecuador — excellent; the stability of the present government, poor; and the chances of war with Peru, good. I spend a day with Jimmie at his home. He lives in a large house with one bathroom located by the front door. He explains that this is where rich Ecuadoreans put their bathrooms as a symbol of their wealth. The next day I watch sacks of copper concentrate being loaded on barges. The sacks are loaded by black stevedores of incredible strength, with muscled bodies worthy of Greek gods. The stevedores make a dollar fifty a day. The barges will be taken down past the mouth of the Guayas, and there reloaded into the oceangoing freighters. Were the freighters, with their steam-driven winches, to load the sacks at the harbor docks, they would run aground on the sandbars at the river's mouth.

The morning of the fourth day we wake at six-thirty and drive on dirt roads to the airfield to take our chartered flight to the mining town of Portobelo. The plane is an eight-seat, twin-engine Focker Transport. Nazi Germany strives to enhance its trade and influence in Latin America. The flight is very rough, bucking, shifting, and slipping. The winds through the Kuna passes in the mountains between Guayaquil and Portobelo average 80 knots, and their galelike gusts tear at the small bimotor. We fly close to one wall of the mountain passes so that if something goes wrong with the plane our pilot can turn or side slip into the valley for a crash landing. The papal nuncio and his aide are flying in with us. The nuncio is being brought to Portobelo to bless the mine. There was an accident in the mine several weeks ago, two people killed, and the workers are scared. The nuncio's blessing will solve that problem. Before he gets very air sick, the priest and I have a pleasant conversation in French. The rest of our party, except for Mr. Tyng and me, are also overcome by the turbulence.

Portobelo itself overlooks scenery that would be the boast of a costly Alpine resort. To the northeast loom the high Andes, their crests shredded with scarfs of white clouds. Scattered before them are their foothills, dormant former volcanoes strewn about the landscape like dice thrown by giants. Their cones point every which way, like enormous medieval cannon mouths hastily abandoned in a galloping retreat. The houses of the mining engineers, the "gringos," are built above the malaria line. The breeze is cool and breadfruit trees with their broad leaves shade these villas. Belladonna and other flowering vines and shrubs twine about them. They are also full of spiders. The first night I have thirty-eight in my bedroom, which remains my trip record. I am warned to watch for tarantulas. The bedposts are set in cans of poison so that dangerous spiders and scorpions will not climb up. You shake your boots out in the morning before putting them on. No one is kidding. One morning I shake out a tarantula. Another time, when I am on the outhouse toilet, a tarantula checks me out. After that I keep a broom near.

In Portobelo I watch a fiesta, play some basketball with the company team, go down in the mine several times, meet and drink with the engineers, and go riding with some of them. They are a great bunch of joking men, much like those with whom I fought the Groton fires. But I am too much of an outside visitor — a guest of the boss — to fit in. I also forget the rules and go out for a walk without my mining helmet. I receive a slight case of sunstroke in return, which knocks me out for two days.

The Marquands, Mr. Tyng, and Henry Luce III leave to tour Ecuador, see Quito, and visit the coast; after that the Marquands will go home. Mr. Tyng and Henry will stay on a while and leave on August 16. Rather than tour, I want to work in a mine as arranged. Our party breaks up. They leave, and two days later I start for a new mine the company owns, Minos Nuevos in another part of Ecuador, where I will become a regular part of the crew. The mine boss there will see that I get to Guayaquil before the fifteeenth.

I, and another miner going to Minos Nuevos temporarily, take the train as far as Lataconga, where a welcoming party awaits us with mules. The enormous snow-covered cone of Cotopaxi looms over us. We ride across a cold, desolate plain covered with giant cactuses and little else. Some spiked cactus leaves are large as a ten-place dining-room table. The Indians take these huge leaves, stack them on one another, and paste them together with mud to make their homes. After a day's ride we descend into the jungle and reach Minos Nuevos, a small village pockmarked by mine entrances that sprawl along the bank on one side of a three-foot-deep slow-flowing river. A large furnace and cyanide-flotation plant dominate the village. The engineers explain to me that there are plants in the United States making a fortune from ore that contains less gold than the tailings (waste) from our plant. But to get more gold we would lose more copper, and we now get a careful mix to maximize profits.

The mine engineers here take me in. I share a cabin with Jack Malcolm, a young, compact, friendly engineer, a graduate of Georgia

Tech. He is glad to have company, and I settle down to enjoy myself in exciting work among interesting people. I spend a lot of time underground making measurements and collecting rock-face samples with a small, picklike hammer in air so damp and hot that you can see your breath as if it were a cold winter day. Depending on where we work the powder fumes from the blasting can leave a mean headache. I learn to take immediate shelter at the cry "Iabajo" to avoid falling rock and broken wooden beams. The "natives" working underground with pick and shovel, and sometimes compressed-air drills, labor without safety helmets for four cents a day. They also push ore carts and lay underground track along the stope (tunnel) floors. Now and then I work in the office, analyzing and mapping ore samples. I continue to make friends, particularly with Jack and Larry, the old-timer among us and the diamond-drill expert. He has the unique skill of being able to set the tiny industrial diamonds into the head of the drill bit so that the drill cuts into the ground with maximum efficiency. I enjoy the life, the jokes, the partying, the work, and the people. I get really drunk for the first time. On days off, we take rides into the jungle to see the amazing flowers, and to look for strange animals and birds, all the while on the watch for snakes.

One hot afternoon, after I've been there about three weeks, Jack Malcolm and I are climbing a cliff across the river from the mine. We are driving markers into the cliff face to help us later map the proper placement of a new flue. The cliff rises more than two thousand feet above the river. I'm climbing first, Malcolm behind me. We climb slowly and carefully to where we are about three-quarters of the way up. A small piece of wood sticks out of the cliff face, and I put my right foot on it for added support. The wood gives way, pulling out of the cliff face to start a small landslide. Jack manages to scuttle left out of the way of the tumbling shale and stones. His shirt is torn but he is not hurt. Sliding, out of control behind the falling shale and rock, comes myself.

Jack moves to his right through the falling stones and reaches out to grab the back of my shirt. My weight and the momentum of my sliding body are too much for his own toehold and we both start to slide toward the bottom. If we keep going, we will end up in the river over a thousand feet below. We learn later that miners, watching from the opposite side, have phoned the hospital for stretchers and ropes in case we should live. We slide and slide, dig at the rock frantically with fingers and boot toes. Finally one of Jack's feet hits something solid and we pull up. Jack looks at me and smiles. His blue eyes could light up all of Ecuador. A man has done his work.

Luck

Luck: That I should misjudge the stick of wood and start the slide. *Luck:* Again, that such a man climbs behind me. I will see such eyes like Jack's once more only. During the Korean War, General George Marshall, worn out, resigns as secretary of defense. He calls us regular Pentagon correspondents into his office to tell us. We number about five. By the time of this his final resignation, Marshall has been chief of staff during World War II, made his famous mission to China, and been secretary of state at the creation of the Marshall Plan that revived war-torn Europe. He retired and finally went home. Then in the Korean emergency, he returned as secretary of defense. There he turns an incipient disaster into ultimate triumph.

Now he rocks back and forth in his desk chair, his hands behind his head. "I have spent my life in the service of the state," he says. "And it has brought me some satisfaction." He smiles. He rocks forward. His eyes light up. They could power Washington. They have the same light as Jack's. This time I think: What a gift to end life with such eyes. As much as I can, I will try.

When people who I believe are serious, ask me why anyone would want to spend their lives in the Armed Forces, I tell them about Marshall's eyes, and Jack's. If I guess they read books, I mention "The Tall Soldier" in Crane's *Red Badge of Courage*. Sometimes I think they get it. At other times, I gather they believe I'm a bit nuts.

Nothing that happens in the rest of my time in Ecuador compares with that cliff-face slide. I visit an open-air Indian market several thousand feet up at the foot of the Andes, and fill several pages of my diary with thoughts on the disconnect between wealth and happiness. I get taken by Ecuadorian friends to a round of nightclub drinking while gunfire sounds outside. The big joke in this friendly group is that I could make any one of them president of Ecuador by telling them where I and another miner have hidden the company payroll. Another night, in a hut on the upper reaches of the Guayas River, I am kept awake by vultures landing on the hut's sloping tin roof. Their talons can't get a purchase on the tin. They slide down the roof with a sound like fingernails on a blackboard, greatly amplified, finally slide off the roof and hit the ground with a great thump. This is a rather unique experience, but hardly life enhancing or changing.

I ride in a tug for two days down the Gauyas River between two large barges laden with sacks of gold. The freighter ride home is uneventful. I return home to family a bright yellow with infectious jaundice. I am worried I may be stopped by health inspectors at dockside, so I cover my face with powder to hide the yellow. Fortunately the jaundice is curable, though it keeps me out of Groton for two weeks.

Sixth-form year, my senior year, is the most pleasant I will pass at Groton. I no longer have French, with its killing grades because of my spelling. Mr. Lowenberg twice has me voted onto the Merit List in spite of a disqualifying mark in German because "with dyslexia a 75 for Hadley is the same as a 90 for the average student" — a thought that has escaped the Groton faculty up to that moment. Thanks to Mr Gallien I have a room to myself off his new-boy dormitory and a single study again down the quiet of Library Hall.

I have managed to wangle two tutorials, one with Mr. Gallien on poetry and one with Mr. Lowenberg on educational psychology. The second offers an excuse to discuss all life with Lowenberg. I am captain of the basketball team, the rebuttalist of the debating team, president of the Dramatic Association, and editor in chief of the *Grotonian*. All of which means I don't get much studying done except for the two tutorials, and English and history and now German. I realize that the positions I hold, except for captain of the basketball team, are largely faculty appointments, with student input, rather than the results of votes by my formmates.

My only testing of authority concerns the basketball team. The new headmaster, the Reverend John Crocker, faces a task that would daunt the most talented and experienced administrator. He must make important changes to move Groton into the future, but most graduates and some of the faculty find the school, as is, perfect. They do not want change, and fight against it. I know just the way to help Dr. Crocker, poor man. We already play two famous Boston public high schools in football — English High and Boston Latin. Why not a basketball team from a local high school? Crocker fails to grasp the opportunity.

I have managed to get the *Grotonian* included in the Central Massachusetts Interscholastic Press Association made up of public local high-school magazines. In this organization I become friendly with the principal of the Litttleton Public High School, Mr. Moran. He thinks it a fine idea for his school to play Groton, good for both schools. So I arrange a game and set a date. I go back to Dr. Crocker to tell him Mr. Moran has suggested a game on the nineteenth of February, just a small pick-up game. And that not wishing to be snobbish I had said yes. Should I cancel the game?

I think Dr. Crocker knows I have set him up, but he agrees we should play. I sense the school is a bit surprised when three busloads of not just players but cheerleaders and fans of both sexes arrive that night. But he and Mrs. Crocker become good sports, and after the game take the team into their home for doughnuts, cookies, and soft drinks. However, I know my hopes of a follow-up game with Fitchburg High are dead. In fact there is some talk by conservative members of the faculty that I should be restricted to the Circle, "campused," for the rest of the term.

Only years later do I realize the extent of the problem Crocker faced in pushing for fairly rapid change. When I do, I wish I had sympathized with him more. The Rockefeller Foundation two years before had sent a scholar around to evaluate a number of private preparatory schools. At Groton he happened to interview myself among others. I gathered he was not too taken with the school. Years later I met him and asked him how he had evaluated Groton of that time.

"I kept my feelings private," he said

"And what were those feelings?"

"Casting artificial pearls before genuine swine."

The school year lurches on. Christmas and vacation approach. Which parties and what dances will I go to, and with whom? Then in comes marching *Chance,* and *Choice* follows On Sunday, December 7, 1941, the Japanese attack Pearl Harbor.

Chance

The news of Pearl Harbor and President Roosevelt's speech next day bring me no *Hellzapoppin* moment. No Paul on the road to Damascus insight. I don't immediately realize that the bombs that have just sunk ships and leveled parts of Hawaii have blown holes in my walls. I do not hear "Out, Out, Out" blast loudly through the window of my room off the new-boy dormitory. Yet slowly, slowly, slowly, I begin to realize, without conscious focus or sudden revelation, that the preordained path ahead may change. Certainty can transmute into maybe, mutate even further from a maybe to a perhaps not. I may become a man with hope.

Christmas vacation is what vacations should be and then better. Father is away in Washington as a deputy director of the Office of Facts and Figures, under Archibald MacLeish. On my second afternoon home mother and I go to Carnegie Hall to hear Dimitri Mitropoulos and Rachmaninoff perform a Rachmaninoff concerto. I am struck not only by the music but by the extraordinary faces of both men. That evening I go the Groton–St. Mark's dance. I note in my diary that this vacation is important because it may be the last Christmas vacation I will have. Yale is planning to start freshman year in June, to hold a summer term, and also cut other vacations. Obviously, at this moment Yale still looms ahead.

Father comes up from Washington with stories of the confusion there. It once took him one and one half hours to get a cafeteria lunch. He predicts an eighteen-year war. I spend a great deal of my time wondering which of the two stunning Haynes sisters I am in love with. Father has a crush on the elder, Phyllis, whom he says is

the most gorgeous woman he has ever seen. Meanwhile a new female, Mary Anderson, entrances my eyes. She is the first of my dates
to stand draped in a towel and point out the dress she wants me to
bring her from the closet. I am amazed at the transformation of the
dress when draped upon her. Christmas comes and goes. One night,
my parents out, I invite my childhood friend from the Glen Cove
summer play group, Larry Hughes, for dinner. We have oysters, rack
of lamb, wine, cheese, and Swedish pancakes, then go on to a play,
Noel Coward's *Blythe Spirit*. Mr. and Mrs. Haynes throw a New
Year's party at La Rue, a popular nightclub, so wonderful that I can
still remember individual moments. I go to Washington and spend
two pleasant days with Father. We take the train together back to
New York. More parties and dances, a final dinner with Mother, a
good night's sleep, and back to Groton.

Choice

Nothing changes, yet, during vacation, something has changed. Like
Sandburg's fog, the fact that war may give me a *Choice* drifts in on
little cat feet. I do not have to go to Yale, I do not have to become a
lawyer or teacher. I do not have to miss life. My diary reports that
three months after Pearl Harbor on March 16, two weeks after returning to school, I am talking to Fred Whitridge, visiting Groton
from Yale, about college or the Army. Two days later, I ask my
friendly master, Mr. Gallien for advice. He strongly urges Yale.

During spring vacation, on March 23, I talk to Larry Hughes. I
explain my fears that if I go to college I will miss out on life. (Judging
from diary entries of that time, "life" translates as "girls," a euphe-
mism for "sex.") On March 24, I go to 90 Church Street in lower
Manhattan to ask the Navy and Army recruiting officers there if I
must go to college to become an officer. The Navy recruiter says
"Yes." The Army officer answers with a definite "No." At the end of
vacation, April 3, I write in my diary, "I am inclined to run around in
great big glorious circles, probably one reason I am going into the
Army." Back at school on April 8, I talk to Ward Goodenough, a boy
five years ahead of me whom I greatly admire. He has been in the
Army five months, is now a corporal, and is back at Groton for a

visit. He assures me the Army, in selecting officers, does not give a damn about whether you have been to college.

Duty and guilt are also part of *Choice*. I know I am privileged. Should I sit this one out? Isaiah heard the Lord say, "Who shall we send and who shall go for us?" And he replied, "Lord, here am I, send me." Should I reply, "Send someone else, Lord. I am going to Yale?" Do I get to live behind Jack Malcolm's eyes that way? Alan Pifer, a friend four years ahead of me and who, like myself, won the poetry prize twice, writes me he is leaving Harvard to enter the Army in tank operations.

Whatever the inner and outer weave my *Choice* is set. A letter from my father dated April 21 thanks me for my "fine letter" on my decision to join the Army. He still thinks I should go to college, but I must make up my own mind. Years afterward, talking with Jane, I once said it was more difficult for her to get out than me. I always had some cash to fall back upon. "No," she said, "you had the more difficult time. Your life was so seductive." This is the first great time I flip the coin.

Now the sixty-four-million-dollar question, my *Gretchenfrage*. How free is my *Choice* of the Army over Yale? Back then I thought and felt the decision totally free. All the power and advice falls on the college side. On April 30, Dean Edward Noyes, the admissions officer at Yale, writes, "We shall be glad to keep your application on file, but I trust that on maturer consideration you will decide to come to college after all." None of my friends are making my same choice. I alone in my class will enter the Army on graduation. William Grey, our class senior prefect and a good friend, thought he might also join up. My diary reports, "Bill Grey's father gives him a brand-new Chrysler convertible with trimmings. Thereby washing out any effective agitation on Bill's part for going into the Army."

Only Robert Lovett, now secretary of war for air, advises rather than exhorts. If I am to join, he writes, he would advise against my choice of the paratroopers. They are fine soldiers, but many of the best college graduates and athletes are choosing the airborne. The competition there for OCS, Officer Candidate School, for everyone, and particularly for someone my age, would be especially tough. On the other hand, the tank corps, newly named the armored force, badly needs officers. They have just completed a large maneuver in Louisiana, where they were lost most of the time. If I enlist in the armored force, I will see just as much combat, contribute just as much, and have a better chance to become an officer.

Still the question remains: Did *Fate* play a part in my "free" choice? If so, how large a part? What velvet-gloved power did the genes in my double helix deploy? Had I been born rebellious? Did those contrary genes, reinforced by eighteen year's experience, now make the Army not the hard free choice that I believe, but the predictably easy way out? Seven year later reading *The Kinsey Report* while at Yale, I will discover that my sex drive is toward the top end of the curve. I mention this not to cast myself as an epic stud. I remain a shy man, happily married in every way for twenty-seven years. But I am trying here to tease out honest answers. Part of my *Fate*, my genes at birth, could lie embedded in some part of my "free" *Choice*. I had heard, and in part believed, that once you put on a uniform you just had to stand on a corner and fight them off. Whoever told me that was a liar.

And from were came the arrogant belief that I would become an officer? A small mouse crumb describes my knowledge of the world. If asked to write anything, my handwriting and spelling would scream "high school dropout" I will turn eighteen the day I enlist. I have never been particularly popular with many of my classmates. While in excellent shape, I am just six feet tall and no poster athlete. Yet I believe I will go in as a private and come out an officer. Did my genes produce that confidence? Had they made the war canoe, the lifeguard's action at the plane crash, and Jack Malcolm's eyes so powerfully important? Neither Groton nor my family had nourished my self-confidence.

Looking back, I believe my *Choice* almost totally free. The length of time before I realized I even had a *Choice* argues for that conclusion. Even if the double helix deployed its genetic tentacles, their threads were few and weak. I flipped the coin. I made a *Choice*.

My choice for the Army set, the rest of school flashes by. I seem to have studied for I get nineties and eighty-fives, except for the usual trouble with German. I pass the last set of examinations that I will ever take at Groton, pack my trunk, help the former new kids pack theirs, and say good-bye to Groton friends, favorite masters, and the school. I have twelve days before I turn eighteen. I plan to take a week's more vacation after that. Swimming, sleeping, eating, loafing, seeing old friends, and debutante parties fill up most of my time. I also buy and study sample tests recommended to help one in scoring high on the Army Classification Tests. They work. I even score well on mathematics and mechanical engineering. I realize I do not know how to make a really neat bed and get the upstairs maid to show me. On the advice of some old-timer I get a short but good-looking hair cut so I will not have to have my head shaved as a new recruit. Robert Lovett comes over for dinner with distressing news about the war's lack of progress. At times I find myself quite depressed and unhappy over the size of the leap I will take.

Aside from the girls, my standout memory of the "deb" parties is the same about two of them, one in Connecticut the other on Long Island. At both these parties town and state police have been hired to watch over things. As the dances break up around two A.M., many of the boys and men come out drunk. The police take their car keys, get their cars for them, and point the cars toward the driveway. Then help the drunks into their cars. You can hear the tires screech as the drunks negotiate the turn from the driveway onto the main road. I guess the cops figured if the rich SOBs wanted to kill themselves, so what?

I have a day of lunch and sailing alone with Mary Anderson. Then a final family supper, all my favorites: soft-shell crabs, straw potatoes, fresh corn, Swedish pancakes, and Champagne.

The next day, a week after my eighteenth birthday, I pass my Army physical. Then on to Governor's Island in New York Harbor. There I raise my right hand and swear the oath. I become Private Arthur Hadley 12091009, a tanker. I have dropped my middle initial: "T" for Twining. One small letter, a tiny part of me, but still, in such a way as 12091009, I begin new.

THREE

LUCK, LUCK, MORE LUCK, NOT ALL GOOD, CHOICE, AND FATE

In the Army, as in any large organization, *Fate* and *Choice* play but a tiny part in life. The Army does not care who you are or what you choose to want. You exist to fill the Army's needs, not the Army to honor your *Choice*. *Chance* and *Luck* take over. On entrance to Army life, one major *Choice* does appear, brilliantly outlined by A. E. Houseman.

> To stand up straight and tread the turning mill,
> To lie flat and know nothing and be still,
> Are the two trades of man; and which is worse
> I know not, but I know that both are ill.

Having herded myself into the Army on flimsy evidence and wishful logic that I would become an officer, I cannot *Choose* "To lie flat and know nothing and be still." However, during the first week at the Army Reception Center, Camp Upton, on Long Island, I do little standing tall. I am too busy on KP, bending over filthy garbage cans to clean them with live steam. Several times, off in a corner of the garbage shed, the eighteen-year-old cries secretly. Not just from the work but also from the way I and my clothes smell at night. I believe I may have fantasized my ability to get to OCS and become an officer. These stinking cans are my Army future.

I do learn new rules. Cleaning garbage cans with me one day is a forlorn young Spanish-speaking man who keeps burning himself with the steam. When it comes time to stop cleaning the cans and pick up dirty plates, he stacks an incredible number of plates on his arm. "Well, anyway," I tell him sarcastically, "you'd make a great waiter."

He looks at me and beams. "You think so. You think so. That's what I tell 'em. But they say I only good for busboy."

"No, no," I say, smiling reassurance this time. "You'd make a great waiter." And as for you, Arthur, shut that Groton-privileged mouth and learn the world. Two weeks later, when I arrive at Fort Knox for thirteen weeks of basic training as a tanker, I have mastered a basic strategy. Keep quiet and team up with older men who understand the rules. In order to survive at home and Groton I have become something of a chameleon. Now I watch the old soldiers at work and on parade, and try, at least outwardly, to become them.

After a few weeks at Knox, I find the Army more pleasant and easy going than Groton. I am not being facetious. The Army has definite rules of conduct and behavior, and punishment for violations is severe; but the rules are few and none are hidden. We get most weekends off. What we are taught and study is important in our lives, even to our life. The World War I Army commander in France, General Pershing, ordered Army trainers in America to send him "Men who can shoot and salute." Following these precepts we train to become disciplined soldiers who are good at our jobs. I find I get along well. Though still concerned about my future, I turn happy.

Fate and *Luck*

Unknown to me, a small portion of *Fate*, and two portions of *Luck*, shower blessings. The small portion of Luck happens the afternoon of my first day, during my enlistment interviews. Everyone in the Army who is not fighting, gets a ten-minute break at the end of every hour. Then everyone can relax, smoke if they want, or just stand around. As I sit down before the officer who will examine my background, a ten-minute break starts. I and the interviewer get to chatting. When the break expires and the examination begins he asks me what I did before deciding to enter the army.

I answer, "I was a student."

"Oh, don't say that," he says. "Students and lawyers, that's what we've got too much of." The interview is taking place on Governors Island, part of New York City. "Haven't you ever done anything else?"

"Well, I worked in Ecuador as an apprentice mining engineer."

"Mining engineer, I haven't seen one of those in the year and a half I've been doing these interviews. I'll have to ask you some questions." He reaches behind his back to pull down a great book. The book is obviously full of questions about jobs to trip unskilled bullshit artists. He asks me the difference between a raise and a stope and what is a work and fill stope? These simple questions I can answer. He puts me down as a mining engineer on the basic card, one copy of which goes to Washington, while the duplicate follows me throughout my service. He also asks me if I know any foreign languages. I answer that I have spent three summers in France and taken a bicycle trip through the French countryside. He puts me down on the same card as fluent in French.

I think no more of either of these answers, but at various times in the next four years I will see people pause as they review my record and say, "Oh, mining engineer, that must have been an interesting job." Or, "You must have seen quite a bit of life before you entered the service." The French answer will redirect my Army career.

Luck

Important *Luck:* The date at which I enter the Army greatly affects my life once inside. The Army is now expanding rapidly and so is short of officers, particularly in the combat arms, tanks, infantry, artillery, and cavalry. Some early military disasters in Africa occur while I am at Fort Knox in basic training. The Army's need for more lieutenants becomes desperate. Two years later, after the disaster of the Battle of the Bulge, when my classmates who elected college are hastily drafted off their campuses, the Army has slight need of officers a but great need for private foot soldiers. Those drafted then are rushed into combat with minimal training and little hope of promotion. Their experiences bear no relation to mine.

Fate

The small portion of *Fate* does not do much for my Army career, but makes my life more pleasant. My mother has a Vassar classmate living in Louisville, the city outside Fort Knox. That friend has a friend, Mrs. James Bruce, wife of Doctor James Bruce, the premier pediatrician of Louisville. The Bruces's have three daughters; the two oldest bracket my age. Mrs. Bruce writes me to please come to stay with them some weekend when I can get off. I do. I must have passed muster, for I get invited back. In the end they even give me a door key so I can come and stay when they are away.

This means that weekends away from Army life, instead of desperately looking for excitement, I find rest and fun. The Bruces are loving and kind; Dr. Bruce one of the wisest and most dedicated of men I will ever know. I meet friends of the Bruces. On weekends I go waterskiing on the Ohio River and to dances at the country club. Interesting people, many with Army know-how, offer me advice and places to stay. One of these, Margie Foresyth, an exciting and wise blond, is daughter of the colonel commanding Fort Knox, an old-time cavalry man turned tanker. I will meet Margie again, when covering the Pentagon for *Newsweek* during the Korean War, I interview her husband, Major James Camp. He invites me to their home, and they both become and remain among Jane's and my very close friends. Margie's tales of growing up as a small girl in the Philippines, where her father commanded a horse cavalry battalion are fascinating and describe experiences from another world. *Luck* will even bring Jim, now a general, and I, a reporter for *Playboy* magazine, to Vietnam at the same time. He helps make my stay "in country" easier and more productive.

At the end of nine weeks' basic training our platoon sergeant, Joe Wolf, lines up our training platoon and we play "Simon Says." Wolf is regular Army and muscular, with some twenty years' experience. He has been a first sergeant several times and then broken back to private for drink, then climbed the promotion ladder again. He is tough, rigid, and does not play favorites.

Simon Says is a game where you don't execute a command unless "Simon" says to do so. This is more difficult than you might think. For example if Simon says, "hand salute," you bring your right hand up to just above your right eye, fingers extended, and then bring it down sharply, slapping your thigh.

But if Simon says, "by the numbers hand salute," you stand still. "By the numbers" and "hand salute" are separate commands. All Simon has said is "by the numbers," which means each part of the command must be exercised separately. Simon said nothing about a "hand salute." The sleepy, the overanxious, or those who have not payed attention in previous Simon says exercises have their hand above their eye. They must drop out. When Simon says, "hand salute," your still don't move because "by the numbers" is on and that makes "hand salute" a two-part order. You must wait for "Simon says one." Up comes the hand. After that it can start to get tricky. The three finalists in this game, of which I am one, Wolf makes corporals.

Does this method work? One of the other new corporals, Andrew Panda, is certainly the best soldier in the platoon, and one of the finest men I will meet in my life. A twenty-two-year-old steel worker, he is athletic, has educated himself, has presence, and wants to be a good soldier. The other man selected is a pleasant and thoughtful man who, in civilian life, was a pianist. As for myself, my command of a squad of twenty newly enlisted soldiers as an eighteen-year-old corporal remains my toughest Army assignment. More importantly, I am on my way. Those who make corporal while in basic training, if they wish and have luck, will soon go before the OCS selection board. Three weeks before Christmas, Corporal Hadley, now an old soldier, a trainer and not a trainee, goes before the OCS selection board.

As an eighteen-year-old I am questioned thoroughly. What job would I like if I graduate from OCS? Answer: "Platoon leader." That is the answer they want to hear and also the truth. Why? I tell them I joined to Army to become a platoon leader. What would I do if someone is bleeding to death in my tank during battle? "I continue the firefight. If I stop to take care of my wounded crew member, many others may be killed. If he is bleeding to death, stopping will not help." I make it through the board. My shoes gleam. I have made it a point to read the newspapers so I know how the war progresses. That I was captain of my school basketball team and now play on one of the Fort Knox basketball teams certainly helps.

Choice

I make a *Choice* before the OCS board that will rearrange my Army career. When asked which Officer Candidate School I wish to attend I reply, "Tank Destroyer at Fort Hood, Texas." As I feared, that surprises the board. The preferred answer would have been Armor at Fort Knox. But I have learned that the schedule of classes for Armor OCS means that I would spend the last two weeks of OCS out in the open, in an individual pup tent, at Fort Knox, Kentucky during February. February is a miserable, snowy, cold, wet month at Knox. No place for an eighteen-year-old still susceptible to colds. I have heard from old timers the February weather in Texas is all right.

Personally I would have preferred the Cavalry OCS at Fort Riley, Kansas. But the Cavalry and Armor branches of the Army are feuding. (Will tanks really replace horses?) There is no room for a soldier from Fort Knox at Cavalry OCS until next June. I understand the Army enough to know a soldier's world can change beyond recognition in six months. It is too dangerous to wait for Cavalry OCS.

The tank destroyer opening is the week after Christmas. I tell the board I hear the tank destroyers are expanding fast and need platoon leaders. They give me tank destroyers. Without knowing, I have not only picked an easy OCS, but reorganized my Army future. In a year tank destroyers will be found a flawed concept and the number of tank destroyer units greatly reduced. Like many unneeded tank destroyers officers, I will be shuttled about to finally end up making loudspeaker broadcasts and firing leaflets at German troops.

But first I have to get through OCS. I follow my rules, get close to those who know, watch, and listen. Three days after Christmas, two days before my OCS class starts, I stand beneath a hot shower at Fort Hood, Texas, scrubbing brush, laundry soap, and boots in hand. I listen to Homer, a fellow candidate from Texas. Homer, an accomplished soldier, has already served six years as a Cavalry Platoon sergeant before he came to OCS. He also has brush, soap, and boots in hand. He has explained to me how to get a super shine on our boots. First we have to scrub out all the dubbing, the grease we have put on our boots previously to make them waterproof, as dubbing inhibits a gleaming shine. Then we will leave our boots on the radiators all night to open their leather pores. Tomorrow, the day before OCS starts, we will put on four coats of two different types of polish. Homer has brought his with him and I have just bought the same polishes at the post exchange. I recall Dr. Lowenberg's warning as I left Groton: my shoes will be more important than my thoughts. My shoes are not found wanting during the entire thirteen weeks of OCS.

The shine on my mess kit draws praise from the old Cavalry sergeant. I do not reveal my secret. I have taken my mess kit to Tiffany's to be shined on the jeweler's wheel. They have warned me there is a problem with the shine. They have sealed it with a special formula to make the shine last. That substance will peal in heat and be poisonous. Thirteen weeks without hot food. I can make it. Fortunately, much of the time we eat in mess halls off plates. At others I make do with a sandwich. I note a few old-time soldiers have an extra plate hidden somewhere beneath their shirts. I am not secure enough to do this.

Groton and Fort Knox combine to give me a fairly easy time at

OCS. Many tank destroyer weapons are the same as those in Armor and I have learned by heart their characteristics. Just out of school, I am more used to studying and memorizing than most other candidates. Debating has taught me to think fast on my feet and speak well. At graduation I learn I have the highest academic average, but to my great surprise, and here that trite phrase is freighted with meaning, "the profound disgrace," the Groton misfit, is elected by his classmates "Outstanding Candidate."

Two of my OCS classmates I meet again after the war. Chris Gaus is the oldest student in the class, at thirty-eight over twice my age. The son of a famous Princeton dean, Chris, a six-foot-two man with grayish hair and a deep base voice, just missed World War I. Determined not to miss World War II he volunteered into the Army. We had met and talked through one whole night back at Fort Knox when we were sergeants of the guard, sharing the same guard room, though from different battalions. He became a lawyer in New York City and we visit occasionally, as we used to eat in the same restaurant.

The other, Hugh McKinley, after vanishing for a time, and his wife, Evelyn, become lifelong friends of Jane and myself. He is the only all-American football player that ever graduated from Reed College in Oregon, a very progressive institution. He is my closest friend at OCS and my choice for outstanding candidate. After OCS we share a tent with two other classmates at the 666 Tank Destroyer Battalion at Camp Hood, to which we and many of our classmates are also assigned. When I am transferred to the 21st Tank Destroyer Group at another post, I lose track of Hugh. Then, on a book tour in California plugging *The Invisible Primary* in 1977, the station conducting my interview takes a phone call. It's from the city manager of San Diego, Hugh McKinley. Am I the Hadley who was at TD OCS in early 1943? We talk.

I stop off to see him. He tells me that Johnson, one of our four tent mates, like himself became an Infantry officer, and was killed a few yards from him during the Battle of the Bulge. Six years later our daughter Caroline leaves teaching in New York City to become part of the publicity department for the San Diego Globe Theater. Jane and I visit her several times a year and the friendship with the McKinleys flourishes.

After I graduate from OCS, 1943 and the first half of 1944 are downhill and difficult for new 2nd Lieutenant Hadley. The newly formed 666 Tank Destroyer Battalion , to which I am first assigned, will never go overseas, and in the end is broken up to become a truck company. The problem with the tank destroyer concept strikes again. For some reason after a few months in the 666, I am transferred out of the battalion into the 21st TD (tank destroyer) Group. The TD Group is another flawed concept. Most are broken up toward the end of the war for officer replacements.

The 21st TD Group moves to Camp Shelby, Mississippi, a heat-baked camp and home of an Infantry Division and two tank destroyer battalions. I, who desperately want to go overseas, am made Special Services Officer, in charge of sports and entertainment. Pictures of me from that time show a sullen, frowning, unhappy face. I am certain Europe will be invaded soon and I will miss all the action. My Groton classmates at least are in college, learning something and moving ahead. I assume that many of my OCS classmates have gone overseas already as replacements. They may have seen or are about to see a great deal of action, and be promoted. I am inspecting athletic equipment.

Fate and Choice

I don't want to die without knowing firsthand about sex. But my methods of finding out are constricted by my upbringing and education.

The result, I marry a young debutante who has just graduated from an elite girl's school. She is a striking woman, crazy, and romantic enough to marry a second lieutenant in Mississippi rather than go to college. We live in a tiny two-room ground-floor apartment in the junior officers quarters, in Camp Shelby, Mississippi, cooking on a coal stove. The heat is constant, even at night. There are no window screens. Little kids peer through the windows. She and the other wives have little in common except boredom. She cries a lot. I do not blame her. I recognize I am in a disaster.

Chance and Luck

Two weeks after D-day both *Chance* and *Luck* strike. *Chance:* The break out from the D-day beaches is not going as fast as planned. The Army finds itself desperately short of French speakers. *Luck:* My interviewer at the induction center in New York City, the one who put me down as a mining engineer, also reported me as fluent in French. The newly created punch cards, great-great-grand-fathers of the computer, find me out. An order from Washington arrives detaching this miserable second lieutenant from the 21st TD Group and ordering him and his wife to the Intelligence Center at Camp Ritchie, Maryland. The order's force is such I even get to buy four new tires for my car, otherwise a wartime impossibility.

I hope this means I will be sent to France immediately. And sur-prisingly, after a few military hiccups, I am. My wife and I arrive at Camp Ritchie, which is a well-constructed, luxurious by Army stan-dards, prewar camp in the hills of northern Maryland. Postwar pres-idents will make their summer homes close by. My wife and I rent a nice, small house near the camp. Then comes the first hiccup: At my interview two days later it is immediately obvious that I do not speak French well enough to qualify as a French speaker. I suggest that since I cannot do that, how about sending me to Europe as a replace-ment tank destroyer or Armor officer? No. I am firmly told I am now in Intelligence and must remain in Intelligence. The second hiccup: I am ordered to train as a photo interpreter. Once trained, I will be flown to Europe or the Pacific to sit safely in the rear, look at aerial photographs and explain to others what they mean. I flunk the eye-sight examination. I again suggest assignment to Europe. No, again. I must remain in Intelligence.

Luck

Two weeks later I am assigned to something called the Fifth MRB, the Fifth Mobile Radio Broadcasting Company. What is that? No one at Ritchie is quite sure, but it is part of intelligence and located in a secret camp called Sharp, just a few miles from Ritchie. The rules say I must live at Sharp on the post. My screams and protests accomplish what lieutenant's screams and protests usually do in the Army: nothing. I say good-bye to my wife of four months. She drives off in our car. The Fifth MRB sends a jeep to pick me up. No whisper on the wind, no change in my heart rate, no prickle of premonition on the back of my hands to tell me that *Luck* has just dealt me an extraordinary gift. In fact, next to meeting Jane, her greatest gift.

To begin, the Fifth MRB is leaving for France in five days. All is confusion. Confusion is endemic to the Fifth MRB, its men and officers. Most have been selected for their fluency in German or radio-repair expertise. Many have not even been through basic training or fired their rifles or pistols. A few like myself are present by pure accident. Others were foisted off on the the Fifth MRB from units wishing to get rid of their foul-ups and oddballs. Orders are usual obeyed in the Fifth MRB, but only after international negotiations. The company has supposedly been trained to make radio and loudspeaker broadcasts to the Germans, and also write and fire leaflets at them.

My second day confirms the unit's uniqueness. Some months before, a civilian contractor has erected the company's eighty-foot radio tower. Now the tower must be dropped and packed for France. The raised tower is bolted together in two-foot steel sections, each section secured to the one above and the one below by four large bolts in each corner. A rigger with his safety belt girdling the tower must climb to the tower's top and take the tower down heavy section by heavy section. The Fifth MRB only has two riggers. They turn out never to have rigged or unrigged anything. They are heroic Norwegian sailors who escaped from Norway in a small boat that they sailed across the North Sea to Scotland. The Fifth MRB captain calls for volunteers. The Norwegian sailors, myself, and two German-language speakers do so. By the end of the day we manage to get down three or four sections. It becomes obvious the tower will not be ready to go to Europe. Not even half ready.

The bottom of the tower pivots on a huge single bolt. Perhaps we can swing the whole tower down side wise on that bolt. None of us knows, but we have no real choice. We are not going to be ready doing as we are. We cannot ask for help because our overseas move is classified top secret. With care we line up trucks, winches, and attach wires to parts of the tower. The massed truck engines roar. The tower swings forward. The tower hesitates. The tower collapses in a crumbled broken mass resembling a heap of gigantic bent and severed hairpins. "There goes somebody's war bond," remarks the first sergeant. The captain gathers a task force to cover the debacle with paperwork. If Adolph Hitler had spies watching the Fifth Mobile Radio Broadcasting Company, he would have had reason to hope for victory.

The Fifth MRB actually makes it to Great Britain safely. After all, we are not in command of the ancient, remodeled tramp freighter into which we are crammed. None of us is let near the engine room. In Britain the Fifth MRB merges with the already arrived Fourth MRB. The merged units then divide up into teams that will be attached to various Army headquarters to do their assigned work. As the war progresses and more of Europe gets liberated, some will go to Eisenhower's Supreme Headquarters in Versailles to write leaflets, some will go to Paris or Luxemburg to run major radio stations, others to various prisoner-of-war cages to provide intelligence on German morale. There is no doubt where I will go. I am both the "new guy" and the "dirty boot" guy of the units. I will go with the Ninth Army Detachment; there I will fire at the Germans the leaflets others write. Also, if the moment is opportune, make an occasional loudspeaker broadcast to frontline German troops.

Luck

There is no way I could know at the time, but I could not have designed a better or more fulfilling military job for myself. I am usually off alone, going where I want to go, firing leaflets over a whole Army front, an area about two hours fast drive in length, and now and then making a loudspeaker broadcast. The job can be dangerous but not continually so. I am more like a bomber or fighter pilot than a ground combat soldier. I have moments of extreme danger, but am safe most of the time. My life has nowhere near the hardship and continuous risk borne by each infantryman in his exposed foxhole under artillery fire and in hostile contact twenty-four hours every day. Of the six of us doing roughly the same leaflet and loudspeaker work in France and later Germany, only two are killed, one wounded. I will do this job, or one like it, for ten months.

I distrust most war memoirs. Battle facts are illusive and the tellers often prejudiced. There are some great memoir-novels. To unfairly single out four favorites of mine, for ground combat: *All Quiet on the Western Front* by Erich Maria Remarque, also *The Forgotten Soldier* by Guy Sajer, and not to slight the Navy *Das Boat* by Lothar-Günther Buchheim, and *The Cruel Sea* by Nicholas Monsarrat. But all too often the loud are heard while those who have done more remain silent. I will make an effort to get around this problem by quoting from military reports or newspaper articles about my work. I will restrict my own descriptions to technical details about how the work was done, the two exceptions being where I am changed by *Luck*.

For the preparation and firing of leaflets, here is one part of a citation from the Ninth Army Psychological Warfare Headquarters:

> HEADQUARTERS NINTH U.S. ARMY
> SUBJECT: Commendation
> THRU: P & PW Officer 12th Army Group
> TO: 1st Lieutenant Arthur Hadley, TD.
> You organized the Artillery section of the Psychological Warfare Detachment and it functioned so well under your direction that many commanders and staff officers praised its efficient operation.

To expand this brief text with technical detail: The firing of leaflet shells begins with finding smoke shells in which to put the leaflets. There are no special leaflet shells. Finding smoke shells gets easier as the war progresses and better records are kept about what kind of shells are where in which vast ammunition dump. Next I must find an officer at Army headquarters who has the authority to release the smoke shells to me and is willing to do so. Next I must find a dry, unused barn for the four soldiers in my artillery section to open up the smoke shells and put in leaflets, without getting the shell's powder so damp they will not fire. Opening the smoke shells requires stands and special wrenches that have to be made. Then the smoke canisters must be removed from the smoke shells and the printed leaflets properly folded so they not only go into the now-empty shells but also come out readable when the shells explode to blow out the leaflets. Then the former smoke shells, now leaflet shells, must get to the 105mm artillery guns that will fire them. Finally the officers commanding the guns must be persuaded to actually fire them.

The methods used by earlier units to do all this have not been successful. In my little sphere of action I am in command. No one really understands what I am doing. I can change what happens and where it happens, and I do. That is mainly what is behind the commendation, but is only part of the work. The artillery units must be persuaded not merely to shoot the leaflets but to fire them accurately at the enemy units for which they are written. This part is also the most interesting. I begin with the Corps Fire Direction Centers, of which there are three to an Army, then go to the Fire Direction Centers of Divisions, of which there are three to a corps, then to the Battalion Fire Direction Centers, of which there are three to a division. At each step down the line, I give a brief explanation of what I am doing and hand out leaflets and translations all around. I also have leaflets and translations stuffed into the tops of the leaflet shell cases to motivate the gunners doing the work.

I end up at the front lines with the lieutenant forward observers at their observation points (OP). There with them, often under fire, I fire the leaflets at specific German targets. In all this my training in armor and tank destroyers becomes an incredible bonus. In an organization of propaganda experts, German speakers and printers, I alone know how the Army is organized, how to talk to the concerns and strengths of officers at various levels of command from the generals and colonels at Army and corps to lieutenants adjusting artillery fire. Or to soldiers helping me get loudspeakers forward to where the enemy can hear them. And at the same time set them in places where no one in the area gets killed when the Germans try to shut up the loudspeakers by shelling them.

I admit to occasional subterfuge. The Germans sometimes fire their leaflets at our frontline soldiers. These leaflets almost invariably picture nude, beautiful women in sexual acts with civilians. Beneath the picture the text reads roughly as follows: "This is what is happening to your wife, Johnny, while the rich stay home." I get Army headquarters to issue an order that such leaflets are to be turned over to the artillery psychological warfare officer for expert study. As I suspected, some Army outfits are so conditioned to obedience that they actually turn in their sexy leaflets. Not many, but a few. I take these leaflets around to the headquarters of artillery units that complain about firing my leaflets. Their officers wish I could get them some of these sexy German leaflets to show the folks back home, after the war of course. I reply that while I do have some surplus sexy German leaflets, I give most of them to units that fire a lot of my own leaflets. I don't mention the ones promised to the guys at Army headquarters who issued the order.

"That's us. That's us. We fire a lot," they say.

"Sir, I'm not sure."

"Oh yes, Lieutenant. We are about to step up our leaflet firing. We like your leaflets. They're effective."

As I have already noted, Army rules are simpler and easier to understand than those at Groton.

Luck and Luck Alone

Mid-September, a straight stretch of country road in the rolling hills of southeast Holland between Sittard and Roermond, just east of a small bend in the Mass River. The autumn mist keeps rising and falling, a cover through which we six officers silently walk. I am looking for a place to possibly get close enough to German lines to make a loudspeaker broadcast or find an observation point from which I can fire leaflets. The other five with me are checking out the ground. They are from a Cavalry unit that has just moved into this thinly held part of the front.

I hear the sharp whistle of incoming shells and throw myself against the grassy verge without even time to make the drainage ditch. When I pick myself up after the shells explode, I see fresh white scars on the already mutilated trees lining the road. Of the five walking with me two are unhurt. One slightly wounded. Two seriously. One of these two is dying. The blue-white death color rising to his face as we, the unhurt, rip open bandages.

My jump had been no faster, farther, wiser than the others. *Luck* had decided. I had already mentally accepted the importance of *Luck*. From now on I physically feel its power. I live in *Luck*'s kingdom. There are actions I can take to move about inside his Kingdom to places more or less secure. But I cannot leave his land. While war lasts, I am his indentured servant.

Choice

In the kingdom of *Luck*, *Choice* is still possible. The Hastenrath church tower dominates both its small farming town and the surrounding fields between the Mass and the Roer rivers. The tower is full of large holes. The Germans realize we use it as an observation post from which to adjust artillery fire and from time to time they pound it with shells to discourage the practice. I climb up the ladders and broken walls inside the tower, carefully avoiding the gaps in the tower walls where the Germans might glimpse me. Crouched on a wooden beam almost at the top is another lieutenant, a forward observer from one of the corp's artillery battalions. I introduce myself, unsling my radio, set up the proper frequency, and tell him I am here to fire leaflets. He is not happy.

As I begin to adjust leaflet fire, the Germans range on the church with high-velocity cannon. One shot hits the towers base and the whole structure shakes. The lieutenant urges me to stop firing the damn leaflets before German fire collapses the whole tower. But I have read several months before, while still in the States, that if taken under fire while adjusting artillery, you should not stop. The Germans will then be certain where you are and shell the hell out of you. I keep firing. After working us over a few long minutes more, the Germans shift their fire to the church tower in the next town. I quit firing leaflets. The Germans clobber the other tower. The Hastenrath tower becomes a strong symbol of *Choice*. Knowledge plus *Choice* helps toward survival. After the war I will read in a speech by

Werner Heisenberg, "We can only use our powers to maximize our chances." I recognize that map.

I am always acutely conscious that my life is easier than those for whom I make broadcasts and fire leaflets. These soldiers are living in harm's way day and night, in fields and towns I only visit. And among those living there are men who by conscious choice are brave. Brave beyond the wildest fictions of Hollywood. One lieutenant colonel of the Second Armored, who became a postwar friend, had five tanks shot out from underneath him in one day. And the bravest were often those killed first. One thing wars do, good wars, better wars, wrong wars is break your heart. As Keith Douglas wrote after the Battle of El Alamain:

> How can I live among this gentle,
> obsolescent breed of heroes and not weep?

I called this land, where others live all the time and I just visit, "The Instant Easy Gone," part of *Luck's* Kingdom where it is routine, "easy," to make or become a ghost.

When I cannot give more help to those living there I experience failure, guilt, and impotence that still haunt me, though my nightmares stopped in the 1960s. The Merzenhausen cross road is such a moment. About a quarter of a mile beyond this cross road, a regiment of the 29th Infantry Division is attacking toward a small group of buildings. I am close to certain I can get the Germans in those buildings to surrender with a loudspeaker broadcast. I have the speaker ready to be carried forward in the back of my jeep. But I cannot get permission from the colonel running the attack to make such a broadcast. I am a young lieutenant he does not know. I lack people skills. Loudspeakers are still new and suspect. Many broadcasts produce no prisoners but draw heavy fire from the Germans. We loudspeaker personnel can pack up and leave. The infantry men have to remain and suffer the shelling. I try twice to persuade the colonel, but get a commanding brush off each time. I still believe I should have been able to make the broadcast.

•   •   •

Lighter moments do happen in "The Instant Easy Gone." One item of my uniform causes stares. By regulation everyone must wear on their left shoulder the distinctive shoulder patch of their unit, usually their division. The Second Armored, the Fourth Infantry, the 75th Infantry, etc. I'm attached to Ninth Army in Germany. But because the 5th MRB, my parent unit, is with SHAFE, General Eisenhower's Supreme Headquarters Allied Forces Europe in Versailles, these regulations dictate that I must wear a SHAFE patch, a flaming sword on a blue shield, as if I were on Ike's staff back in France. To put it mildly, such patches are seldom if ever seen in the circles where I travel.

In Julich, the Germans hold out for several months in a sports stadium. I have my usual hope that maybe I can get them to surrender some night with a loudspeaker broadcast. I visit that section of the front in daylight to find if there is some way I can sneak my loudspeaker close. It's a quiet day with a bit of mist bringing safety. I run, zigzagging forward, taking cover from time to time in someone's foxhole. One such hole is occupied by a grizzled and very senior first sergeant. He has one of those unique Southern, Scotch-Irish farm faces that radiate tough, no-nonsense power. When you see one of those sergeants you know he will take good care of you, but do not ever cross him. As I jump into his foxhole he checks me out with an unfriendly stare. Who, or even what, is this strange young lieutenant who has leapt into his hole? Then he spots the SHAFE patch. He throws himself theatrically against his foxhole side.

"SHAFE, Jesus Christ Lieutenant, SHAFE. Does General Eisenhower know you're lost?" Later, covering Eisenhower for *Newsweek*, I tell this to the president. He has a great laugh.

The cold winter of 1944–45 drags on. The Germans are repulsed at the Battle of the Bulge. Their Siegfried line is finally breached, the Allied Armies reach the Rhine. A heroic OSS agent, Alex Samarepa, mounts a loudspeaker on a Third Armored Division tank. He is unfortunately killed two weeks later. I mount a loudspeaker on a Second Armored Division tank. If only I had been able to a mount a loudspeaker on a tank in June of '44 not March of '45, how many lives might I have saved? Along with the loudspeaker and spares, I have two fine sergeants: William Plice, an electrician who keeps the speakers working, and Walter Freund, a German speaker. Both courageous men. Plice will leave the safety of our tank to save my life. Freund has quit a soft job in Versailles to work on loudspeakers with me.

Again, to quote official documents appears a reliable way to describe the "talking tank." The first is from the Headquarters Ninth U.S. Army report quoted before on the work of the Artillery Section:

> During the drive to the Elbe River in Germany as Commander of a light tank Public Address you contributed greatly to the rapid advance of the armored spearhead by your initiative, sound judgment, and coolness under hostile fire. The rapid reduction of road blocks and the prompt surrender of towns and villages was facilitated by your actions, thus reducing casualties.

The second report, less official in sound, is from the American Army newspaper *Stars and Stripes* of April 13:

> WITH THE NINTH ARMY SPEARHEAD
> First Lt. Arthur Hadley is assigned from Ninth Army to a Corps as a Psychological Warfare Liaison Officer. "I interpreted my orders to mean that I should do as much for psychological warfare as possible," said Hadley. "Now you can't do much of that back in Corps Headquarters can you?"
> So he rigged up a tank with a loudspeaker and started "Hadley's war."
> It was some war too. Whenever the rolling tanks met some resistance, they'd send Hadley's tank to the head of the column. Hadley's assistant Sgt. Walter Freund would start some smooth talking. Almost always the Germans would come out from behind the roadblocks or the buildings and surrender. In cases

where they didn't, the tanks would shoot up the works for a little while and then Hadley and Freund would take the air again. "You'd be surprised how it worked," said Hadley. He talked whole towns into giving up, brought about the surrender of single snipers. The Second Armored credited him with capturing more than 5,000 of its prisoners.

Personally, I learn the way tank officers judge their peers. They watch the speed with which a man's head shows above his turret rim, after that first reflexive duck when taken under fire. The quicker the head pops up, the better the leader, the finer the man. I also remember exactly how I feel when told by a Second Armored colonel that I will be awarded the Silver Star medal for my loudspeaker broadcasts. I recall the Biblical line from Matthew: "Lo the stone that the builders rejected has become the head stone of the corner." I had not changed as much as I believed.

The Silver Star remains an important public symbol of those times. More intimately, I remember my joy. Yes, joy. I sing in the tank. The world sings back. I pound the turret armor. The fullness of my heart makes me lightheaded. I see the look of relief on the tankers' faces as at Allen, when the town surrenders and we have no casualties. Most war novels, the conventional wisdom, and literary criticism overlook, or even deny this joy. But joy was there. I felt it then. I still feel it. It still brings tears. I am in history. I have a part to play. Like a true medieval monk, I serve not only myself, but the welfare of others. I am behind Jack Malcolm's eyes. Not till thirty-five years later, when I realize Jane and I will marry, do I again become so explosively happy.

Three brief, dissimilar moments in the war also leave marks on my life.

Luck

It is early April and still cold, somewhere close to the Elbe. The lane winds, deserted and compressed by tall pines. The "talking tank" is number three in the column, the two point tanks ahead of me. We turn a sharp corner and before us are barbed wire walls. I'm alert expecting to be fired at. The two tanks ahead of me traverse their guns. Then I see dead bodies, all withered hanging on the wire. I am amazed that men could be so barbarous as to string up corpses. Then some of the corpses on the barbed wire move. A few actually half wave. Not with their arms, just wiggle and flop their wrists. I am not looking at the dead but at the starved living. Every horror I had seen or imagined fell short of this reality. My *Luck* is that I am one of the first few to come surprised upon this nightmare. Since then, I reject as totally false any belief that mankind are born good.

We could not stop. The Piper Cub overhead tells us German tanks are going into position on the far side of the ridge. We did pause. The lead tank breaks down the concentration camp gate. I, and the other tankers who have followed, climb on the backs of our tanks, loosen the ropes that bind our ration crates to our tanks and throw the cases off. Then we pivot and grind on. As we leave I see men crawling, not walking, crawling toward the food. I wonder how they will get the cases open.

Luck

One afternoon in the last weeks of the war, I huddle down and peer around the door frame of a shattered factory in Magdeburg on the Elbe. From the next factory across a narrow street come the sounds of a rough firefight. I have never run loudspeakers with this unit before yesterday. They are a good unit, legendary good; they are treating me well, but we do not really know each other yet. One of their tanks still burns before that next factory. I want to race across the narrow street, through the side door of that factory and learn how close I can bring my "talking tank." But the sounds are wrong. Fingertip-feeling, past experience, says don't go. But I should go. I unholster my pistol, load it, and rise to a crouch, prepare to sprint. A big red-headed lieutenant I've met just minutes before shoves me aside and races across the street. He gets stitched; parts of him crumbling to the street at different speeds, like a marionette with its strings cut at random. I am left with survivor's guilt, a trauma often found among concentration-camp and combat survivors. I have not done what I should have done. I have failed.

Survivor's guilt, unlike combat fatigue, is not understood until several years after the war, when Robert Jay Lifton publishes his groundbreaking study. Before that I and many others, including several friends at Yale, are more disturbed by this trauma than we realize. We feel basically we have no right to be alive. We failed and survived while our betters died. I suffer its powerful effects again after Jane's courageous fight against cancer. Parts of me know I could not do more to save her. Other parts shout I could have done much more.

Luck and Choice

Somewhere in France during the early months after D-day I meet an OSS agent who is a Russian interpreter. I don't remember his name, or where, when, or how we meet. I tell him that it is quite possible that I, with my loudspeakers, will be one of the first soldiers to meet the Russians when the two armies link up. Can he give me a phrase I can use on my loudspeakers to tell the Russians we are Americans and not to shoot, and do something to show they are Russians? I write the sentence he gives me phonetically on a slip of paper that I put in my wallet.

Almost two weeks after Magdeberg I hear that a Cavalry unit with which I have done some leaflet work in the past is going across the Elbe on a long-range patrol to meet the Russians. I pull the piece of paper out of my wallet, detach "the talking tank" from the Second Armored Division, and with its crew of three plus myself drive across the Elbe to catch the Cavalry.

One day and some sniper fire later I am broadcasting my Russian message into woods that I hope contain Russians. Nothing happens. Several hours later the Piper Cub above us, watching our advance, assures me that there are Russians two hundred yards ahead. I have already made a white flag out of looted German sheets. Now I walk with it in front of the "talking tank," while my German-speaking technician repeats my Russian message. I hope the airborne spotter is right. It is a long, tense walk. But when I shake hands with the Russian officer and say "Comrade, Hitler kaput," I feel my war is over. I am out the other side, unhurt.

I am wrong. Two months later the Second Armored invites me to rejoin my by now famous "talking tank" for their march into Berlin. I chose to go. As an honor, the Second has been chosen the first America unit to garrison Berlin. I get permission from Psychological Warfare Headquarters to rejoin the division. Driving between parts of the division one night on the march to Berlin I am ambushed by a wire stretched across the road. Fortunately it only bashes and knocks me from the jeep. I remember flying through the air toward a great, dull, red void. Then just black.

When I wake my first thought is, *Doctor Peabody and the clergy were right. There is life after death.* I look around to see if I have made heaven. I do not exaggerate. That is what I did. I find Heaven quite dark. My left heal is touching the front of my left knee. When I recover enough to sit up and look about, Heaven resembles a small German road with a battered jeep lying on its side. *They will come to finish you off,* I think. *They will come to finish you off.* I try to get my pistol out of my holster. I can't. I start to straighten out my leg. I realize I must not do this, but do it anyway.

My pants leg is torn and wet with, I guess, blood, but not soaked through. Moving my foot has not started arterial bleeding. I focus on my jeep lying on its steering wheel side. If I could pull myself over there I could reach the horn button. I push with my hands and good foot and wiggle my tail and make it. I believe I tap out an SOS on the horn but the world goes gray, then black again. I wake for a moment to hear someone say, "Don't bother with the morphine; start the plasma." A patrol has found me and takes me to an aid station.

From there I go to an aviation evacuation hospital. My main memory is that the shock has made it difficult for me to pee. I keep trying and nothing happens. Finally the ambulance stops, I get out and can do it. When we get to the evacuation hospital — a bunch of tents in a clearing — my stretcher is placed before the surgical tent. Doctors come out with flashlights to look us over and I wave to them frantically to show I am in good shape and not by any measure a candidate for surgery. As I am wheeled into the operating tent I ask the surgeon, "Am I going to loose my leg?"

"You'll know when you wake up," he says. I feel better. I am in the hands of a professional.

From the evac, I along with several other patients are flown to a general hospital outside of Reims, France, for more surgery. I stay in the hospital over a month, sometimes on crutches, sometimes in a wheelchair. From the hospital's upper floors I find I can see the Reims' cathedral spire. The week the war started my mother myself, two sisters, and my younger brother passed our first night here. Wheelchairs are more dangerous for us than crutches because of the temptation to bet on wheelchair races. One warrant officer misses a turn, chair and he cascade down a fire escape, injuring himself further. The staff is unhappy.

I write my father that "the old Hadley luck has finally run out," that I have a mangled left leg and will have to spend some time in the hospital. I give my new address. In his letter back he replies: "I cannot tell you how glad I was to read the second sentence of your letter, 'that you had been badly wounded.' When your letter began that your luck had finally run out I assumed you had been court-martialed." He continues on with gossip from home.

Patients come and go. My leg is operated on three times but its bones will not unite. By now the only the patients who remain are those like myself with serious problems. The worst off are the unconscious men with head wounds. They pierce the hospital walls with their agonized screams when their pain killers wear off. They exist in a world beyond horror. The word "live" mocks what they are. The surgical staff finally decide they can do no more for me. I will be moved back to a more sophisticated hospital in the States.

Now *Luck* intervenes. Again not life-changing *Luck* but one of those unbelievable glitches in the military system that always are just about to happen. The United States has just commissioned a new hospital ship, the *Frances Y. Slanger*. She is much faster than the others, more comfortable, and has on board all the latest surgical and medical equipment. Because my case is so serious my orders read that I am to be transported back to the United States only on board the *Slanger*. Those who have been in the service know what now happens. The *Slanger* bends her propeller shaft on her maiden voyage and is laid up for repairs. The slower hospital ships come and go, come and go, several times. My orders say I must go on the *Slanger*. Two months pass and I wait for the *Slanger*.

I am at a transient hospital. There is no library, or books, scant medical facilities, the officers club is for staff only. It is hard to get into town on crutches. I make friends with one or two other officers also doomed to wait for the *Slanger*. We play a lot of hearts and Monopoly. I climb Mont Saint Michel twice on crutches, I cadge a few drinks, finally the U. S. *Slanger* limps into France. I am on my way home; or rather to Ward 3-D, Officers Major Surgery, Halloran General Hospital on Staten Island, New York. One of my fellow patients in the ward, Jerry Levy, becomes a lifetime friend. His wife, Penny, will be one of the six people who, at Jane's request, speaks at her memorial service.

Luck and Chance

Now *Luck* takes over with a bow to *Chance*. The war has brought into the Army and Navy some of America's finest doctors. The orthopedic surgeon at Halloran Hospital is Colonel Frank Stinchfield from Columbia Presbyterian Hospital in New York City. He looks at the leg that no surgeon in France has been able to repair and studies the X-rays. He thinks he can get union, repair the leg. He does.

Frank Stinchfield returns to teach at Columbia Presbyterian Medical School after the war. In the 1970s and 1980s it is said that half the heads of orthopedic surgery in major hospitals throughout America are trained by Frank. We become friendly acquaintances, sharing several interests. When he dies, I make certain I attend his funeral.

Much later, in 2005, I am having some perennial trouble with my left leg. I take myself, my leg, and its X-rays to my orthopedic surgeon. He looks at the X-rays.

"These pictures are old."

"Yes. 1945, in an Army hospital."

"Do you know who did this work?"

"Yes."

"Frank Stinchfield?"

"Yes."

The doctor shakes his head at the arrangement of screws inside my leg. "I thought so. Nobody could do such work back then. Very few now. A masterpiece."

I am walking around with some surgical *Mona Lisa* inside my left leg. I could do without that. I now wake every morning in some pain. Not much, just a little, that grows slightly as I age. A painful and important reminder of the war and its mix of *Chance, Luck,* and *Choice.*

I spend one year plus one day in Army hospitals. Just before discharge, I go before an Army medical board to determine how much pension I should receive. They look at my records from the day I enlisted to this day, the day of my discharge.

"You were a mining engineer," the colonel in charge says, reading my record,

"A what!"

"It says here on you records 'mining engineer.' "

"We haven't seen one of those yet," says another doctor on the board.

In the immortal words of Yogi Berra, "It's deja vu all over again." I remember my first-day interview at Staten Island

"Yes, yes. That's where I had worked."

"This lieutenant will have to be retrained," opines a member of the board.

"From the ground up," I say. They give a feeble laugh. I get a helpful pension.

After four years less three days, Captain Arthur Hadley, 01824612 no longer exists. "How easy it is to make a ghost," as Keith Douglas wrote the first time he killed a man with his tank gun. I expect that when I shed my uniform, I will find beneath a new, strong, and complete man. One totally capable of handling life. I and Lady MacBeth, who believed just a little murder and she would be Queen of Scot-

land, both get our predictions wrong. The first time I enter a store in civilian clothes to buy razor blades I fail. I had never bought razor blades when at eighteen I enter the Army. For four years I am supplied them by Uncle Sam. When I ask, "How much?" the shopgirls look at me and titter. I am still quite thin, walk strangely, and use a cane. Feeling completely alone with no place to go or friend to ask for help, I flee the store, bladeless. After that I keep twenty dollar bills on hand for items whose cost I don't know — like a cup of coffee, a bottle of milk. The ghost of Captain Hadley does not have an easy time.

Fate and Choice

If *Fate* determines any part of my life, it is going to Yale. I remember joking to Jane that the sperm that bore me was blue. My great-grandfather taught Latin, Greek, and Roman law at Yale, my grandfather was president, my father served on the Yale Corporation. To jump ahead, my wondrous marriage to Jane hinges on Yale. As I start Yale, I make some less than perfect *Choices*.

Choice One: With two summer terms and military credit I can make it through Yale in three years. I decide to do so. A mistake. I am at a great feast and end up wolfing the meal. Some of the best parts of the feast happen senior year. I never have a senior year. I know why I make such a choice.. After four years in the Army I feel, and indeed am, well behind my peers. I am in a hurry to try the civilian real world.

Choice Two: To live off-campus. Really a Choice without a Choice. After a year of living in a hospital ward, my every bodily action and pain observed by others, followed by six months of a painful marriage, plus a continued interest in girls, there is no way I can live on campus. However, moving through college in three years plus not living on campus means I make few friends. I spend one year in a small room with bed and desk in a funeral home. There is only one advantage. I can drive the hearse to take girls to football games. The police find me a place to park and the girls are impressed. The next year I know how to apartment hunt. I find a nice, two-room

attic apartment with bath four blocks from the campus, on Dwight Street, then a pleasant, tree-shaded location. I study and entertain there, leading an independent rather than a college life.

Choice Three: Yale has a new program called "Scholar of the House." If you have good grades in freshman and the first semester of sophomore year, and have a coherent program, you can take graduate school courses instead of undergraduate work. You will not be graded in these courses but must produce a final paper and face an oral examination. By choosing this program I miss some hard early slogging where I would have picked up some needed intellectual discipline. But I also get to do fascinating work in the graduate school at a level that I would have missed as an undergraduate. But again as both an undergraduate and in the graduate school, I don't fit anywhere. I am viewed as rather a "rara avis," Latin for "rare bird" — read "oddball" — by many. My tendency to be an outsider is unfortunately reinforced: A mixed bag of a *Choice*, but on the whole I benefit.

Another choice of great fun that adds to my "rara avis" image, the Reserve Officers Training Corps (ROTC) course at Yale, that turns out those wishing to be artillery second lieutenants, has a week devoted to psychological warfare. I volunteer to teach that week of the ROTC, and the colonel in charge accepts my offer, if I can find the money to pay myself. I visit the Military District Headquarters in New York City and a friendly colonel finds the money. I put on my captain's uniform and for one week of each of my last two years teach the Yale ROTC. This technically puts me on the Yale faculty, which makes me the third generation to teach at Yale. Some thirty years later my son, Nick the quark finder, as a Yale physics instructor will become the fourth.

I understand that an important part of Yale is the forming of friendships. I know by heart the words of the Yale song: "Time and change shall naught avail / To break the friendships formed at Yale." But I have not digested the meaning. Never connected the song to the fact that one of my favorite uncles, Nick, is married to my father's sister because my other favorite uncle, "H," roomed with Nick at Yale. "H" introduced Nick to his sister, Laura. They have a very happy marriage. Nick is a great fly-fisherman and takes me fishing

when I am ten and eleven. He builds into my life a love of fly-fishing that lasts. But no one ever took me by the hand and said, "That's what Yale friendships do." I don't recall anyone, other than Jane or my children, taking me by the hand. No wonder I tear up at Robert Burns' "Auld Lang Syne."

My focus at Yale is different from so many. They have come for the full Yale life. I have just come from "The Instant Easy Gone." Throughout my Army life I had been troubled by my lack of knowledge, starting with self-knowledge in particular, but including other questions. What phrases best made men surrender? Why? What made men fight, some so much better than others? Where in history do we go wrong to let wars happen? Or are they a natural part of life? What I want from Yale are those tools for life that Dalton talked about. That's my dream of Yale: knowledge first, friendship second. I never realized back then there is no need to rank them.

I begin to understand that I entered the armed services for reasons far different from my other classmates', even veterans who, like myself, volunteered. They see their time in the service, whether in combat or not, as a gap in their lives, a necessary interlude that had to be endured, but now should be put aside. They have no wish to dwell on or explore their service experiences. For me to enter the Army was a *Choice* integral to my purpose of "out, out, out." A *Choice* for independent growth made possible by the *Chance* of war. I have not changed as much as I had hoped, but I have started. I wish to constantly explore what happened, to keep alive my experiences, not put them aside. Those experiences are not an interlude in my life. They are my life.

Keith Douglas wrote after his first weeks of tank combat in the western desert:

> Under the parabola of a ball,
> a child turning into a man,
> I look into the air too long.
> The ball fell into my hand, it sang
> in my closed fist: "Open." "Open."

•   •   •

In my closed fist that same ball sang "out, out, out." I want to grip that ball tight.

Friendships are also difficult because of my age and the date on which I entered the service. This is that *Luck* that set me in an expanding army with opportunities for promotion. Other classmates may have seen as much or more combat than I, but *Luck* had placed me higher up the ladder with different experiences. I had what the British call "a good war." My military career had been interesting, had garnered medals and press clippings. I am more apt to find friends with shared experience among students in the art or law schools whose age gave them a war more like mine. Also there are women in New York City on weekends. I have more fun, learn more, and wish to spend time with them rather than with many of my Yale classmates.

I publish a short story, more a death story than a war story, in the Yale literary magazine. The story wins the Freshman Writing Prize. But when I try and deal with my survivor's guilt in a poem, I get laughed at. The editors, too young for the war, chide me.

"This poem says that the dead may be the more fortunate than the living. That's nonsense."

The poem doesn't say exactly that but I withdraw it. An argument will go nowhere.

My important writing at Yale takes place in the college news paper, the *Yale Daily News*. Proudly advertising itself as "The Oldest College Daily" or the "OCD" for short. Things old are very important at old Yale, most of them good, some not so hot. I write a column each Wednesday for the OCD called "The Old Fox," after Rabelais's adventuresome and lecherous long-tailed animal. I report on the crazy nature of the Yale I see. I give out prizes each term. The William H. Skunk Memorial Prize for the worst-managed student enterprise. The Old Fox Challenge Cup for the worst faculty or university management screw up.

I report on how White Shoe Yale — prep schoolers whose fathers went to Yale — see Black Shoe Yale — everybody else — and then on the poor Brown Shoes who want to be White Shoe but are seldom mentally deficient enough to grasp the concepts. The column is so popular that at the end of my third and last year the *Yale Daily*

News prints a collection as a book: *Three Years of the Old Fox*. In some manner this book falls into the hands of Charles Morton at the Atlantic Monthly Press and I graduate with a book contract. Also my classmates elect me one of their two speakers on graduation day. Not enough to please my family but quite okay for "the profound disgrace."

Luck and a Bit of Fate and Choice

At Yale I do start two lifetime friendships. The first is not even at Yale, but in the Pentagon. I usually check the new book room of the Yale Library once or twice a month. By *Luck* this time I see upon a table *Airborne Warfare*, by the parachute general, James M. Gavin. I know of Gavin as a charismatic leader and hero of Sicily, D-day, and Arnheim. With a tanker's mix of appreciation and suspicion of the airborne, I pick up the book expecting a panegyric in praise of airborne operations. What I find instead is a thoughtful exploration of the uses of air power as an international instrument that rivals the naval classic, Mahan's book on sea power. I read the book carefully and take notes, then type a thoughtful letter of praise to the general. I include personal thoughts on how to exploit the shock value of airborne forces with loudspeakers and leaflets, both directly and indirectly through deception and the exploitation of battle fears.

I don't expect an answer. At best a secretary-typed reply or thank-you note. What general is going to reply to a Yale student? Instead I get a four-page, handwritten letter discussing my ideas, carrying them further, and even giving then-still-unpublished details about the British use of deception on D-day.

Covering the military for *Newsweek* before the Korean War, I meet Gavin at Swarmer, the first large, postwar airborne maneuver. He actually remembers the letter, and back in Washington we have lunch. For reasons I still do not fully understand, a friendship begins. He lends me his book about choice and coin-flipping. During the Vietnam War our friendship deepens. He is one of the first generals to publicly argue against the war. I help him with his book explaining his beliefs about the war and America. I also manage his brief anti-war Democratic presidential campaign. After Jane and I marry, the friendship deepens as our two families become friends. We visit each other several times a year, on Martha's Vineyard, at Cape Cod, and in Florida. In the end, at his and his wife Jean's request General John R. Norton and I deliver Gavin's eulogy at Arlington National Cemetery. In between, from my Pentagon coverage to Vietnam to politics, I try to help Jim as I learn from him. Jim needed help at times. As Robert Lovett, General Marshall's right hand and later secretary of defense himself, remarked: "Jim's great problem is he expects everybody to treat him with the same honesty as he treats them."

I feel *Fate* as well as *Luck* is part of the mix between James Gavin and myself. Gavin, an orphan, had no father. Neither, in reality, did I. Also Jim, who would have liked to have a son, has four daughters. We filled each other's needs. Jane, a psychoanalyst, agreed. When asked about our friendship by people I think care, I reply: "I started off with a hero I admired and ended with a man I loved."

Luck

In the summer of my second year at Yale, the year before I graduate, I go to Europe with two friends. But when they leave Paris to visit Rome, I decide instead to go to Norway to travel by steamer, bus, and on foot up the coast and through the Jotten Heim, the central mountains. I still need time alone.

I walk into the apartment in Oslo of a friend of a friend, whose name I have been given. There on the wall is an Edvard Munch lithograph, Jealousy. I am literally transfixed, or in the modern phrase, "blown away." Not since Epstein's *Bomb Thrower* have I felt goosepimples rise from a work of art. The work is of a naked woman whose diaphanous layers of robe envelope her like the lips of a vagina. She is tremendously alluring and men around her stare at her, their faces distorted by jealously, lust, and want. I learn that the artist, Edvard Munch, is a famous Norwegian who died in the last year of the war.

The next morning finds me at the Norwegian National Gallery — in 1948 the Munch Museum is not yet built — where I find the haunting paintings, *Puberty*, *The Red Vine*, *The Cry* — now world famous — and *Vampire*. In the late 1950s, through Norwegian friends I am able to buy a major Munch oil, one of the three Vampire paintings. Jane and I are captivated by its power daily. One of our close friends would only sit with her back to the painting, the power affected her so. Other's knees truly buckled the first time they came through the door and saw it. Unfortunately, the painting so increased in value that eventually we realize we have a large portion of our wealth hanging on our living room wall, generating no income, and with the insurance rising. We love the picture, but we have to sell it. I miss it still.

Luck and Choice

The friend I make at Yale who works the greatest changes my life is a professor of anthropology, Clellan S. "Joe" Ford. Joe Ford is twelve years older than I, a tough, short man with a great sense of humor and like most field anthropologists absolutely unflappable. As a student before the war at Yale, he and his roommate, John Whiting, later the head of the Harvard's Anthropology Department, were both on the Yale wrestling team. Together they perfected an infamous parlor trick. Picking a room several stories up, one or the other of them would pretend to be drunk and disgusted with the conversation or behavior of those in a room. Yelling, he would climb out the room's window, stand on the ledge, wave good-bye over his shoulder and jump. The other man would rush to the window, look out, and say to everyone such words as "Oh, my God. Stand back. No one must see this." At that moment, as people screamed, the grinning face of Joe or John would appear in the window. Both men were in such superb physical condition they could twist in the air, turn around, and grab the window ledge with their fingers to arrest their fall.

I first meet Joe Ford when, as a Scholar of the House, I audit his by-invitation-only course on Yale undergraduate social structure. I ask him for help in a paper I plan to do on Fear in Battle. He tells me about the Cross Cultural Files, where I can study battle fears and taboos and magic against such fears among the most ferocious tribes of the present and immediate past, from the Latin American Ick to the Western Apaches. With his superb advice and counsel I produce a paper on "The Creation of Fear in Battle," which helps me graduate magna cum laude. Unfortunately, I later send my only copy to the Psychological Warfare Department of the Army. They classify it so heavily on a "need to know" basis that I have never been able to read it again. My time in the files also teaches me to be very careful about cross-cultural value judgments.

When I graduate in 1949, Joe finds my wife, Mary Hill, and myself a two-room cabin at $500 for the whole summer, on Tisbury Great Pond in the town of West Tisbury on Martha's Vineyard. I enjoy West Tisbury, its untroubled uniqueness and interesting people. I start my first book in that cabin. Later, in the days when wives disappeared from June to September, Mary and I and the children summered on the Vineyard. In 1960, with the money from my first novel's paperback sale, plus a large bank loan, I will buy 350 acres and half a mile of beach in West Tisbury. Without knowledge of what I do, I so determine a large part of my emotional and financial future.

Several months after meeting Joe, while studying as he suggested in the Cross Cultural Files area of the graduate school, I hear a commotion outside. The Anthropology Department rooms are across a narrow street from Grace New Haven Hospital. I look out my window and see across that street a red-headed young woman in a hospital gown standing on a window ledge. She screams she is about to jump. Behind her I see the safety grating that covers her hospital window. Men in white jackets mill about in the room behind her; I assume they are doctors, probably psychiatrists. Several times these men approach the window and say, "Now, Helen, you don't want to jump." Each time they repeat this ridiculous rubric she screams louder that she does and leans out, seeming more determined to leap.

The street between our buildings is one-way and quite narrow. The girl is directly across from me and one story below. She is on the fourth floor; I on the fifth. In the room behind her the white jackets come and go. They have obviously screwed up and let her get out the window. I alert Joe Ford in his office. He calls the fire department, something the hospital has neglected to do.

I open the large window in the files area. The jump down and across is far, but not impossible. I'm back to running again and in fair shape. But how will the bad leg respond? I suppose Jack Malcome's eyes and the Magdeberg red-headed lieutenant float somewhere. I look out the window across to the woman. The words of the great black ballad, "John Henry," come to mind.

> John Henry said to his shaker
> "A man ain't nothing but a man."

I take off my shoes to get a better purchase on the window ledge with my toes. I crawl out the window, carefully stand up, and turn around. I jump hard. I crash into the woman and pin her against the security mesh for a long few minutes. She struggles and bites me until the firemen arrive, put up a ladder, and get her down. I squeeze into the room behind her through the hole she made to escape. I am exhausted, bitten, shoeless, my shirt ripped. I expect praise. Wrong again. The psychiatrists berate me as a show off. They yell I did it for publicity. They had her talked back in. Because of me she almost committed suicide. Now it will be in the papers. They storm out.

For several minutes Joe Ford has been standing in the back of the room. He has my shoes. The last doctor leaves. "Well," says Joe, "now you've learned about psychiatrists. How about a martini?" A mere friendship becomes a strong friendship that will include his wife, Eddy, and later my children. He dies of cancer before he can meet Jane.

In the '50s the Martha's Vineyard to which Joe Ford introduces myself and Mary remains a magic world. Still hard to reach, the Vineyard has not yet been discovered. The tiny town of West Tisbury, on whose pond we live, is truly an Athens. In the town each summer live and work Joe and Eddy Ford; John Whiting, Joe's former roommate and his wife, Bea, both anthropologists at Harvard; the famed psychologist, Leonard Doob; alcohol expert Seldon Bacon; the artist Stan Murphy and his wife, Polly Wolcot; Phileo Nash, the anthropologist in Harry Truman's White House; and others.

Everett Whiting, of the old island family and brother of John, runs the town. Everett likes to recount how, on his first day at Yale, his economics professor told the class, "Now if you young gentlemen pay strict attention in this class, someday you can retire to a farm and keep sheep." Everett says he thought: "Hell, I already own a beautiful farm and keep sheep. What in God's name am I doing here? So I shut my book and left Yale." A wise, kind, generous, upright man.

All of us except Everett live in small to tiny cabins beside Tisbury Great Pond. We come together with our different outlooks and disciplines to laugh, talk, dig clams, net crabs, swim, eat, drink, plot the future, argue ideas. A magic time.

I receive a note in my Yale mail box that if I think I might like to work for the CIA I should report at a definite time — neither earlier nor later — to a certain room in one of Yale's buildings. I go there to find a paper with my name on it. If I wish the interview to preceed I must sign the paper. Otherwise leave. The paper, a security clearance, commits me to never mention any details of the interview to come. I sign the paper. A woman collects the paper, and at the designated time leads me into another room. There sits a man I know well who describes dangerous work that everyone by now knows about. But since I signed the paper and my friend has denied he was ever connected with the CIA, I will say no more. I am not selected for the job. Through a rather extended grapevine I later learn that a member of the "vetting team" on the Yale faculty insisted I was too much of a loner to fit the organization. Later I am asked twice more to join that type of work, once by the legendary Colonel Landsdale. By then I know enough about myself and that organization to say no.

I meet "B," a woman I first knew in my Groton days. She was always energetic and beautiful. Now she has grown exciting and does fascinating work. We are thrown together for some time on the New Haven–New York train. I have an intense feeling we want to see each other again. If we do it will be no casual affair; whatever happens will take time. I ask for a phone number. She gives it willingly and not only says we should meet again but adds that "let's meet again" smile. I never call. I do not flip the coin.

Luck

A friend and writer at *Vogue* has introduced me to Mary Hill, the *Vogue* shopping editor. We are living together on weekends. *Luck* struck on our first date, when a gigantic snow storm shut down New York City. Instead of going to watch professional tennis, for which I have tickets, we go to bed. On weekends and during spring vacation she helps me with my college work, now going well. An English paper of mine, "Laughter in Shakespeare's Tragedies" wins the Curtis Prize, the most prestigious English prize in undergraduate Yale. If I don't goof up or blow the final Scholar of the House interview, I will graduate magna cum laude, which will be important in finding a job.

Not only do I find Mary interesting and supportive, all my friends like her and urge me to hang on to her. Even my mother and father like her. To call "B" may well destroy the difficult balance I have achieved. I've had enough of risk. Since I asked for and received "B's" phone number and address, I must have come close to a coin flip. But the coin stays in my pocket. In later years I sometimes hear about "B" and wonder what would have happened had I flipped. My life might have been very different. I could not possibly have been more happy.

Mary and I drift on together. I get a Fulbright scholarship to teach English at Anatolia College in Greece and coach their basketball team. Mary does not want such a major move and lifestyle change. Mary is Catholic, which will make problems with my family and myself, particularly over raising our children. Her father, George Washington Hill, the Lucky Strike tycoon, had promised her mother when they married that he would raise their children as Catholics. Mary's mother dies in childbirth. Mr. Hill marries another Catholic who enforces his promise. Mary quits the Catholic Church. I get the book contract, so I will have a writing job for at least three-quarters of my first year out of college. Mary has money of her own. I have some also. We come more and more together. Marriage moves from a possibility, to a definite possibility, to a certainty. In the winter break of my final year we marry and honeymoon at a dude ranch in Jamaica.

Fate

My *Fate* drives me to settled down. All around me friends are settling or have settled down. My father and mother were married at my present age. Now they continually ask, "When will you settle down?" Since early childhood people have looked at me and said,

"Hey, Hadley, settle down." My brief affairs have not been happy. Except for "The Old Fox," I am not writing. If I am going to accomplish anything, write a book, I must be settled. "The Instant Easy Gone" stays close. Order is important. I do not wish to become again that undirected "messy boy." From loudspeakers to Scholar of the House, I have been too much outside the system. Settle down Hadley. Settle down.

Jane hated to hear me call myself Hadley. "You are Arthur," she would say, either annoyed or with a smile and kiss. "You are Arthur. Do not let them do that to you." But that comes later.

Mary and I get married, a small ceremony with my family and just about ten Groton, Army, and Yale friends, some ten of Mary's friends, two aunts with their husbands, several of her cousins and, her two brothers. Her stepmother does not come because the ceremony is not Catholic. We spend the summer in the tiny cabin in West Tisbury, whose living room looks out over Tisbury Great Pond to the ocean. I work daily on my book. When we invite up one of Mary's *Vogue* friends she says, as we drive up to our tiny cabin, "You've got to be kidding. Where is your house?" In the winter I rewrite the book in our two-room fifth-floor walk-up near the Metropolitan Museum. One of the four moving men who sweat Mary's enormous, family dining room table up the five flights remarks, "When Christopher Columbus sailed over in this thing, he should have carried it up these stairs."

Unfortunately my book finds no takers, including the publisher who furnished the advance. Mary is pregnant. I need a job.

Fate and Luck

My college and Army record, plus the Yale book *Three Years of the Old Fox* and people I have met, mean that my job interviews are not only friendly, they end in offers. *Time* magazine, *Life*, the *Herald Tribune*, the *New York Times* all offer me an entry-level position. One night my mother happens to dine with Malcolm Muir, the publisher of *Newsweek*. I interview there. I am called back to be reinterviewed by Denver Lindley, the Washington bureau chief. I spend a day in the New York Public Library reading Lindley's two books.

Disraeli, once asked how he got on so well with Queen Victoria, re-marked, "I laid it on with a trowel." At Yale I developed Hadley's corollary to Disraeli's trowel: "Never use a trowel if there is a dump truck handy." I have *Luck*. Lindley, who was a Rhodes scholar, has money in his *Newsweek* Washington bureau budget for a young Rhodes scholar friend. That man has decided to become an aca-demic. This means that in the Washington bureau instead of starting as a fact-checker, intern, or copy boy, a reporter's job is open. Would I be willing to relocate? I would.

My family puts Mary up in the guest room of their apartment and I move to Washington. During her pregnancy, Mary is discov-ered to be quite ill with ulcerated colitis. I fly to New York on Tues-days and Wednesdays, my *Newsweek* days off, for meetings with Mary and many doctors. With fingers crossed, all agree that the in-testinal operation can be put off until after our baby's birth. Though I am new at *Newsweek*, Mr. Lindley gives me a week off for the birth and operation. All goes well. I have a cured wife and a healthy daughter. They will join me in Washington in several months.

I start out as a general-assignment reporter covering the Orga-nization of American States, unimportant congressional hearings, and hastily called press conferences. Some stories take me to the Pentagon. There I meet several colonels who had been in the same Yale Graduate School seminar on international relations as myself, others for whom I had made loudspeaker broadcasts or fired leaflets. One interviewee, Major James Camp, turns out to be the husband of Margie Foresyth, my Fort Knox dancing partner. They become another pair of longtime friends. My inside Pentagon knowledge produces several "Periscope" items. "Periscope" is a unique and im-portant part of *Newsweek*; Mr. Lindley congratulates me.

Chance and Luck

Chance and *Luck* then combine to give me an extraordinary lift. *Chance* that the North Koreans, poor but fanatic communists with a powerful army, decide to conquer Democratic South Korea. *Luck* that they launch their invasion on a Sunday in June. The *Newsweek* Washington bureau is closed on Sunday and Monday except for the junior member who is there for last minute fact-checking and emergencies — that's me. Also in June, the reporter covering the Pentagon is on vacation. As I start my work that Sunday I am glum. Tomorrow is my birthday and I am working then also and my wife and daughter have not yet arrived.

When the first news comes over the Associated Press ticker that there may be an invasion in Korea, I cab over to the Pentagon in the bright sunlight to find a few of my friends and learn what is happening. "In Those High and Far-Off Times, O Best Beloved," as Kipling begins some of his wonderful *Just So Stories*, you didn't need a pass to get inside the Pentagon, even on weekends. Officers are beginning to drift in as puzzled and confused as I. That we are totally surprised by what is happening is too evident to require comment. The fact that Pearl Harbor also happened on a Sunday receives much comment. In the International Branch of the Army staff are several officers, friends from Yale Graduate School. In the Operations Branch are two more friends with whose outfits I had run loudspeaker missions. What strikes me now as I look back, though my notes do not reflect the feeling, is our complete innocence. This is the first war of the nuclear age. A limited war of a type future studies will forecast, but is then unpredicted. We sit there, drink coffee, and talk or stare out the window at the green Pentagon lawns, and ask ourselves what's going to happen. Is this the start of World War III? Will the United States resist? Use our atomic bombs? Are the reports even true? From time to time some wag sticks his head in the door to ask if we have called up and federalized the National Guard yet.

It becomes obvious that my friends know as little as I. I wonder if the CIA knows more. The editors in New York are holding up printing the magazine, desperate for late information. No one in the Army has heard from the CIA. Sitting in the Army's International Affairs Office, I pick up the phone to call Admiral Roscoe H. Hillenkoetter, director of the CIA. I recite this not to make myself out as some hotshot reporter, but to show how different that Washington is from today's. I explain to the admiral's aide who answers the phone who I am, where I am, and my plight. Hillenkoetter comes on the phone. He says he hasn't been able to see the AP wire. Do I know what the AP says? I read him the AP wire. He indicates that he is as much in the dark as we at the Pentagon.

I call *Newsweek* and give them my non-information. They don't think much of it. I don't either, though with hindsight, how little we knew should have prepared us for the disasters that followed. By the time the *Newsweek*'s regular Pentagon reporter comes back from vacation two weeks later, I have been able to produce two cover stories. I am made the second Pentagon reporter. I am not senior enough on *Newsweek* to go to Korea. I continue to cover that war and the start of NATO from the Pentagon.

I spend six years at *Newsweek*, two covering the Pentagon, three covering President Eisenhower, and one as editor of the "Periscope" page. Throughout this time a learning process makes me less judgmental and more aware of the complex mix of power, ideas, and people that create decisions. I also learn, after several close calls, to distrust all unchecked stories, and all single-cause explanations. I take to heart the mantra of Hal Levine, one of our senior New York reporters: "More good stories are ruined by checking than by anything else."

Concerned that the older reporters have a small group that meets secretly with government officials to get inside information, I create a small group of us New Kids to do the same thing. Unknowns then, many of them go on to be national figures. Rowland Evans and Charles Bartlett, as major columnists; Phillip Geyelin, as chief editorial writer for the *Washington Post*; Ray Sherer as White House correspondent for NBC; Alistair Buchan, a British foreign correspondent, will become the first director of the Institute of Strategic Studies; Tom Winship will become editor of the *Boston Globe*; Ed Dale financial reporter for the *New York Times*; Douglas Cater, president of Washington College.

Two stories and one moment illustrate news gathering in those times and the effect on myself. The stories were difficult to get. They changed the way at least some people viewed an event or an issue.

They may even have helped the Republic prosper. The moment I did not report, and should not have, I was a guest if an uninvited one. But the moment shows how a trivial instant can provide insight into a person and shape future stories. And why, even in this electronic age, the use of shoe leather is important to a reporter.

First: the nuclear weapons story. The original atom bombs dropped on Nagasaki and Hiroshima were enormous, cumbersome objects, about the size of a four-door sedan and could only be carried by specially equipped heavy bombers. As soon as World War II ended, efforts begin in deepest secrecy to shrink the size of the bombs. In the second year of the Korean War, I cover a miserably cold winter maneuver in upstate New York. By the third day of the maneuver I still have no story, though I do have scribbled in my notebook an extraordinary military speech. It was given by the senior army doctor at the maneuver, a brigadier general to about ten other junior doctors.

"Now we have another parachute jump today. I want you doctors who will be standing by at the drop zone to be sure and carry your casualty report papers underneath your arm inside your shirts and combat jackets, in your armpits. In the jump two days ago, a lot of you didn't. As a result, as I warned you, the carbon paper in your report forms froze. We left several badly injured soldiers lying out there on the frozen ground for some time. Did not get them into ambulances, because you couldn't fill out the forms in quadruplicate with the frozen carbon paper." One of the joys of reporting is learning how the world works.

Today's event is an infantry attack coordinated with air power. As I watch a mock battle I see a jet fighter, engine roaring, bore in on an infantry unit. But it suddenly cuts its engine power, shoves it nose into the sky. Then instantly goes back to full power, does a barrel roll, and disappears fast. I ask a watching Air Force officer wearing a fighter-pilot patch, "What the hell was that maneuver?" "Oh you'll have to ask my general that, sir" The officer looks intelligent and is well turned out and decorated, so why the cautious answer? He tells me his general's location on the post and I drive on over. After a short hesitation, the general tells me an extraordinary story. The atomic bomb, or nuclear weapon as it is now called, has been greatly shrunk in size to where it can be carried by a jet fighter. But the fighter pilot on releasing the bomb must throw it up into the air instead of dropping it toward the ground. This maneuver gives the fighter pilot himself time to escape the nuclear explosion.

Further, the general continues, the nuclear weapon will soon be shrunk further to where it can be fired from a large cannon or ride on a rocket nose. This will change the nature of warfare because these smaller weapons can be used against troops or to take out enemy airfields instead of, as now, being dropped on cities where they kill thousands of civilians. The whole effort to shrink the weapons and use them this way is slowed and discouraged by SAC, the Strategic Air Command. SAC's reason is to keep nuclear weapons solely in their possession so they can gain a near monopoly of defense funds and promotions. I thank the general. I assure him I will never reveal his name. His name is not even in my notes. I leave with one hell of a scoop.

The story carries two major problems. The first, how do I check it's true? The second, America is presently in both a hot and cold war. If the story is true and I break it, will I damage American security? After two weeks, while pretending to do a story on new jet engines, I have been able to check with enough people to be sure that the story is true, and by breaking it I will in fact enhance American security. *Newsweek* ran the stories. After the story breaks, Air Force Secretary Thomas Finletter calls me in and tells me he is doing his best to put me in jail for security violations. My friend Lieutenant Colonel John R. Norton, who as Lieutenant General Norton will later join myself to deliver General James Gavin's eulogies at Arlington National Cemetery, tracks me down in a Pentagon corridor. Norton tells me to talk to no one on the phone because there is a full field security investigation targeting me. This means my phones are tapped and perhaps some rooms of my house bugged.

Several weeks later Jack Norton again tracks me down in the Pentagon. He asks if I have told anyone about the full field investigation. I say certainly I have. I am angry. "Oh," he says "you shouldn't have done that, Arthur. Now there are two 'full field investigations' against you. The first to find out where you got the story on small nuclear weapons. The second, how you found out there was a full field investigation." After other news organizations pick up the story, the heat dies down. I never think of Finletter, who later out and out lied to me about something else, without remembering Dean Acheson's description of him: "Those mummies standing at the entrance of the Egyptian Wing in the Metropolitan Museum in New York. They always remind me of Tom Finletter come to life."

Meanwhile NATO has been created and the Americans and Europeans are about to hold its first joint maneuver: Main Brace, with the Norwegian Army, British observers, the U.S. Navy and Air Force, all in far northern Norway. The rest of the Pentagon reporters will cover the exercise from a U.S. Navy aircraft carrier. I convince *Newsweek* that to really cover the story I should be on the ground. The press on the carrier, with nothing to go on but the twice-daily Navy briefings, report Main Brace as a series of triumphs. On the ground I report back to *Newsweek* a series of foul-ups. Chief among these is that the carrier planes flying in support of the Norwegian troops on the ground can't talk to those troops. The Navy airplane radios do not mesh with the radios of the U.S. Air Force forward observers supporting the Norwegians. As a British observer put it bluntly: "This is a damn long, cold way to come to find out that your fuckin' Navy and fuckin' Air Force still can't talk to each other."

I miss some big stories too. On this maneuver I looked through a window of a hangar on Bodo, north Norway, and saw a most unusual aircraft. The plane had long tapered wings and practically no engine. I assumed that the Norwegians had invented some new low-powered, ultra-light glider for the mountains. I was looking at a U-2 spy plane. Bodo was where they landed after overflying the Soviet Union from Formosa.

More importantly for my life rather than my career, while stopping in London I rent, for the first time in my life, a week's fishing on a salmon river. The river, a small one in the far north of Scotland, the Brora, while not too productive of salmon seems the best I can afford. I had always wanted to salmon fish and Mary had grown up salmon fishing in a camp in Canada owned by her father. I find I not only love salmon fishing, but my intense concentration and, for me, unusual patience make me remarkably successful.

Luck

The fishing on the Brora turns out to be owned by Charles Jansen, a classmate at Eton of my close friend in Washington, the *London Observer*'s reporter Alistair Buchan. Alistair's "heads up" letter to Charles and his wife, Lisa, lead to a strong friendship, plus years of exciting and therapeutic fishing on the pure fly rivers of the Highlands.

During the two years I cover the Pentagon there occur two outside moments that, had they gone another way, would have greatly affected my life.

Luck

In the early days of the Korean War, the Army calls Captain Hadley out of the Individual Reserves to go on active duty with the Psychological Warfare staff in the Pentagon. Fortunately, the ankle of my damaged leg is laterally immobile. Immobility is something the Army can measure. I flunk the physical examination. I am told that the only way I can go on active duty is to sign a paper that says I will not hold the Army responsible for any further damage to my leg. Nor, if the leg is damaged, will there be an increase in my disability pension. I do not sign. I cannot be called up. I remain *Newsweek*'s Pentagon correspondent.

Luck

The Army becomes dissatisfied with its propaganda efforts in Korea. What to do? I have become friendly with Frank Pace, the secretary of the Army, and I make a suggestion. The excellent strategic leaflets produced during World War II were under the supervision of C. D. Jackson, now publisher of *Life*. He is a thoughtful, energetic executive with great publishing and people skills who could pull things together rapidly. He should go to Korea with the simulated rank of brigadier general. As for the loudspeaker problem, I should go to Korea along with Jackson with the simulated rank of lieutenant colonel and use my experience to soon have the loudspeakers producing prisoners.

Much to my surprise, first Frank Pace and then C. D. agrees. Since the assignment is special, the orders to put it into action are forwarded to the White House. Jackson and Hadley get briefings on the Korean situation and our medical shots. Truman turns the proposal down. He feels Jackson is such a strong Republican that he will never get to Korea. Instead he will stop in Tokyo to help MacArthur run for president. That's unfair to C. D. Yes, he is a strong Republican. But he is a patriot first. Without C. D. at the head of the ticket, Hadley lacks the clout to be sent to Korea alone.

Had *Luck* in the form of Truman's veto not intervened and I had gone, what would have happened to me? I cannot be sure. I suspect, having fallen still further behind my contemporaries in the private sector, but at the same time moved further ahead in the public sector, and with a high civil service rank, I would have chosen to stay somewhere in government. That would have been an unhappy *Choice*. I would have led a totally different life and, for me, with no writing, one less challenging and rewarding. I would not have changed so much, and never met Jane. But back then my *Fate* would have prevailed. I must climb the ladder of success, a ladder I still saw as only vertical. Horizontal achievement did not exist. And as for the satisfactions of wedded happiness, they were a distraction from life's purpose. I don't think I'd have flipped the coin. My disastrous *Choice* would have been government.

Some six months later *Newsweek* rewards me with the coverage of the White House in the last few months of Truman's stewardship. After that I have the opportunity to cover parts of the Eisenhower campaign. The implication being that if I don't fall on my face, I will become the magazine's White House correspondent. Eisenhower is elected. I become a White House correspondent. I even had, much to the delight of my editors, correctly predicted the exact number of electoral votes Eisenhower would receive. I forecast two states wrongly: Oklahoma and Mississippi. Fortunately they have the same number of electoral votes. I do not publicize my error. My basic reason to perceive an Eisenhower landslide is that I see his and Nixon's pictures draped all over New York City firehouses in the Irish sections of Queens. That is a tectonic shift.

Between my first Eisenhower campaign in 1952 and Ike's second in 1956, campaigning and campaign coverage enter the age of the airplane and the long-distance phone. The change is so complete that campaign coverage becomes almost a different animal. The campaign train was magic. The campaign plane is a bore. As the train whistle-stopped across the nation you could get a feeling for America. The difference between southern and northern Illinois, between eastern and western Ohio. I would stand on the tracks at some small station watching and listening to Truman or Eisenhower. I scribble notes, get individual and crowd reactions. I learn from the old-time reporters. There are a few who still use railroad slang: "riding the yellow" for taking a risk. "High-balling the white" for writing a story fast.

At each stop a new set of local politicians, and often local reporters, board the train and make for the club car to swap information with us national reporters. These contacts are vital for both locals and nationals. Back then there are no effective political public relations firms that handle national and local candidates and issues. The word "spin" has yet to enter politics. What is said can be incorrectly seen or biased, but is reasonably honest. The long-distance telephone is still slow, erratic, and expensive. The names, phone numbers, and information exchanged in the club car between local politicians and news people and national reporters are gold to both. The locals wish to get their news and views out, and we wish to learn what is hot locally in a still largely parochial America.

I take to riding in the photographers' truck immediately behind a candidate. There I can feel and judge crowd reaction far better than reporters in the bus farther back in the caravan. I persuade an older Groton renegade, Stewart Alsop, to do the same and we become firm friends. I stand on some small-town railroad tracks, or talk in the club car, or ride in the photographers' truck and think: What a job. To watch power, to see America, to take part in this process. I'd pay to have this job. And I'm getting paid. I have not yet noticed the strains placed on my marriage by all the time away, including much of the summer when Eisenhower vacations in Denver.

Luck and One Quick Moment

I draw the lucky straw to be the pool man to cover Eisenhower's inaugural ball for all news magazines. Mary and I have a limousine to ourselves in the Cabinet convoy to the party. Through some lucky glitch in Secret Service procedures, we get ushered into seats at the back of Vice President Nixon's box. Some of the Cabinet members already seated there are surprised to see a reporter and his wife. However, they know *Newsweek* is friendly to the president and make no fuss.

Nixon and his wife, Pat, stand in the front row of the box to wave to the crowd on the ballroom floor below. The president and his wife, Mamie, arrive on the ballroom floor and the band strikes up "Hail to the Chief." Nixon hears the music and comes to attention. His wife does not hear the music and keeps waving. Nixon reaches over with his right hand and pinches his wife's buttocks hard, just below the end of her girdle. She winces. "Shut up," he says. "Put your arms down. They're playing 'Hail to the Chief.'" I think: At a moment of triumph like this, to treat your wife like that. There is a man without grace or limits.

Luck and Choice

A long-lasting period is when I work both sides of the Senator Joseph McCarthy story. I report on him while trying to build strength against him and end up in the White House lobby literally coughing blood.

I start with my Eisenhower White House years with some good contacts in place. C. D. Jackson is a member of the president's staff as psychological-warfare adviser. A friend, Hugh Farley, remains on the National Security Council. And a new member of the council, whom I met on the campaign train, is living in Mary's and my Georgetown house until he finds a house to buy for himself. Brigadier General Pete Carroll, who worked for Eisenhower at

SHAFE, is a friend of friends and is secretary of the White House staff. Secretary of the Army Robert Stevens, a Yale stalwart, becomes a friend. Though he is only a sub-Cabinet member, destiny will force the unprepared Stevens center stage in the coming White House battle with Senator Joseph McCarthy.

Stevens's front office is run by an extremely close friend, the one-legged Colonel Ken BeLieu. BeLieu, a powerful six-footer with uncanny people skills, was a decorated officer in the Second Infantry Division in World War II. He volunteered for Korea, where he lost his left leg. On his desk, Ken keeps a picture of his father in police uniform walking his beat in Seattle to remind himself where he came from. He is also a reasonably good amateur artist, especially of Pacific landscapes. His humorous stories were justifiably legendary.

On February 1, 1950, Senator McCarthy made his famous — or infamous — speech to the Women's Republican Club in Wheeling, West Virginia. "I have in my hand a list of 205 individuals who appear either to be card-carrying members or certainly loyal to the Communist Party." By the time Eisenhower runs for president in 1952, the senator has grown so powerful that he attacks General George Marshall with impunity. In October, on the advice of his traveling campaign staff, Eisenhower takes his defense of Marshall out of his campaign stop in Milwaukee. McCarthy is splitting the country and the Republican Party. Eisenhower's strategy, based on his experiences handling power, is to let McCarthy destroy himself. He feels that for himself as president to attack McCarthy raises the senator to presidential level. He and some members of his staff believe in Harry Truman's often-quoted advice: "Never get into a pissing contest with a skunk." The problem is that a number of people are getting hurt and McCarthy's self-destruction seems far away.

Eisenhower leaves no doubt as to his own personal feelings. I cover his famous June 14, 1953, Dartmouth College speech, "Don't join the book burners," a passionate statement he delivered with fire. I tell *Newsweek* I feel the speech merits major play. Nothing happens. I interview all my White House sources to see if there has been a shift in Eisenhower's strategy. I find none. Some, like C. D. Jackson, tell me off the record they are working hard to change that strategy, but nothing overt happens. McCarthy and McCarthyism continue to grow. National polls show that 50 percent of the country believes McCarthy's charges, while 20 percent are undecided.

Then on February 18, 1954, comes a decisive moment. An obscure dentist, Captain Irving Peress, at Camp Kilmer, New Jersey, who has declined to sign a loyalty oath, receives through bureaucratic ineptitude an automatic promotion to major. McCarthy finds an issue he knows he can exploit for news coverage and power. He calls before his committee the commander of Camp Kilmer, Brigadier General Ralph W. Zwicker, an officer with a distinguished combat record. He berates Zwicker for coddling Communists. "Don't be coy with me general." "... anyone with the brains of a five-year-old child can understand that question." "Then, general, you should be removed from any command." Two days later the *New York Times* publishes a verbatim transcript of how McCarthy bullied Zwicker. Secretary Stephens, with a bit of help from generals on the Army staff plus Colonel BeLieu and myself, gets out a written statement that he is not going to let officers testify without a guarantee of fair treatment.

Pressure on Stephens and advice comes from all directions, to stand firm, to compromise, to put the Army first, to fight, to remember they are all Republicans. A great many of these conflicting solutions come from the White House. One of those always urging compromise with McCarthy is General Jerry Persons, Eisenhower's chief of congressional liaison. Now Persons and Nixon arrange a "secret" luncheon meeting between Stevens and McCarthy in a Capitol room next the vice president's office. Also present will be the other Republican members of McCarthy's committee: Senators Karl Mundt, Everett Dirksen, and Charles Potter. Stevens accepts. When he gets to the "secret" meeting he finds ten or so reporters already outside the door. Still he opens the door and goes in — goes in alone, no aide to back him up, no notebook, no tape recorder. An exceptionally innocent lamb, blindfolded by good breeding, entering a renowned slaughter house.

They all eat fried chicken for lunch. McCarthy and the senators also eat the secretary of the Army. Without realizing what he is doing, Stevens gives in and signs a paper offering up Army personnel to testify without restrictions.

"Stevens ate red meat yesterday. He ate chicken today," crows McCarthy to the press. Stephens goes home exhausted.

When the press ticker begins to report what the document signed by Stevens says, the phone calls start. Colonel BeLieu, plugging holes in the dike with fingers and toes, asks me to come to Stevens's house to help. There I find a shattered Stevens who is drinking too much. I listen on another phone to take notes as senators, friends, and White House staff phone to give him conflicting advice. He tries to call his two bosses, the secretary and deputy of defense, for support and advice They can't be reached. BeLieu and I get Stevens upstairs and into bed, where he goes to sleep.

Ken and I go downstairs to talk. What happens now? The phone keeps ringing. Sometimes BeLieu answers it, sometimes he doesn't. We know this is a mess. Stevens will probably be destroyed and McCarthy become bigger than ever. The Army is in for a long, bad time with falling morale. The White House may get involved. Ken wonders if we can get a statement out to the press that Stevens does not feel he gave in and that he intends to fight. I believe we can at least try. We will say he drafted the statement just before he went to sleep. We write up a statement. First I read it to Rowland "Rolly" Evans, then with the Associated Press. I tell him Stevens signed it just after talking to the White House. Rolly accepts the statement.

Next I call a friend on the *Washington Post*. He thanks me and asks what sort of shape the secretary is in. "On the record, worn out and tired but ready for battle. Off the record he is really beat and exhausted but okay." Finally, I call John Finney, then covering the Pentagon for the United Press, later a star on the *New York Times*. I know John will be the tough sell. He is the type of reporter who will check inside the Pearly Gates before he decides to enter.

"Arthur," says John, "I can't take that story without talking with Stevens."

"I'm not sure just what he is doing now, John. Colonel BeLieu is here. He should do."

"Stevens."

Belieu and I go upstairs to wake up Stevens.

Belieu, his hand over the phone's mouthpiece, says to Stevens, "Mr. Secretary, It's your old friend John Finney. Tell him you are going to fight." He holds the phone in front of the recumbent Stevens.

"I'm going to fight, John."

"How you feeling, Mr. Secretary?"

Belieu mouths "I'm going to fight."

"I'm going to fight."

In the background I hear a number of bells strike on what sounds like a press ticker. Six bells mean a major scoop. There is a pause. Finney comes back on the line.

"Mr. Secretary?"

"It's me, John."

"The AP has the story. Can I talk to the secretary some more? He doesn't sound so good."

"He's dead tired."

"Okay. The AP is running the story. I'll go with it."

I hand Stevens's bedside phone back to BeLieu, who rests it on its cradle. We look at each other and smile. We're off to the war. And we are. We have helped turn the tide. Within the week, official documents are released that tabulate and quote the many threats used by Roy Cohen, McCarthy's chief aide, and the senator himself to get an illegal commission for a former McCarthy committee staffer, now an Army private, J. Myer Schine. They contain threats to investigate the Army for communists if a commission is not forthcoming. A Senate committee is ordered to investigate the Army-McCarthy battle. To defend its position, the Army chooses a soon-to-be-justifiably-famous Boston trial lawyer, Joseph Welch

While all this is happening I cover and report the Army-McCarthy story and help BeLieu and Stevens. I also cover my White House beat. I have problems. Not just the amount of time and strain it takes to do my work and help keep the heat on McCarthy, but *Newsweek*'s congressional correspondent, Sam Shaefer, keeps reporting to New York things that are not true. This is not Schaefer's fault. He is reporting what he is being told by his sources, right-wing senators on the McCarthy committee. They tell Sam what they are telling Stevens and what Stevens has told them and what the strategy of the hearings will be. They are lying. I know because I am listening to their conversations and taking notes on another phone in Stevens's home. They do not say to Stevens what they are telling Sam they said.

I can't reveal my sources because what I am doing is illegal, and news of it would certainly leak out in the supercharged atmosphere of these days and it would hurt myself, BeLieu, and Stevens. Around six one evening, I sit in one of the deep leather chairs in the White House lobby. I am waiting for a call from the president's Counsel Bernard Shanley to come up to his office. I want to ask him about the limits of executive privilege should the committee ask Stevens about conversations with White House personnel. I already know most of the answers from illegally listening in on the phones or reading the phone logs being kept by Ken BeLieu. BeLieu has been ordered not to make such transcripts, but this is no time for a wise man to uncover his ass and obey stupid orders. I need some quotes from Shanley that I can legally use in *Newsweek*'s report on the McCarthy story. As I relax in the deep chair, I feel a huge cough coming on. I get my handkerchief to my mouth before the cough breaks. There seems to be a good bit of phlegm behind it. I get the phlegm into my handkerchief and bring the handkerchief from my mouth. It is bright red. I am terrified.

I cancel the appointment with Shanley and take a cab home and crawl under the bedcovers. Mary calls our doctor. He comes, takes a look and orders an ambulance. There are no private rooms left in the District General Hospital, so I go under an oxygen tent in the emergency ward. I have double lobar pneumonia. I am out for three weeks, the last two of which I spend in Florida, slowly recovering my health and gaining back strength and weight at the small house my Uncle Nick and Aunt Laura have built in Boca Grande.

The self-destruction of McCarthy is still some way off. The Army-McCarthy hearings do not begin until April 22, 1954. Counsel for the Army Joseph Welch's famous destruction of McCarthy with his "Have you no sense of decency sir" speech comes on June 9. The Senate vote of censure, 67 to 22, will not come until December 2. McCarthy's final booze-besotted death is in May of 1957.

At one moment during the TV hearings, Secretary Stevens reports that only BeLieu and Art Hadley of *Newsweek* were with him the night he issued his famous fighting statement. BeLieu and I get subpoenaed. BeLieu testifies. I want to testify, but I have a wise lawyer who is also a good friend, Walter Skallerup.

"You are not important enough, Arthur. I'll just keep shuffling the dates when you can be available and you will be passed over."

"I want to testify." He and his two partners finally beat some sense into my head.

The TV remarks of Stevens greatly increase my status at *Newsweek* and at the White House, both with Eisenhower's staff and among my fellow reporters.

I am tremendously happy in my White House assignment and with *Newsweek*. I love my work, I am learning a great deal, and I find time to write a book. I have two more children whom I love, with another planned. Mary and I live in an old, ten-room house set on a small hill at the corner of O and Dumbarton streets in Georgetown. The house boasts a brick-walled terrace for cocktails and cookouts, a small garden, a children's play area, and a reserved parking space in the alley in the rear. We have a live-in nurse for the children, Voicey, who brought two small Dutch children safely through the war after the mother and father were jailed as suspected Resistance members. A cook and maid come in by the day. We throw parties and even a dance in our large, sunken living room. The dance, our "New Year's Recovery Party" on the Saturday after New Year's, takes off each year with a lively mixture of friends from the press, Congress, old Washington, CIA, State, and the Pentagon.

In the summer Mary, nurse, and children go to Edgartown, a quiet, exclusive harbor town on Martha's Vineyard. After renting there for three years we have finally bought a five-bedroom house overlooking Edgartown harbor. The house has a basement, a back yard, and a tiny dock, suitable for a small dingy with outboard. Next to our ten feet of beach is the harbor boatyard, an ideal neighbor, interesting by day, silent by night. I join Mary and the children on weekends and for my three-week summer vacation.

I am too busy to worry about my marriage, which on the whole, while not great, remains quite possible, certainly compared to that of my parents. I assume "passable" applies to many lasting marriages. As David Riesman wrote, "Most men lead lives of quiet desperation." My life at least is interesting, exciting, and noisy. Yet, I am about to make a completely unwise *Choice*. One that takes me from Washington, with a full life, close friends, and fascinating work, to set me down in a new place, in a job I find frustrating, unpleasant, and unimportant.

Because of my fine work at the Eisenhower White House, *Newsweek* offers me a salary increase and a major promotion to New York, where I will become the "Periscope" editor. "Periscope," two pages at the front of *Newsweek*, is a unique feature of the magazine, vital to its image and circulation. The two pages are full of crisp paragraphs, each of which purports to give the inside truths about news events and prophesies about what comes next. Some of the "Periscope" items are examples of insight and great reporting. Others are somewhat dubious.

Fate and Choice

I once asked a grizzled Highlander, my guide on the Helmsdale, a salmon river in the way far north of Scotland, what the old Duke of Sutherland, long deceased, had been like. "Auch," the Highlander replied. "He was born na good. He was raised na good. And when he came into man's estate, he fulfilled the promise of his birth and breeding." I don't believe *Fate* ever controlled me so completely. But at this moment *Fate* laughed at the "free" in my free *Choice* and struck. I choose as *Fate* programmed me. I elect to climb the ladder that I have been taught to regard as close to sacred. Editors and TV anchors are more important and happier than reporters. They have more orderly lives. They sit at desks and make more money. I negotiate a caveat: that I can stay in Washington and commute two days a week, Saturday and Sunday, to New York in order to both gather material for "Periscope" and edit the page. *Newsweek* accepts. I do not realize that what I have asked has once again put me outside the normal pattern of an organization. I go to New York and "Periscope," while I continue to live in Washington, neither fully a reporter nor an editor.

I have a miserable time. As a reporter, if I uncover an important piece of information that bears on the future, I would much rather write a full piece than a paragraph for "Periscope." Reporters not on the *Newsweek* staff are paid for the items they submit. Many do so for the extra money. Often such items, to be charitable, are inaccurate, some, I suspect, made up. These outside reporters also send in information from off-the-record briefings that would cause a reporter trouble if the information appeared in his own paper. I sit at my desk and negotiate. I realize that in coming to "Periscope" I have made a mistake from which it will be difficult to recover.

I do have two pleasant memories from that brief year.

First, I cannot understand when I come into the Saturday editorial conference in New York why so little attention is paid to my excellent inside news from Washington and so much attention paid to reports of others. I decide that something about me does not say Washington. I watch the comings and goings at the White House. The comers and goers all wear hats. I don't. I do have in my closet a wonderful homburg given me by my late Grandfather Blodget. The next Saturday conference I arrive just as it is about to start. I take off my homburg and place it on the table beside my briefcase. I give them the same stuff I've been giving them for weeks. But this time I am congratulated on the excellence of my inside information.

Second, "Periscope" is the last department of *Newsweek* to be cleared for printing on Sunday afternoon, "To go to bed," in journalistic argot. This means that I can usually make the American Airlines five P.M. flight back home to Washington. The shuttle does not yet exist.

The flight is comfortable, with wide seats, the stewardesses ask your name, free drinks and tea are served. Nelson Rockefeller, then Health Education and Welfare secretary in Eisenhower's Cabinet, and I often take this flight. We know each other from press conferences, meetings, and are sometimes at the same parties. We get into the habit of sitting together on the flight to talk problems and politics.

On one such flight the stewardess comes by and as usual asks our names and what we would like to drink. I give my name and order a bourbon on the rocks. Nelson gives his name, "Rockefeller" and orders tea. The stewardess vanishes for a long time. When she comes back she has on fresh lipstick, her sleeves are tastefully rolled up, her blouse open to the navel, she has hiked up her skirt and done something with her bra. She is so excited by the possibilities she spills tea all over Nelson.

After she has wiped him off I say, "Nelson, you must get a lot of girls."

"I get a lot of tea in my lap, too."

With only my homburg and Nelson's tea the two most memorable events of my *Newsweek* life during that year, I use the spare time "Periscope" gives me to create a television pilot for a news program. I know nothing about television, but the coin flipper plows blindly ahead. My theory is that TV news is too like an extension of radio news, just talking heads telling the day's events. What is needed is animation and puppets to dramatize the news with all its humor and conflicts. I put up some money and enlist the help, and some more money, from two of the ablest journalists my age: Phillip Geyelin, who will later become chief editor of the editorial pages of the *Washington Post,* and Douglas Cater, later president of Washington College. We hire Bil Baird of Baird's Puppets and UPA, the animators, who created Gerald McBong Bong and Mr. Magoo. Baird summers on Martha's Vineyard and becomes a friend.

The creation of the pilot film for our TV news show *Insight* requires a steep learning curve. The three of us rush through roller-coaster days of delight, despair, and hair-tearing disappointment. Geyelin will later describe the time as the most exciting part of his life outside of the Marines. We end with absolute failure. We are dead before we start, but we don't know that. After much labor, we put together a challenging half-hour pilot. Then the Stage Hands' Union rules that each of our three puppet stages, individually about the size of a family card table, are full stages under the terms of their contract. Each will require eleven men to operate. No amount of negotiation changes their minds. The show is too expensive to even consider. TV continues to be talking heads. I learn two old lessons: excessive power corrupts whether wielded by management, government or labor, and look before you leap.

Choice

The look before you leap message does not stick. In a mix of euphoria and confusion after the *Insight* failure, I resign from *Newsweek* determined to try to write a play. I scarcely take the time in which a coin could rise and descend. I just leap. I enjoyed the excitement of working for myself while producing the failed *Insight*. My Yale class yearbook lists my future occupation as "playwright." At Yale I had taken a battery of tests to discover occupations for which I would be psychology well suited, types of work where my profiles matched those who were successful in such careers. The tests reported the job I most certainly should avoid is that of a counselor at a "Young Mens' Christian Association camp." That made perfect sense. The area of work where I would be the happiest was that of a writer. Unfortunately there was no test to find out if I could write. Why not now find out if I can write a play? Since I know a great deal about the intelligence and military world, I take as my plot the protection of the top-secret tunnel dug by the CIA beneath Soviet headquarters in Berlin built to listen electronically to phone calls and conversations inside.

I go back to my old Underwood typewriter, a possession close to my heart, which I used at *Newsweek* and with which I wrote *Do I Make Myself Clear?* my second published book. The Underwood is so ancient that the keys drop rather than the roller rises. I will peck away at this machine through two unsuccessful plays and four successful books before its melt down in the fire that destroyed my West

Tisbury home. I write slowly, even today on a computer, as my dyslexia prevents me from typing fast. When I speed up the letters either get omitted, reverse themselves, or just jumble.

Chance, Luck and Choice

I am writing my play in the guest room of our house in Edgartown. The phone rings. I answer and hear a voice that sounds much like one of my heroes, Dean Acheson. Acheson says he relies on my ability to keep a secret and tells me the following: Former President Truman believes that Adlai Stevenson is not the man to run for president a second time against Eisenhower. He will go down to defeat again, as will any Democrat who runs against the extremely popular president. What is important is that whoever runs be strong enough so that in defeat he can keep the Democratic Party out of the hands of its conservative wing, led by Senator Lyndon Johnson and Speaker of the House Sam Rayburn. Stevenson has shown he is not strong enough to do this. Governor Harriman of New York is. Truman wants Averell Harriman to win the nomination. Truman will come out for Harriman at some decisive moment during the Democratic convention. This is all secret. But right now Harriman's campaign is not running well. Would I be willing to join it as press secretary?

I have gotten part of my play written. Should I not finish it? Bring some regularity into my life? Mary is concerned about the length of time my writing has already taken. She thinks it keeps me out of the real world. But to be part of a major presidential primary campaign. To be inside looking out, not outside looking in. And suppose we win the primaries and go against Ike? There is a book in that if the play does not work. And to be allies with Acheson and Truman, I join the Harriman campaign.

The Harriman campaign is strangely skewed from the beginning because it is based on the idea of eventual defeat. Its true objective cannot even be hinted at: to keep the conservative Southern wing of the Democratic Party from taking over the party machinery. Only six or seven of us know this strategy. Further, the campaign is staffed almost 100 percent by New Yorkers with limited knowledge of the rest of America. Harriman himself largely finances his own campaign. Most of our fund-raising effort is a front designed to disguise that Averell is paying for Averell. Among other problems, and my particular concern, is that most of the press, including the New York Times, much favors Adlai Stevenson. Stevenson a likable man, is a master of the quotable nugget and press contacts. Avrell, though strong in a press conference, can come across as stiff and humorless, and also has few press contacts.

The first two days in my new job I spend much of my afternoons and evenings in the New York Public Library and in the archives of the *New York Times*. I want to make sure that there is nothing in Harriman's past that can blindside him. I find that he had a love affair with Dolores Del Rio, and financed a picture for her, an Eric Ambler spy thriller, *Journey into Fear*. I rather hope that leaks out. My candidate needs the humanization.

I have heard via the grapevine and jest that, like many rich men, Harriman is inclined to believe that those working for him are not earning their pay. He makes early-morning phone calls to find out who is on the job. The first week I am at work at Harriman headquarters in the Beverly Hotel in New York City, I arrive at my desk at a prompt six each morning, already having scanned several newspapers. Sure enough, at six-thirty on Thursday my phone rings and the governor is on the phone. Have I seen the unfair article about the campaign in the *New York Times*? I am able to reply that not only have I seen it, I have already called the *Times*'s city desk, left a message, and also written personally to the managing editor. "I will make sure a copy of that letter is on your desk today, Governor." I never get bothered again by the early-morning Harriman. We Grotonians know that sleep after six is profligate luxury.

The governor's miserly ways have become the stuff of legend. One story concerns the hire of a steamboat on Lake Ontario for a friendly outing of upstate politicians and friends on a trip around the lake's shores. The boat fills up rapidly, but the food and booze disappear more rapidly. Mike Pendergast, the Democratic Party boss of New York, is standing by the governor.

"Mike, there are a great many people on board. This is getting expensive."

"Yes, it is, Governor. And the worst part is half of these people are not going to vote for you anyway."

"Well get them off, Mike. Get them off!"

"Oh I couldn't do that, Governor. I don't know which half they are."

I myself get a taste of Harriman's legendary impecuniousness. The early Democratic primaries had been a three-way race. Stevenson, Harriman, and Senator Estes Kefauver, the crime-fighting senator. Then Kefauver drops out, unable to compete with Stevenson's popularity or Harriman's wealth. The day this happens, Harriman is flying into LaGuardia Airport on a private plane from upstate New York. I go out to the airport to go aboard the plane to brief Harriman before he deplanes on Krefauver's withdrawal and what the press is saying and predicting. He will then be ready with answers for the five or six reporters waiting in the airport terminal.

After Harriman talks with the reporters, he wants to call his headquarters in the various states where he has a chance of winning. But he has no money to put in the coin phones. I race around the terminal changing my dollar bills into quarters. I never get repaid.

On the inside of politics I learn three new truths. Politicians can keep secrets as well as secret agents or the Mafia. At least seven people in Harriman's headquarters and in the New York Democratic Party know that Truman will forcefully declare for Harriman at the Democratic convention in Chicago. The press never hears the faintest whisper of a leak.

The next more widely known truth: campaigns are totally disorganized. There are titles but they have no meaning as power indicators. You can seldom be sure who is the real boss. Are you checking with Charlie, when you need to put the fix in with Fred? There are no keys to the executive washroom. And if there are, someone is forging more. Campaigns are full of powerful people trying to get the candidate to go their way. A path that they are sure will guarantee his election, and of course protect their interests. Successful candidates need to be self-assured and tough. The distance between those qualities and blind arrogance can be frighteningly small.

The final truth I report sadly. The prejudices of reporters can badly distort the news. By this I emphatically do not mean that reporters deliberately distort news. All but a few extreme ideologies try to tell both sides fairly, usually with success. The problem comes because, without their realizing what they are doing, reporters' sympathies cause them to emphasize one fact and overlook or slight another. I see that defect in myself. Because of my Army experience and as a military reporter I believe passionately in the need for a just draft. The poor should not be put in harm's way to defend the rich. People, politicians, and others who are against a fair draft, and worse those who avoid the draft, I tend to minimize as cowardly schemers.

Jack Germond, an old-time shoe-leather reporter with a wise and sympathetic understanding of politicians and people, has written a lovely book, *Fat Man in the Middle Seat*. In his book Jack takes an insider's look at how the press handles the dilemma of sympathy versus bias. "For the press (Robert) Kennedy's campaign of 1968 posed a special problem — how to keep a proper distance, how to maintain a professional detachment. Most of us also liked Kennedy and the people around him. He was a wiseguy and so were many of those closest to him. . . . One of the true tough (old-time) guys on the story, Richard Harwood of the *Washington Post*, worried enough about his own objectivity that he suggested to his editors that he should be replaced for a time."

The press favoritism for Stevenson comes naturally. He is a liberal, thoughtful man with an off-beat sense of humor and fun to be around. Harriman remains distant. My constant refrain is: "Look guys, we're not talking about which person we'd like to have dinner with. We are talking about the best man for president." I don't get very far.

To win the nomination Harriman must peel off some Southern states from Stevenson, while picking up more Northern states. But Stevenson is holding on to his Southern support by waffling on integration, while the press keeps stressing Harriman's commitment to that issue. I ask several well-respected reporters to put tough questions to Stevenson to expose the free ride he is getting on integration.

The author at age three, hogging the ball from a future soft drink heiress.

(From left to right) John, age 6; Barbara, age 9 months; Katharine "Winks," age 9; and the author, age 12.

The author as the captain of Groton's first ever basketball team.

(Left) The author at age seventeen, about to be a sixth-former at Groton, and *(below)* at discharge from the Army four years later in 1946.

Kate and George aboard the *Queen Mary* watching crepe suzettes being prepared.

A lifetime of press coverage.

The author after a B-52 low-level training mission.

The author and General James Gavin, a friend and mentor.

(Top to bottom)
Our wedding. Life changes.
From left: Caroline, Kate,
George, the author, Arthur III,
Jane, Nick, and Elisabeth.

Jane, an expert fisher, with
an Okyel River salmon.

An aerial view of the West
Tisbury house and the three
cabins.

The Vineyard house.

Jane and author with Dr. Ernst Lowenberg and his wife on the Vincyard. Ernst, a refugee from Germany who asked exploring questions, came to teach at Groton in 1940. He and the author became lifelong friends.

The Vineyard house
after the fire.

The author and Jane in the kitchen of the ancient farm-house we rented for six summers in the Dordogne.

The author and an old-time British colonel talk over a great many NATO maneuvers since 1952.

The author in Vietnam.   Jane at age sixty.

Grandchildren: Austin Thies, Ali Wheeler,
Angus Thies, and Ben Wheeler.

Together in the New York apartment.

Merry Christmas • Seasons Greetings • Happy New Year

from two once upon a time 21 year olds

Miss Chesterfield

01824612

still together in memory and spirit

My 2004 Christmas card.

No response. One goes so far as to say, "Look, I love that guy. He should be president. I'm not going to ask those questions."

Truman's endorsement is not enough. Harriman does not get the nomination. His headquarters closes immediately. My last memory is some of the more mobbed-up members of the New York delegation rushing through the headquarters pushing huge post office baskets on wheels, stealing typewriters, telephones, radios, everything else not securely nailed down.

Fate and Luck

In the pressure cooker of campaign politics I find inside me an alarming self-image. I do not see myself as fully grown up. When I am with others I am usually standing back. I have difficulty speaking at the right time. Several times I lose important arguments through this hesitation. I kneel on one leg to hand senior politicians a paper. I see myself as looking through a window at events, not part of the action, not a major player. I lack the psychological strength, the self-confidence to force my way. My school debating prowess, my Army leadership skills, have gone. Where is the Hadley of the war canoe? I stay out of meetings to which I am not asked but know I am needed, rather than just enter. Now that I recognize this problem, what comes next?

Luck now blocks what would have been a major change in my life. During the Harriman campaign I become friendly with Jim Mc-Conaughy, the Washington bureau chief of Time-Life. We eat together and freely swap ideas about politics, social trends, reporting. Just before the end of the Harriman campaign Jim asks me if I would like to come back to Washington to cover politics for *Life* magazine. I realize that would be a perfect job for me. *Life* does not put the spin on politics that *Time* and *Newsweek* do. I have an ally of sorts at *Life* already in C. D. Jackson, who used to be *Life*'s publisher. I accept. Jim says we will have to wait to write the contract till later in the election when everyone no longer goes all out. Four weeks later Jim McConaughy is killed in the crash of an Air Force transport plane.

He was on an Air Force VIP flight with several other well-known reporters. The trip was so important that a senior Air Force general rather than the regular pilot was at the plane's controls. The general could not handle the aircraft, a tanker converted into a VIP transport.

Had the reporting job materialized, I would have returned to Washington and been happy in that work for some time. Probably I would have made reporting a lifetime occupation. Never reached the crisis in my life. Never met, and after much bungling, married Jane. I would never have wept for joy, loss, and love. Three short, trite nouns, but they apply here. I go back to writing my play.

Then an interlude with an upside-down ending. My friend Walter Skallerup, the lawyer who had me wisely lie low and not testify before the McCarthy-Army committee, now is one of those in charge of finances for the Stevenson presidential campaign. The symbol of that campaign is a small silver pin in the shape of a shoe with a hole in it. The pin can go in a man's buttonhole or become a woman's dress ornament. A few are sold in select stores but mainly they are sold at large Stevenson rallies. Each pin costs a dollar and at a large rally — say twenty thousand people — there is a lot of loose cash floating around. Multiply this by four or five huge rallies a campaign trip; that's real money. Walter is looking for a new person to handle shoe pin sales. Would I be available to join Stevenson's traveling campaign staff in charge of shoe pin sales?

Sure.

From the first day out I find there are problems. There are a great many shoe pins on the market. Our pins are made of silver at a cost of about fifty cents apiece and sell for a dollar. The others on the market are made of lead. They cost about four cents apiece to make and sell for fifty cents. There is a problem with these cheaper pins. The Stevenson campaign gets no money from their sale. The wiseguys making them, reportedly in Brooklyn, keep all the cash. I find the lady in overall charge of the Stevenson shoe pin effort. I suggest we make ours from lead also, to gain the campaign more money. I am told that lead is not in keeping with the personality of the candidate. The lady in overall charge of shoe pins is Stevenson's aunt. That solves that problem.

The other worry is more complicated. Most of the large rallies are held at night and this is where the sales of shoe pins are made. The campaign plane usually leaves for the next city at nine in the morning. I have roughly $6,000 to $10,000, mostly one-dollar bills with a few fives in a suitcase from the rallies. I would like to exchange these ones and fives for a bank check. Is there anyone in any local bank who will do this for me at one in the morning? No. How early can someone be at the bank to count the bills with me and issue a check? Eight in the morning. Even with a car waiting, that gives about fifteen minutes to count $8,000 to $10,000 worth in singles and fives. It can't be done. As the fortnight goes on I have more and more ones and fives in my new suitcase. I have bought this second suitcase that I personally carry on board the aircraft and leave in hotel strong rooms.

Back in Washington with some $30,000 plus in small bills, I dump the whole problem in Walter's lap. He knows the manager of the Riggs Bank near the White House. I will go there to count the money with one of the bank's officers. When we agree on the sum, the bank will issue a bank check. I will walk the check over to the Stevenson headquarters and give them the check as a gift. Making the money a gift was the only way to transfer it to the campaign legally.

Several weeks after the election, the *New York Times* publishes a list of major contributors to the Democratic Party. Low, and unfortunately behold, up there with the nation's richest Democratic families and financiers is Arthur T. Hadley, writer. My life does change a bit. I get more phone calls from strangers. Senator Lyndon Johnson, who has found but little time for me when I was a reporter, now takes to crossing the street to greet me and introduces me to his friends as "The Honorable Arthur T. Hadley, a great force for good in this country." Three years later Robert Kennedy chews me out for not giving more to his brother's presidential campaign. I explain the shoe pin situation. I do not think he believes me. After his brother's election I listen, but hear no siren call from Washington.

I go back to writing and finish the first draft of my play, a CIA drama about hard choices in the real world. I put that aside and, while the experience is fresh, start my first novel, *The Joy Wagon,* a humorous (I hope) political satire about the first electronic calculator to run for U.S. president. The book benefits from George Orwell's dictum, "There is always room for one more custard pie," does well in hardcover and later becomes a paperback. The paperback sale money, plus a mortgage, enable me to buy the land and beach in West Tisbury.

Mary and I take a three-week vacation to Europe. A week's salmon fishing and two weeks in France. Mary leaves first by boat. She has trouble flying even short distances, some secret pact she made in adolescence with her God. In France we explore the cave paintings of Lascaux in the Dordogne. They had not yet been closed to the public, indeed they had not even been much discovered by the public. We have them to ourselves, guided by a flashlight held by one of the two men who had discovered the caves. From the paintings and carvings the outlines of the great beasts blaze out in striking colors to become almost abstractions of animal power, their 15,000-year-old glory absolutely intact.

While at Yale my interest in language had caused me to read the Polish philosopher Alfred Korzybski and his theory of general semantics. My self-assured ego had dismissed his work as some simple truths obscured by complex language. As I emerge from the explosive experience of the 15,000-year-old cave paintings I realize instead that Korzybski exemplified Isaiah Berlin's dictum, "The fox knows many things; but the hedgehog knows one great thing well." Korzybski distinguishes between two types of knowledge, "time bound knowledge" and "time free knowledge."

"Time bound knowledge" is that which mankind can build on from generation to generation. Copernicus builds on Galileo, Newton builds on Copernicus, Einstein builds on Newton, Fermi builds on Einstein, and so on. But the other type of knowledge, "time free knowledge" or "emotional knowledge," stays the same from generation to generation. There is nothing we can build on that makes us more kind, loving, and forgiving than our fathers and mothers. And nothing our children can build on to make them more kind, loving, and forgiving than ourselves.

Between Picasso or Brancusi or Munch or Rembrandt and the 15,000-year-old cave artists exists zero time. They have the same amount of emotional knowledge and artistic skill. The cave artists see and experience their world the same way we see ours today. Yet I stand at the mouth of their Lascaux cave and watch cars drive by in the age of atom bombs. I have a son who will later find part of a split atom: the top quark. And all I have, and all he has, to handle the immense problems created by "time bound nowledge" is the "time free knowledge," the emotional knowledge, possessed 15,000 years ago by Lascaux's painters. Nothing more. There is no emotional time bound knowledge. Since that instant I have not given myself or mankind much hope.

> Gather ye rosebuds while ye may,
> Old Time is still a-flying.

Fate and Choice

I am back in Martha's Vineyard in my house in Edgartown working on my political novel. The phone rings. (Perhaps I should write a book about my life called *Summoned by Bells*.) It's another job offer. By now I should have learned from being "Periscope" editor, the abortive television show, the Yale psychological tests, the Harriman campaign, being White House correspondent, and from the play in my typewriter, from all of these, that my life fits about me best when I report or write. And that I am unhappy, troubled, and function with strain when I issue orders and sit behind a desk. On some level I do know this, but not deeply enough to even consider a coin flip. My *Fate* again dictates the decision I make in this supposedly free *Choice*. I ask for a month to finish my book. When that is arranged I agree to become an editor at the *New York Herald Tribune*.

I hold various titles at various times with the paper but basically I am the assistant executive editor. Or as one wag put it, my job is "to improve the paper without changing it." He is not far wrong. A person with different genes and brought up differently, his *Fate* might have understood how power works on the *Herald Tribune*. He might have done well and benefited both himself and given the *Tribune* more help. I did not. I soon learn what should be done — make some small improvements — but have no clue how to effect the major changes needed. I could not have devised a more unpleasant, even dangerous, job for myself.

I know the publisher, Ogden "Brownie" (or simply "Brown") Ried. We were at the same summer camp and at Yale together, where I helped him in one of his courses. I was an usher at his wedding. But I do not know how to cultivate him or, more importantly, how to handle his mother, the paper's true ruler. Brown is neither abusively arrogant, nor stupid, nor a drunk like his father. He does have two serious problems. He has no way of relating to people, and he lacks filters to separate the nonsense he hears from friends, sycophants, and outsiders from the nuggets, mostly unpleasant, he gets from his able staff. Brown relies on a man he personally picked to be his second in command, Frank Taylor. Since I and others who cared for the paper fought with Taylor continually, it seems fairest for me to leave describing Taylor to Richard Kluger, who wrote *The Paper*, a masterful history of the *Herald Tribune*. Kluger paints a more flattering picture of Frank Taylor than I might. "Frank Taylor was a washout almost from the moment he arrived," writes Kluger. "Whatever professional competence he once possessed had been consumed by alcohol. He was detected drinking vodka out of a water glass during *Tribune* working hours...Taylor was grossly deficient in education, manners, and culture and the editorial people rated him a blowhard who tried occasionally to throw his weight around and then retreated glumly in the shadows of dysfunction."

Taylor's ally on the editorial floor was Luke Carroll. To quote Kluger again, "Carrol was often a brutal, bullying ruler....(his) news judgment fell far short of the *Tribune*'s traditional standard. He retained a police reporter's mentality, which had its uses, but in an age when the news was growing increasingly complex, something more was required to direct the daily operations of a sophisticated metropolitan newspaper...journalism to Luke Carroll too often meant being guided by sensation; history to him was for libraries not newspapers."

Overly kind again, but fair. I would add that his brutal ways caused some of our ablest reporters, such as Homer W. Bigart, to leave. With such commanders and short of cash we are going to take on the *New York Times*?

Besides its management, the *Trib* has other basic problems. First is the rise of television, and second the excellence of the *New York Times*. More people are getting their news from television, fewer from newspapers. That cuts circulation for everyone and makes competition between newspapers more intense. The *New York Times* sits on top of us with more pages and more advertising. They are a great and inclusive newspaper but also a dull newspaper. With a little hustle, and we have a hustling city room, we may not take them, but we can keep pace. Our motto, "They have a man at every rat hole, but we have a rat at every manhole," expresses a fighting truth. But can management bring this truth into battle?

Those who run the *Times* would like New York to have but one serious newspaper — theirs. To accomplish that, while they publicly praise diversity and differing viewpoints, their private policy is "kill the *Trib*." I recognize this is a perfectly legitimate business policy, though their Uriah Heep insincerity annoys me. Were I top dog, I would probably do the same, though, I hope, without phony bleats of sorrow. One of the *Times*'s chief strategies to kill the *Trib* is to hold the cost of the daily paper at five cents. On the daily paper circulation we hold our own. We are behind but not by a killing amount. At five cents, both we and the *Times* lose money on the daily. But while that slowly kills us, the *Times* is not bothered. With their circulation and advertising pages, they take in more advertising on their daily than we do. They have their mammoth Sunday paper, section on section, a huge moneymaker. Their Sunday paper rightfully buries us completely.

To stay alive we have to take on the *Sunday Times*, the paper of the future or dinosaur of the past, depending if you are selling its ads or fighting it. Our own Sunday paper is a small wasteland, littered with wrong past decisions now fiercely defended with pride and prejudice. Old friends of Ried's mother dot its dreary landscape, along with faithful, long-term employees past their prime and put out to Sunday pastures. To even suggest change brings on a nightmare of long knives. I construct a new and lively Book Review. I line up two able publishing executives willing to come aboard as Book Review editors. Across America several other major newspapers agree to buy the new review to insert in their Sunday editions. Management friends of Mrs. Ried destroy that project. I argue the weekend is now two days, Saturday and Sunday, not just Sunday. To take advantage of this social change and beat the *Times*, our Sunday paper should come out on Saturday, now a major shopping day. That gets buried under cries of "tradition, tradition." I suggest we need a strong, local Sunday magazine and work up the format and a prospectus. Management lets the idea slip away. The concept later becomes *New York Magazine* and prospers under the able editorship of Clay Felker.

All this while I am conscious that I have placed myself in moral jeopardy. I try to persuade fine reporters and editors, some who are my friends and others whom I only know by work and reputation, to come to work for the *Tribune*. But if the *Tribune* fails, as it well may, I have put them out on the street at a bad time in their lives. But unless I get some of them to the *Trib*, the paper's chances grow less and less. To recruit people, I am not telling the whole truth. Most of the hires I make or reporters already there whom I promote are fine. One of the best is Peter Braestrup, who wins a Nieman Fellowship at Harvard for his reporting of racketeering in the garment trucking industry. He also gets shot at, which just increases his enthusiasm for the story. (Many years later Jane will remark that Braestrup's only problem is his tendency to swing naked from a dining room chandelier with combat boots on, while kicking wine glasses off the table.)

One of Braestrup's scoops stands out as a sad example of the *Trib*'s basic management problems. The Algerian war is going on between France and the Algerian Arab rebels. All the reporting is from the French side, which may be losing. I find the money to send Braestrup to Africa to cover the war from the Arab side. A reporter from another paper who went out with Braestrup on one Arab guerrilla raid describes Braestrup, a wounded and decorated Marine officer, as showing the Arabs where to place their machine guns to inflict maximum carnage on the French. "No, not there, sergeant. They'll escape that way. Put the other machine gun more to the east to cover that draw."

The French learn who he is, that he is in the desert, and what he is doing. They send scouting planes to locate him. When he is found, a platoon of French paratroopers stand by their aircraft, ready to jump on his position, kill him, and secretly bury him. Braestrup lies covered with desert sand by Arab friends, and escapes. When he returns his copy is Pulitzer-Prize caliber. No other paper has such reporting from the Arab side. His story will lift our circulation, provide Sunday pieces, and show up the *Times*.

His story never gets published in the *Tribune*. The French government informs Mr. Ried that if the story runs they will find ways to shut down the *International Herald Tribune*'s printing plant in Paris. The *Tribune*'s Paris office may be vandalized by loyal Parisians. If the story does not run however, Mr. Ried will receive the Legion de Honor as a true friend of France. Ogden Reid receives his buttonhole red ribbon. Compare this with the *Washington Post*'s courage during Watergate and the *New York Times* with the *Pentagon Papers*.

> Just for a handful of silver he left us,
> Just for a riband to wear in his coat.

I visit my doctor for my annual checkup. My blood pressure has suddenly become dangerously elevated. "I hope you know what you are doing," says my doctor. He is the family doctor and also mine since I was at Yale. "Because you are not doing yourself any good." He gives me some pills and a sad look.

As an editor, one of my jobs on many nights is "putting the paper to bed." This means going down to the pressroom floor, an enormous block-long room that contains the presses, the Linotype composing machines that set our type, and the machines that fold and package papers. There I keep out of the way of pressmen, Linotype operators, and proofreaders while I try to help the process run without glitches. The other executive on the floor with me night after night is Lester Zwick, the *Trib*'s dedicated chief of circulation, an observant realist, full of hands-on experience and human insight. He covers his concerns for the *Trib* with his pose as a gruff, up-from-the-streets circulator, only interested in selling more papers filled the with "Blood, Money, and Sex." As the only two executives regularly on the press floor we talk, drink a bit afterward, and become friends. We find that from totally different backgrounds and news experience, we agree completely on ways that possibly might save the paper; beginning with a total makeover of the Sunday paper.

One night as Zwick and I are talking over the roar of the presses, I hear a phone ring at the far end of the block-long room. That phone stops and a phone a bit nearer to us starts to ring. That one stops and a phone still closer to us rings. The phones are gaining. I hope when they catch us the call is for Zwick. I'm tired. The call is for Zwick, from one of our truck drivers at the Pennsylvania Railroad Station.

"What?" I hear Lester bark. "One of our trucks ran over one of our circulators? Backing up? And he is bleeding to death. Where is he bleeding? No. Not what part of his body? What is he bleeding on? He's bleeding on our papers! Bleeding on the *Herald Tribune*! Move him over and have him bleed to death on the *Times*. If we don't make the ten o'clock train to Washington, the *Times* don't make the ten o'clock to Washington." That's a circulator. That is the *Trib* at its best. That is pure Lester Zwick.

Outside of the *Trib* I am reaping the supposed benefits of success. I am far up that seductive ladder, ahead of most of my classmates from Groton and Yale. I am asked to serve on many charitable boards; quite a few of these I accept. I become a trustee of the Brearley School, the Town School, a director of the Park Association of New York, and of the Public Education Association of New York; my wife, Mary, becomes a trustee of Vassar College. I accomplish little. As on the *Tribune* most of my suggestions seem out of bounds.

I arrange for a grant from the Rockefeller Brothers Fund to pay for a Russian teacher at the Brearley School. At the urging of the headmistress, the board turns it down. The only way to find room for Russian in the curriculum is unthinkable: not to teach Greek. Perhaps Greek could be made optional for those wishing to take Russian? No. I warn another organization not to take back a professional staff director they once let go. I have interviewed him and he carries chips on both shoulders. They rehire him. It's an expensive disaster.

Sometimes it becomes humorous. When Yale or Groton hold high-powered fund-raisers I am now and then included. One time I sit in the back of a meeting room next to a friend, Dr. Paul Russell. He was a year behind me at Groton and now is a leading surgeon at Columbia Presbyterian Hospital, famous for his technical skills and inventor of the liver transplant. Later he will become chief of surgery at the Harvard affiliated Massachusetts General Hospital. The fund-raiser on the dais makes his pitch to the group. "The next time you gentlemen are walking down Wall Street and see an old schoolmate coming toward you, remind him of how much we all owe Groton." Paul and I chuckle.

Luck and Choice

Two potent moments of *Luck* and *Choice* now start to work their slow significance. The first aids, and in part determines, much of what I will write, and also plays an important part later in a pro bono act. The second, which I label the "The Luck that keeps on Lucking," has what reporters call long legs. It keeps on marching and lucking and changing my life, even till today.

In the mid-1950s a number of us who thought about, wrote about, or held military command become concerned over the Eisenhower doctrine of "massive retaliation," the reliance of America and therefore of the free world on atomic bombs as the answer to all military threats. Those of us who question the doctrine are not against a strong Air Force and nuclear weapons, nor do we minimize the Soviet danger or that the doctrine saves money. However, to think of atomic bombs as the sole answer to all military challenges we find both reckless and dangerous. The Air Force has a slogan: "To be strong enough to win the peace, we have to first be able to win the war." That does not help to formulate national policy.

Concern over the massive retaliation is greater in Europe than in the United States. A retired British admiral, Anthony Buzzard, starts a newsletter that examines other ideas and options to massive retaliation. I'd written on this subject for a magazine, *The Reporter*, and so get on Buzzard's list. I send the admiral more of my articles and some money to help keep the newsletter alive.

As a published "expert" in this arcane area I am occasionally invited by friends to travel somewhere and lecture on military problems. In one lecture at Texas A&M on the dangers and difficulties of relying solely on atom bombs, the speaker after me, an Air Force general, tears into me as a chicken-hearted liberal. I am not sure if I have successfully defended my argument against relying on nuclear weapons to do everything. Suddenly a small fire breaks out in the ashtray on the speaker's table. An audience member yells from the back of the room: "For God's sake someone get a fire extinguisher before the general drops an atom bomb on it to put it out." I have never heard the basic problem expressed more cogently.

The number of those of us concerned over a military posture that relies almost exclusively on nuclear bombs keeps rising. Doubts, even fears, increase over where such a policy leads. The debate is particularly intense in Britain. There an interesting and diverse group consisting of leaders of the church, theologians, Royal Air Force air marshals, several admirals and generals, plus a few influential politicians, reporters, and academics decide to call a conference to search for alternative ideas. They form an an impressive group. Several are heroes of the British air battle, Eisenhower's former British chief of staff is one, a future candidate for prime minister another, plus younger officers, clergy, and academics obviously on the way up. Because of my articles and my presence on Admiral Buzzard's list, I am one of the two Americans invited. I convince the *Tribune* that this is an important event that I should cover.

The now-famous Brighton Conference was held in Brighton — where else? — on a weekend in November of 1956. At that moment

Britain, France, and Israel are waging a brief war against Egypt over the nationalization of the Suez Canal. A perfect example of a military challenge where nuclear weapons have no value. Tensions ran high in Britain that cold, wet week. Many Europeans objected to Eisenhower's opposition to the French-British effort. On Sunday I bundle up to go out on the stormy beachfront to buy my favorite British newspaper, the *Observer*. The news vendor hisses at me from his frozen kiosk: "I won't sell no bloody Commie paper to a lousy Yank."

Inside we are united. We agree that, while the conference has helped our thinking, some structure should be created to keep us in contact with one another and to provide thoughtful direction on military affairs independent of government. A committee of roughly seven of us is appointed to stay behind to draft a proposal and statement of purpose for such an organization. I am asked to be a member of this committee. Another member is Michael Howard, who will become a lifelong friend, and a major historian who will hold the prestigious Regis Professor of Military History Chair at Oxford. The Oxford chair, plus seeing the number of junior Pentagon officials who traveled to Oxford to study military history there, inspires me years later to create and raise the money for Yale's Robert Lovett Chair of Military History. The Lovett Chair will be the first chair of military history in America outside of the service academies. Michael Howard will leave the Regius professorship to become the first occupant of Yale's Lovett Chair.

Another friend in that group is Alistair Buchan, the British Washington correspondent who was a member of a small group of younger reporters I created in Washington. There was also a British ground general, an Air Force marshal, and, importantly, Canon Booth, an influential member of the Anglican Church. After three days of write and rewrite we produce the doctrine and the blueprint for the Institute of Strategic Studies, the ISS. Now the IISS, "International" having been added to its name. At its founding and for many years afterward the institute was successfully headed by Buchan. Recently it has grown more academic than I believe we founders intended. A priesthood of experts on nuclear weapons and use of force has grown up inside and outside of government. These people often dominate its discussions. The hard-edged realism of the serving soldier on war, weapons, and casualties has been lost.

As General James Gavin often remarked, "No man who has spent much time in a foxhole looks forward to the next war." The year before the war on Iraq is declared, Jane and I were not just the only civilians at a distinguished Army cocktail party; except for the aides, we are the only ones not generals. We meet no one in that room, some of whom I have known for many years, who are in favor of going into that war. Thy were certain the war had nothing to do with 9/11 and that we were ill-prepared. They understood both military history and harsh reality.

The combination of *Luck* and *Choice* that lead to my going to the Brighton Conference grants me status in both academic and military worlds. When I freelance, reporting on military affairs without a powerful organization behind me, being a founding member of the IISS means I am still a person to whom officials will talk, and I still get invited to important conferences. The institute's meetings, papers, and contacts have kept me current in emerging ideas and defense problems, while making me new friends.

Now *Luck* combines with *Choice* to start a chain of results profound and unexpected. The sequence I call *"The Luck that Keeps on Lucking"* begins.

After my happy times at Dalton, I send there both Kate, my oldest daughter, and George, my middle son. Nick, my youngest son, is a year away from school. My former wife has custody of my eldest son, Arthur. He lives with her and her new husband in South Africa. Interested in both the school and my children, I visit their Dalton classes at least once a term. I begin to be concerned that the unstructured nature of the school, so beneficial for me who grew up in a totally structured world, may not be so ideal for them with their more free-and-easy life. I worry I may be closing down their later educational choices.

One winter day when Kate is seven and George five, I visit their classes. George's class is building a great castle out of blocks, learning cooperation and planning. They have also dispatched a classmate to go down a floor to the class below them to warn that if they hear a great bang it's nothing going wrong, it's the upstairs castle falling down. Kate's class is writing a letter to an absent, sick member. They tell him they miss him and what they are studying. I'm enjoying a slightly unruly but thoughtfully organized class.

A girl comes up to the teacher to tell her she wants to write about studying the Arctic Ocean but does not know how to spell Arctic. "That's easy," says the teacher. "It's what I always tell you. Spell the word as it sounds: art tic; arttic"

Oh, no.

That the child asked that question on a day I am there and I overhear the answer is pure *Luck* . What follows is *Choice*. Mary has not been entranced by Dalton and for some time wanted to move the children. I've been worried. The spelling of "arttic" adds to my doubts. Next year we shift Kate to Brearley. George moves to St. Bernard's, run by William Westgate, a thoughtful headmaster who believes in children, loves learning, and hires sympathetic teachers. That same next year Nick is ready for kindergarten. St. Bernard's has no kindergarten. Where should Nick go? Mary and I look at several schools with kindergartens and decide on the Town School. I do not know it but *Luck* is playing about me like heat lighting. The next fall, a month after Nick begins kindergarten at Town, Mrs. Crane, a strong, thoughtful headmistress, asks me if I would like to go on the school board. I accept. It is a pleasant, small, informal board, all interested in the school rather than in social clout. I make many friends there. One of these is Robert Heilbroner, the economist and writer. He becomes the first part of the *"Luck that Keeps on Lucking."* He will introduce me to Jane.

Another is Nancy White, wife of Theodore "Teddy" White, already a successful author. Nancy and I enjoy each other on the board where we share the same humor and ideas. I meet Teddy and he and I also become friends. The Whites and Hadleys come to each other's houses for dinner or eat out. Teddy's faith in my ability will later lift me out of a desperate time.

Before all this future takes place as a result of an overheard remark at Dalton, life at the *Tribune* does not improve. The Rieds, desperate to save their family Republican newspaper, sell the *Herald Tribune* to Jock Whitney, a multi-multi-millionaire, then President Eisenhower's ambassador to Great Britain. From England Whitney delegates some of the staff members of his risk-capital firm, J. H. Whitney and Co., to study the paper. They sit in on our staff meetings, take part in story planning and the late-afternoon editors conference that makes up the front page and some of the rest of the paper and also does some picture selection. They are concerned and nice people. They have just turned around Minute Maid orange juice into a profit maker. They seem surprised that expertise in orange juice does not help them solve the paper's problems. They all wear suits, some of them even vests. They hire an expert in management organization as a consultant. He admits he too is puzzled by the paper, but he understands it better after lunch when he has talked to his psychoanalyst. When this news leaks, as everything does on a newspaper, hysterical laughter and dark depression grip the newsroom.

In the midst of this multilayered, unfolding management debacle, various teams of us *Tribune* executives are formed by Whitney management to look over different problems of the paper. We are to report back to the J. H. Whitney team. For some reason, undoubtedly as cockeyed as most of the others happening then, Lester Zwick and I are the two-man team to look at new directions for the *Trib*. He and I totally agree. The problem is the changing nature of news in the TV, suburban age, and our Sunday paper. The *Times* has an enormous lead over us. We need to produce a totally redesigned paper that comes out on Saturday. Estimated start-up costs are $10 million. If we cut into the *Times*'s Sunday circulation and use political heat they will probably go to ten cents on the daily. Then we have a chance. We label the two of us "The Boiler Room Bunch" "The Boiler Room Bunch" does not rate highly their chances of success.

The day comes when we have to brief the Whitney management team. I tell Lester, "Let me bring up what we tell them and carry the ball. I can afford to get fired more easily than you. And if they ever let me run this paper — which grows more doubtful every day — you know who will be at the right hand of the WASP who marches without a hat."

Lester nods. The Whitney people open our meeting with a sweetener. They want us to know that Mr Whitney is serious about saving the *Tribune*. They do not want the number talked about; but Whitney has pledged to invest $2 million a year in the paper for five years.

"Two million a year for five years," I say, "you are going to lose your money. Five million a year for two years, you have a fighting chance." The Whitney people do not like what they hear. They keep asking questions about the daily paper, which is not the problem. After we leave the room Lester asks, "Arthur, where did you ever learn to flip the dime?"

This question, put by Lester in his direct and breezy fashion, is basic to this book, basic to my life and basic to the life of anyone who believes some degree of free *Choice* is possible. Why are some people coin flippers while others shudder at the thought? Does *Fate*, as used in this book, design the brains, hearts, and perhaps even special thumbs for coin flippers? Or rather did we have free Choice and flipped, found we liked what happened, and flipped again and again. Or most probably, is there a mixture of both possibilities? *Fate*, both genetic and early training, must play some part to predispose some people toward risk taking, while scaring others away. But after a child's first ten years, life experience must play a part, if not the major part in producing coin flippers.

I look at my close friends and find mostly coin flippers. They come in all ages, sexes, jobs, and lifestyles: Generals James Gavin and John Ralph. Dr. Robert Sorley. Actors Adam and Susan Kennedy. Writers Kevin and Gail Buckley, Matt and Phyllis Clark, Theodore White. Newspeople Peter Braestrup, John Chancellor, Lester Zwick. Costume designer Patricia Zipprodt. Artist Stanley Murphy. Public servants, the Honorable Robert Lovett, Gloria Pleasant. Lawyers Stanley Pleasant, Walter Skallerup. Psychoanalyst Jane Hadley. Jane —now there was a coin flipper. To become my fourth wife.

I last see Lester at a theater in Boston eight years later in 1967.

He has moved back to his hometown where he consults and serves on various prestigious boards. Patricia Zipprodt — we are still partially together — is doing the costumes for *Plaza Suite* and I, living fulltime on Martha's Vineyard, have flown up from the island to see her. Lester is at the preview and I introduce Pat to Lester. We all talk briefly and move away. After we walk a few steps, Pat looks over her shoulder and says: "Arthur, Arthur, look around." I turn and look. Lester's vast smile is likely to break his jaw. He is looking at a happy coin flipper. "That man loves you," Pat continues. I can think of few men or women I would be as proud to be loved by as Lester.

Shortly after "The Boiler Room Bunch" have briefed the Whitney management team, I have another "Paul on the road to Damascus" experience, as powerful as the first at *Hellzapoppin*. What I describe I actually saw. I can still faintly see traces of the event in memory. But what I saw I could not possibly see and it could not be real. The event remains real to me. Real, not as a feeling but as an actual sighting. Real as his spider to Robert the Bruce. Real as the universal law of gravity revealed by Newton's real apple.

Mary and I are guests at a lavish benefit ball, held for the New York City Ballet in a hotel ballroom. Members of the corps de ballet and quite a few benefactors are dancing. I sit with Mary at our friends' table and watch both the dancers and my fellow watchers. Suddenly I become aware of a line running around and through the room like some crazy Balkan Border. That blazing serpentlike barrier, invisible to all but me, divides those in passionate contact with life, the warm and the alive, from the others, the removed and the cold. The line twists and writhes democratically. It includes and excludes members of both groups, ballet dancers and benefit supporters alike. Sometimes it even splits couples.

I sit on the lifeline's dead side. I must have put myself here. I know I have been programmed from birth to be on this side. That is no excuse. None. I have been trying all my life to bring myself, to fight myself "out." I thought I had been at least partway successful. But I am on the dead side of this line. Why? I do not want to be here. Do I look like the others on this side? Well, like some of them. And like some on the other side. What have I done to sit here? Have I just spun round and round like a twirled string, thinking I am changing places but always attached to the same center? How do I cross to the other side? I want to go there. I belong there. How do I cross? If my play gets on, will it do that for me? Exit signs glow on the ballroom walls. Maybe I should count "one potato, two potato, three potato, four," choose an exit sign, get up, and go through it to see where it leads. Yeah, and end up lost in the basement with alarms going off and called crazy by my friends. Somehow I must flip the coin. Where I am now I do not live.

As Mary and I silently taxicab home from the ball, I have no idea of what to do next. No knowledge of how long my hopes will remain in doubt, beyond my reach. How far I have to go. How much vital help I will need and receive from my friends.

Luck

Then during the next year *Luck* coils and hits twice with force. Both strikes help me venture across the line and greatly complicate my life. The first hits almost immediately. A new editor of the *Herald Tribune*, knowing I had been considered for editor, fires me. The second, an even more powerful strike, follows almost a year later.

The *Tribune* management does not bid me a fond farewell. A fingertip feeling for what may happen on the paper had caused me to insist on a special clause in my new, two-year contact. This clause obligates the *Tribune* to pay my salary for the contract's length, unless I leave the paper voluntarily. Management feels I slipped this one by and it would only be fair if I tore up my two-month-old two-year contract. I don't do that. While management does not actually boot me out the door, there is no farewell party, not even a handshake. The reporters in the city room who have in part been working for me are incensed at this treatment. They pass the hat to throw me a party and present me with a desktop silver cigarette case. It is inscribed: ATH FROM HIS FRIENDS AT THE TRIB. It sits in a place of honor on my desk. A pleasant reminder that perhaps for the few years I am there I did a few things right.

Four

LUCK AND THE LAST
GREAT CHOICE

Joining the unemployed gives me a great opportunity to rearrange my life. I do not rush to seize this chance. I feel a failure. Out of work. In a depressing someplace where I never wanted to find myself. I scramble to find a job. My agent at William Morris, who had handled the ill-fated TV program, agrees to handle the just-finished play. He sends it to friends, directors, and producers who might be interested. Most just make suggestions. A few even talk about options. An even fewer take me to lunch. Others who worked on the TV program or are in television or the theater read *Winterkill* and also make suggestions. In a cramped attic room of our East 74th Street house I try to fit their suggestions into new drafts. I yoyo up and down from elation to despair. I search harder for work. Friends like Stewart Alsop and Phil Geyelin try to interest magazines in my story ideas: *The Saturday Evening Post, Collier's, The New Republic.* No interest.

The summer of '59 ends and Mary, Kate, George, Nick, and housekeeper return from Edgartown. Tension rises between myself and Mary, who believes I have gotten way off track: "You don't know what you want, Daddy. You lack purpose." Since they are back from the island, I decide to try writing up there. Perhaps the play will go better in a quieter place.

A mistake. I rattle around in our big house on the water overlooking Edgartown harbor. Its affluent size is a constant reminder that I am nowhere and out of work. I put my typewriter in front of a window in the large back second-floor bedroom overlooking the harbor. The play is not improving and I see no way out. Much of the time I sit and stare at the little two-car ferry, *The On Time,* that shuttles back and forth across the harbor. Occasionally I break out in tears.

Even cooking, which I enjoy, turns sour. I began to cook the second summer after my discharge from the hospital and Army. I am writing an epic poem as credit for a summer course at Yale, and living alone in a friend's farmhouse in Littleton, New Hampshire. The poem, "Cobra Blue, The Day in the Life of a Tank Battalion," was written in the ancient Norse style of the Eddas, where the rhymes occur on the first syllables of words instead of the last. "The World Wolf's whelps, weaned one murders' marrow bones, swallow the sun." "Now as each tanker tracks towards the enemy, the tart taste of history thickens his tongue." "Cobra Blue" never gets published, but the term credit comes through. The love of cooking also remains.

Remained until now. Here, this fall, in Mary's and my Edgartown house, to cook becomes a monotonous chore, my kitchen oppressive. The food I force myself to eat has no taste and seems always mushy and thick. The kitchen wallpaper from the *Fireside Cook Book* should have been hung so its images jumble together in fascinating combinations. Instead the paperer has carefully lined up the images, a spoon above a spoon, a plate above a plate, a salad above a salad, a roast chicken above a roast chicken. The same one on top of each other, dull files of marching images. They force me to keep burning myself. I don't know how. I also drop things.

Choice

One night as I add spices — Tabasco, A-1, cumin, and curry powder — to a can of chili that I will eat over rice, along with some yet-to-be sliced tomatoes; the top of the curry jar falls off the counter. Then it disappears into the toe in. I don't know why or how. I get down on hands and knees to find the damn thing. I grab it. I start to stand. I can't get back up.

The kitchen turns a twilight gray. A black cloud, spongy and with a soggy heaviness, has formed inside my kitchen. Sinking lower, it presses against my back. I let the curry top go, spread out my hands, and push hard against the floor. I still cannot rise. When I push harder or try to straighten my back, the cloud grows heavier. I'm trapped in this baby crawling position. If I stay still, I find my cloud lets me alone. But each time I try to rise I am forced downward. My arms grow tired and shake. How long before my cloud has me on the boards, my kitchen boards. My breath comes in heaving gasps, but I never draw in enough. Perhaps I can crawl out from beneath my cloud. Escape that way.

Carefully and slowly I move my left hand slightly forward, follow by my left knee. Then carefully and slowly repeat the moves with my right hand and knee. I crawl. My cloud lets me crawl. It stays heavy but grows no heavier. My kitchen opens onto the hall. I crawl into the hall, then turn slowly left toward my bedroom. Suddenly I grasp where I am going. I am crawling toward my bedroom closet and the 12-gauge shotgun with the shells beside. No. I stop crawling. I will not go this way. I will not become a ghost. Not now. Not ever. With great care, because I cannot see too well, I face around and start the crawl back into my kitchen. I can take in more air. Inside my kitchen I notice for the first time the five chairs around the circular kitchen table. I crawl over to the nearest and pull myself up. My cloud slowly vanishes.

I never see or feel my cloud again. Even on the floor howling, through tears after Jane dies of cancer, the cloud does not appear. I am in despair then. But who I am by then has become totally different. I have been married to Jane for twenty-five years. As I so often heard her observe about some unnamed patient who was improving: "To cope is a marvelous verb."

The chili smells burned and sticks to the bottom of the pan. I scrape what I can into the garbage and put the pot in the sink to soak. I don't try to cook anything else. I go to bed with milk and three doughnuts like a little kid. I do not dare risk a scotch.

Finding it even harder to write in the Vineyard than on East 74th Street, I come back to New York. I put on a happy face, walk Kate and George to their school buses in the mornings and Nick to his school. I keep working on drafts of the play and hoping.

Luck and Choice

I happen to meet Teddy White at the musical *The Sound of Music* and he asks me to have lunch. Over lunch he explains his unique, groundbreaking idea of a book that will cover the presidential campaign in depth, stressing what goes on behind scenes. The book would report from both camps, starting just before the first primaries. It will reveal all the small intimate details of staff decisions, technical operations — such as advance men and polling — local politics and personal character that finally decide the winner. He asks me if I would be willing to take the gamble and collaborate with him for two years on such a book with the tentative title of *The Making of the President, 1960*. With two of us we can cover the many candidates in the primaries and after the conventions have chosen the final two candidates, report simultaneously on both campaigns.

The idea sounds new, important, and intriguing. I like Teddy, a humorous, tough-minded, hard-working elf of a man. We get along well. We see the world in much the same fashion. I admire him, his record, and his book *Fire in the Ashes*. I stick out my hand. We shake.

The plan falls through. Teddy's publisher does not come up with enough advance money for the two of us to live on and work. If

I finance myself out of my own pocket, we could do the book together. Teddy can't do that. And he and I are wise enough to realize
this will strain both work and friendship. At the same time Teddy
has been asked by physicist friends at Harvard and MIT to sit in on
their Summer Study on Arms Control, and write a popular book on
the subject. The summer study is to include leading scientists and
will be funded by the Twentieth Century Fund. Teddy replies that
unfortunately his commitment to *The Making of the President*
makes that impossible.

However, he has a friend who covered military affairs and the
White House for *Newsweek* and also writes on them for the *Reporter*, who would fit their need. I fly to Boston to meet with some
members of the scientific team lead by Professor Victor Weisskopf of
MIT. Here the *Choice* and *Luck* that made me a founder of the ISS
reassures the physicists. I am not only a writer, but also somewhat an
academic, more like those vetting me. They ask me to do the book.
There are no strings. I agree. I fly back to New York. I have a job.

I look back on the book that becomes *The Nation's Safety and Arms
Control* as my first grown-up book. In it I explore a number of complex questions about which wise and concerned people strongly dis-
agree. The challenge is to make the complex understandable, then
reach a conclusion I can believe in and that most of the study members
will support. Besides the ideas explored, the summer study's members
make my work exciting. I listen to and sometimes argue with member
scientists and weapons experts such as Hans Bethe, Harold Brown,
Leo Szilard, Victor Weisskopf, and Jerome Wiesner. Beyond the study
group I interview, among others, Dean Acheson, Retired Air Chief
Marshal Sir Ralph A. Cochrane, Michael Howard, Paul Nitze, and
Robert Oppenheimer. And of course Robert Lovett and General
James Gavin. I am blessed with a superb research assistant, Nancy
Hoepli, who was with me on the *Herald Tribune*. Our name for that
time of heady experience is: "The summer we saved the world."

The meetings take place outside Boston in a delightful mansion
with a swimming pool. Taking part in a different study in another

part of the building are a number of scientists and submarine officers working on the problem of underwater communications. The interaction between the two groups would have fascinated anthropologists. Particularly the mix of disdain and terror with which the submariners regarded us arms controllers when we shared the swimming pool. Will these "nuts" determine America's military future? Could the submariners have seen accurately the military future, they would have found we arms controllers will save their jobs. One of the summer study's most important conclusions is the need for "a secure deterrent," nuclear weapons that cannot be knocked out by an enemy, but survive to strike back. It turns out that among the best places to put such weapons, to secure the deterrent, was beneath the sea aboard nuclear submarines.

The following summer, 1961, Mary and the children leave as usual for Martha's Vineyard, while Nancy and I stay behind to put the final touches on the *Nation's Safety*. My play gets optioned for a two-week run in Philadelphia. Producer and director want more rewrites. That January, though I have good tickets, I do not go to President Kennedy's inaugural. I feel so inadequate. I am unhappy and constantly worry about what will happen if both play and book are unsuccessful and I cannot find a job.

Late in the summer, *The Nations Safety and Arms Control* is published to favorable reviews as an important and pioneering work on a complex subject. Only a few total disarmers slam the book. One, unfortunately, in the *New York Times*. The Book-of-the-Month Club takes it as an alternate. I get letters of thanks from such knowledgeable senators as Henry "Scoop" Jackson and Stewart Symington. President Kennedy praises the book on television. I am suddenly a reasonably successful author. Not on the Yankees or Red Sox, but no longer struggling in the minors. Surprisingly this does not mean as much to me as I had thought it would. I feel the subject carries the book and that I took too long with my writing.

My first novel, *The Joy Wagon*, has also become reasonably successful and enjoys a paperback sale. I take an office — well, two nonconnected rooms — one very small, the other extremely small, both five flights up on West 53rd Street close to the Museum of Modern Art. The building is an ideal place for a writer. Legend claims that Five West 53rd was once a notorious high-class brothel. Supporting this thesis, the walls and doors are exceptionally thick, making the place almost totally soundproof. Good places to eat and drink are close. A wonderful French bistro — too French for most New Yorkers — the Café des Sports becomes and remains my refuge. One night I grab the arm of a knife wielding drunken customer and save the life of the owner. After that I have a second home. Pat Zipprodt and I eat there. Jane and I court there. My youngest daughter has her wedding supper there.

Luck, Choice, and Chance

With the $20,000 from *The Joy Wagon*'s paperback sale, I take an equal bank mortgage and a second mortgage from the seller to buy 350 acres on Martha's Vineyard, with a 30-acre pond and half a mile of ocean beach, all in West Tisbury. My friends in finance implore me not to be crazy and throw my money away on acres of scrub full of ticks and under water. Instead put my money in the stock market. Martha's Vineyard, like the Hamptons, becomes the summer home of choice for the "new rich and chattering classes." The island is ruined, West Tisbury no longer the Athens of anywhere, but the price of oceanfront land skyrockets. I had bought the acreage for love. It becomes my annuity.

More Luck

My agent at William Morris departs to become a schoolteacher. *Winterkill* becomes the barely alive child of his fellow agent, Mardette Perkins. She invites me to dinner with her husband at their West Side apartment.

When Mardette opens the door I see a woman sitting inside. To twist Gertrude Stein's remark about Oakland: "There is no there, there." This woman brings an "I am here, here" to where she sits. Mardette introduces me to her Wellesley classmate, Patricia Zipprodt, already known as an unusually talented theater costume designer, if a bit far out. In coming years, her career will include four Tony Awards and also raise the artistic status and financial rewards of costume design. Now she sits straight up and out from her chair back. She wears a brown medium-length dress, designed and sewn by herself, with a barebacked halter top that descends in eye-catching line from neck to waist to create a sensuous, striking presence. As drink, conversation, and even food relax the evening, her wit and insights into life appear. One remark intrigues me: "Certain gifts are better never given than given late."

Pat does not wish to be escorted home to her Greenwich Village walk-up with bare brick walls. I remark that I have brick walls, too. This is like calling an aircraft carrier a canoe. My town house off Lexington Avenue in the seventies boasts a two-story living room whose walls are brick. I suggest dinner soon. We agree on tomorrow night. We will meet at my house. She will select a place in the Village for our meal. We say good night.

Choice

How much free *Choice* do I have in asking Pat to dinner? In the taxi going back to Seventy-fourth Street. I try to look my *Choice* in the eye, and fail. Is this the challenge and excitement I wanted when I wrote my play? And if it is, and I get it, do I really want it? At what cost? I am thirty-seven, already with a second wife and four children. I want out. I want to be on the other side of that line. But, in ways, I am out. My marriage is dull and strained and sexually unexciting, like many I know. But it's okay. We don't fight often. In public we are fine. There are ways of moving farther out that are foolish. I can feel their foolishness in my stomach. I don't need my mother or father or books to tell me what is right and wrong. I'm not going to end up chasing chorus girls. Or blonde bombshells in fashion magazines.

Pat is no blond bombshell. That is a big part of the problem. If what I wish to happen, happens, I am going against the behavior patterns *Fate*, family, and Groton drilled into me. But I have seen myself on the dead side of that ballroom line. So what? Safety, maybe finally happiness may lie on the dead side. "Why does your brand so drip with blood, Edward, Edward?" Poor Edward, he gave his mother the "curse of hell" for her council. What are you going to do, Hadley? I am not sure. I'm not going to cancel the date. I'll see what happens.

I am not even sure what will happen after dinner the next night as we walk up two flights of stairs to Pat's apartment. She has two rooms with bare brick walls One serves almost exclusively as her studio, with its large sloping desk/easel. The other acts as her bedroom and sitting area. Other than a double bed against the connecting wall, that room's main feature is a large floor-to-ceiling white pipe in one corner with a red armchair in front. In winter, that pipe bangs loudly as it carries heat somewhere upstairs. Pat thinks drug sellers may previously have used her apartment. People who are high sometimes bang on her door, even try to break in. As she fixes the secure Fox lock from door to floor, I still am not sure what may happen. What I should do. I walk around to look at pictures she has painted that hang on her walls, along with photographs of costumes and stage sets. Also a boyfriend, I presume, in a sudsy bath.

Pat and I look at each other. She gets out a paper Japanese parasol, points it at me, opens it up with a click, and spins the rim with fluttering eyes. Goethe is right once again. "If you really want to know what is going on, ask a wise woman." We go rapidly to bed. The night is wonderful. Next morning when we wake, the sunlight has never shone as bright. I can smell the Hudson River's fresh water ten blocks away. I feel Pat's softness. I delight in her warmth. I am alive.

I eat her delicious scrambled eggs. As I start to help by making her bed she says, "Leave it alone, love. I made it yesterday. Beds are like women. They need to be well made twice a week."

The next night I arrive with a poem. I have not written one for a long time.

> Now parasols are dangerous
> For little girls of thirty plus.
> An open click, a twist of rim
> And little her, spins little him.
> To live a life both safe and right

Keep your parasol furled tight.
But if the lad be braw and tall.
Why then deploy your parasol.

Choice and Luck

Through our particular combination of *Choice* and *Luck*, we begin an affair that lasts in various degrees of intensity for seven years, until I marry Susan. The affair changes both of us, myself more than Pat. Seventeen years later when, through almost unbelievable showers of Luck, Jane and I finally wake up and marry, she becomes a friend of us both. We have her to dinner and parties, she has us to hers. In 1997, when she marries her 1940s boyfriend — not the man in the bathtub — we take part in her wedding. We comfort her after her husband's death, and when she is stricken with cancer. Jane and I treat her to a fine lunch every other week on the day before her chemotherapy begins. She dies from her cancer in 2003, a year before Jane dies from hers. Two wise, exciting, exceptional people.

Passion, problems, and change fill 1961. Sometimes the problems come first, sometimes the passion, often the change. Sometimes all three hit with force in the same moment. Fortunately, I belong to a very discrete club. If the worst comes to the worst, I can always be there if I am not at home. I certainly do not appreciate the comments of my Martha's Vineyard tennis-playing friends that writing plays must be tough because I appear so tired on the court during weekends.

Pat's days are full creating a new show: *She Loves Me*, opening in the fall. We spend as much time as we can together talking, eating, in bed. I show Pat *Winterkill*, which has just been optioned once again. This time for a tryout next summer in Philadelphia's Playhouse in the Park. She reads it later and shakes her head. She believes my play too romantic and melodramatic to work. I try more rewriting. Meanwhile, the sun stays brighter, sounds and smells more intense, food tastes better, even the sight or thought of Pat brings smiles and indrawn breath. Our sex is vigorous, intense, knowledgeable. Our sleep afterward deep, our waking happy and playful.

One morning Pat remarks: "This is the best fucking I have ever had."

"I also. My wife tells me I fuck like a truck driver."

"Tell her she is Goddamn lucky."

My winter will be difficult.

Penny, brown penny, brown penny
I am looped in the loops of her hair.

The winter is difficult. I stage one constant, long pretend to save my loveless marriage and stay with my children. Nick falls out his window, but fortunately hits the fire escape landing one flight down. He, George, Kate, and I build a complex electric train system in the large attic room on which two trains can run at once to different commands — most of the time. I fly out to Hollywood and with help from my agent land Richard Carlson, a leading man with enough stature to guarantee that in July *Winterkill* will be a two-week reality in Philadelphia. Pat is out of town much of the winter with rehearsals and fittings. When she is in New York she is exhausted and I have an extremely limited number of excuses I can use to be out all night.

At the end of June, *Winterkill* goes into rehearsal at the Playhouse in the Park, in Philadelphia. I learn what it is like to be an author at the center of competing egos: the producer, the director and various actors, and the union regulations. Pat comes down several times to give advice. Unfortunately she is right about the play. It is too melodramatic and romantic to work. The audience laughs at the wrong moments. The reviews are discouraging. My parents and Mary fly down for opening night. They don't think much of the play either. Members of the cast and my agent all ask me how I survived with such parents.

I learn from *Winterkill* how little I know of playwriting. Back in New York I join several play writing classes. I make two good friends, both actors in the play: Larry Gates, who had created the roll of Colonel Purdy in *Tea House of the August Moon*, and Adam

Kennedy, a star of daytime television. Unfortunately Larry, a New Yorker, dies all too soon. Adam's friendship and that of Susan, his wife, last as long as both he and she live. They, Jane, and I spend some wonderful moments together, either on Martha's Vineyard, or after our house there burns down, in the sixteenth-century farmhouse Jane and I rent in the northeast corner of the Dordogne. Before those good days, in times when I was far down, they made it a point to be always on call.

Winterkill, in changed form, will be optioned twice more. Once in Britain where it comes close to having a tryout, the leading man dropping out a month before rehearsals, and once, not so close, in New York. However, the play never sees the stage again.

Pat lands two new shows — one for this year one for next — which assures her of at least two year's income. She and I are going to celebrate this evening. She has bought two tickets for *The Boys from Syracuse*. When I arrive at her flat, Pat sits on the chair before her work table hugging her knees, her body tense, face white. Her younger sister has committed suicide. Pat is afraid she may do the same. Her skin is cold and wet. She has a strange smell. Has she called any of her friends? She has not been able to use the phone.

I make tea. Get her to bed with her clothes on, and with her address book call two of her close friends, David Hayes, the stage designer, and his wife, Leni. They are both out. I try another close friend, also out. I set a pillow up against the wall and settle down for the night, leaving a light on for comfort. Pat sits up now and then or the phone rings and I make more tea. By nine next morning four of us, I, the Hayeses, and a dancer, Mary Ann Larkin, have set up a twenty-four hour suicide watch. We are later joined by a fifth, a college friend of Pat's, working in Philadelphia. Coordination is difficult, all of us with jobs and myself in a marriage, but we bring it off. Pat is never alone. After two weeks she thanks us and tells us we are no longer necessary. She is enough of her old self that we, self-christened "the motley five," believe her and part, though we continue to check in by phone.

In the early fall, just before Mary and the children come back from Martha's Vineyard, Pat and I are having dinner at a Village Italian cafe. The restaurant interior is very red. Red walls and bright red tablecloths. I have written a new one-act play about one of my favorite subjects, Odin's encounter with the Völuspá, the wisest and most cunning of the nine worlds' witches. Pat does not like the play in the least. "Arthur," she says and repeats "Arthur, you are never going to be a playwright, one of us, until you bring two ordinary people together in an ordinary situation and write their dialogue as they live it. And make it interesting. That's it."

The tabletops with the red checked tablecloths start to spin, the colors all run together. The red walls press in. The corners of the restaurant recede. The tabletops turn more rapidly, like children's pinwheels. I know I hear the truth. I am terrified. I am being asked— no told — to write beyond my ability. How will I begin? How produce not stereotypes, but real people. I wait for the whirling tabletops to calm down and the room to return to normal size. I look at Pat. She is intense and focused. I manage to force out a "yes" and, after a pause, a second "yes." Pat watches me closely. Waits for more.

The alive side of the line has problems too. Did I romanticize how life there would be? Maybe I am not out yet?

The next day in my office I bring two paper people together. I keep them together for several weeks, pushing dialogue at them. Nothing happens between them. I create another two people. Nothing. I try four people. Worse. I keep forgetting who they are. I read plays, go to classes, and curse a frustrated self. I leave the city and fly to the Vineyard for two weeks. Two paper people become a little more active. Pat joins me for four days. Her visit is tense. I am overly concerned about my work, and worried about prying friends and neighbors. As she tells me afterward, "I was not really wanted."

I go back to the city. Mary is upset. "It's not another play, is it Daddy?" Since Kate was born, she calls me Daddy. When my friends hear her and the tone she uses, I sometimes catch their surprise. Following Pat's mantra about works of art taking time, I write and rewrite the two-character play as I try to feel and think my way inside the people and find out what happens to them. The play becomes *The Four Minute Mile* and will later run for two weeks in an experimental theater in Greenwich Village. I don't make a nickel. But I watch two wonderful actors Marian Seldes and my friend Adam Kennedy, bring two interesting, real people to life with passion and tension. Adam switches his TV schedules to do the play. No one laughs in the wrong places. Pat likes it. I draw some excellent reviews.

Choice and Luck

Later that winter, I announce to Mary that I am taking time off to fly to Greece for three weeks to relax and think about what I do next. Afterward, I will meet her in Inverness, and we can drive north together for our two weeks' fishing. For years I have wanted to spend time in Greece. The ancient plays and legends fascinate me. Recently, I become further excited by new books on life and travel there by Kevin Andrews, Robert Graves, Patrick Lee Fermor, Henry Miller, and an old, 1903 Baedeker Grecian guide book.

Pat has always wanted to go to Italy, but could not afford to. For Christmas, I give her a round-trip plane ticket to Rome. Sometime later she tells me she has tacked a trip to Greece on to her Rome ticket. Neither of us knew the other was going to Greece, let alone when. I change my Greek dates. I will go to Greece a week before Pat to set things up and meet some people who know Greece well and to whom I have letters of introduction. Pat will meet me and we will have a full two weeks together. I can fly from Athens to Inverness to join Mary on Swiss Air with a transfer to British Air in Geneva and another switch in London. I realize I push the edge of the envelope. That is my *Choice*

After the fishing, Mary wants me to fly to Italy with her to meet Frances Randolph, a friend who serves with her on the Vassar Board of Trustees. I know Mr. Randolph; I used to dance with his daughter before the war. She died during the war of the same rare disease, ulcerated colitis, that almost killed Mary when we were first married. Mr. Randolph was a year ahead of my father at Yale. He is a highly successful stockbroker with a villa on Lago de Como. The fact that Mary, who fears flying, is willing to fly to see Mr. Randolph raises a marker in my head to which I pay no attention.

The plan works. I arrange places to stay and boat trips (there were no internal air flights in Greece then) first in Peloponnisos, then on Mykomos — still undiscovered with only one small hotel — and finally on Samos in the small port of Tyagana opposite the Turkish shore. I find the people to whom I have letters and drive through Peloponnisos for a week, trying out the Greek learned in a month at Berlitz. On the advice of Vince Skully, the architecture historian who is among those I have just met in Athens, I visit the temple to Apollo at Bassae, designed like the Parthenon by Ictinus.

To visit the temple then requires a half-hour walk from the road over a mountain trail. The temple surpasses its reputation. Pausanias, a traveler in the time of Caesar Augustus who carefully described everything he saw, wrote that the temple seemed to float toward the sea through the surrounding giant oaks. The oaks are gone. Now the temple seems to levitate above its hill, waiting to drift toward the distant blue waters of the Messenian Gulf. (Twenty years later when Jane and I visit, a road has been built closer to the temple, but we still walk the final quarter mile, though on a better track. In the rainfall of that day we could not see the sea, but the temple still rested on its hill lightly in grandeur. Three ragged shepherds, looking rather like robbers in a B movie, invite us into their hut to get warm. I hesitate but Jane marches in. They give us feta cheese and raki and a place by the fire. In my broken Greek, I thank them. With ancient Greek hospitality, they thank us back for coming so far to see their mighty treasure. If anyone reading this is as enthralled by Greek temples as Jane and I, let me briefly become a travel book. Bassae in its lonely magnificence is worth a journey.)

Back in Athens, I find a pleasant taverna located beneath the Parthenon walls in the Palaka, the old quarter. I plan to take Pat there for dinner. My world falls apart. Pat, an on-time person, does not arrive. No word. That evening I walk the narrow streets of the Palaka to the taverna where I had planned to take Pat. I have walked this route from hotel to taverna alone three times before, and never been hassled by a woman. Tonight I am continually a pick-up target. Do my self-doubts and concern show that much? Maybe I am on the far side of the line after all. A day later Pat arrives. Plane trouble.

Delos, with its justly famous ruins, lies twenty minutes from Mykonos. A voyage made once a day each way by a caique, a small, open Greek fishing boat with a one-cylinder diesel engine. There are no hotels on Delos. In Athens friends have told me that one can sometimes get permission from the National Police chief on Delos to spend nights on the island in the police station, after other tourists have left on the four o'clock caique. The police chief on Delos, after laughing at my Greek, gives Pat and me permission to spend two nights in the station house, along with himself, his wife, and the two policemen on night duty. Pat and I spend a large part of two days and all of two nights alone on Delos. We check carefully for adders, which come out at night to bask on the warm stones.

Using Pausanias as a guide, we locate the well that Agamemnon drank from on his way to Troy. Though fenced off, the well appears to have a rope tied to it. Perhaps the rope's other end possesses a bucket. I climb the fence. The bucket fashioned from an empty olive oil tin is not from Agamemnon's time. We drink from it anyway. How could we find it and not drink from Agamemnon's well? The police chief's wife feeds us delicious suppers of lamb, artichoke hearts, tomatoes, and fried potatoes. We drink tea and retsina. We have never gone to bed together by candlelight, nor either of us made love in a police station. Obviously we have led sheltered lives. We risk some quiet sex. The last afternoon alone, we climb up the smaller of Delos's two hills to watch the sun set over the ruins. As the sky reddens a helicopter circles over us to check us out.

"Don't wave," says Pat. "It's my mother and your wife."

On Samos we walk, swim, climb through the ruins of the totally destroyed temple to Hera, once rated one of the seven wonders of the world. The temple was badly damaged in an earthquake. During World War I the Germans captured the island and German archaeologists restored much of the temple. Several days after war's end, the resistance blew up the restored temple because they wanted nothing left to remind them of the Germans.

Pat feels badly with headache, fever, and upset stomach, which the local doctor brings under control. She recovers, and after a final breakfast of Greek coffee, apricots, bread, and honey, we take the boat for Athens. One night in Athens. The next in Inverness. I am having trouble handling the change. Where am I? Who am I? I'm not sure.

Luck

My problems could have become worse. Four days into fishing, it is raining hard and Mary has forgotten the toilet paper she usually carries in her waist pouch. "Do you have any Daddy?" I do, and laying down my rod, go to stand beneath the nearest tree so I and the paper won't get soaked. I unzip my rain jacket to get into my back pocket. I haul out some toilet paper, and look down at it to see that I have pulled out enough and that the paper is still dry. The outside sheet contains, in bright red, the lipstick the blotted outline of lips belonging to one of New York's best-known costume designers. I check further. That first sheet is the only one. I stow it in my side pocket.

Throughout the rest of the year, marriage to Mary becomes more difficult. This has nothing to do with wanting to marry Patricia. She has said she does not want to marry yet, and that in any event I remain too romantic for her to marry. We remain friends, have occasional pleasant sex, but the constant need and exciting contact is gone. My understanding remains of Pat's talent, and also how she saw and felt the world and how her talent could consume her.

As fall lurches toward winter and I start another play about American presidents, the tensions in our home become worse. I make another *Choice*.

Choice

Over Christmas vacation in the Edgartown house, our children upstairs and perhaps asleep, I tell Mary I want a divorce. She cries and tells her friends. The long process starts.

About the basic reasons for our divorce I write no further. I have kept quiet, even with old friends or when verbally being beaten up by Mary's friends. Mary was someone I loved for a time, married, shared moments of laughter and life, and with whom I have three children. Mary married the person I seemed to be while at Yale. I appeared to be aimed at goals Mary desired. At that time I partially was that person, though not thoroughly, as witness my debate over whether to flip the coin about "B's" offer on the train between Yale and New York. Through *Luck* and *Choice* I changed. I am now miserable with Mary. She is unhappy with me, disappointed in me, and furious at me for bringing this all about.

Quite naturally she tells my father. He makes a date to see me at our house on 74th Street. When he arrives he does not want to come downstairs. We talk in the hall. After the usual questions about do I know what I am doing have been asked, and answered, he says. "If you go through with this I will disinherit you and never talk to you again."

Choice

I have not expected this; not done my math. After a few moments, I put out my right hand and say, "Good-bye, Father." I open the front door. He leaves. We do continue to talk. He phones several times to berate me. My removal from the wills of both my father and mother stands. He draws the wills himself.

Separation is easy. Forging an agreement that will govern our separation and serve as a divorce agreement, difficult and tedious. The lawyer who represented me in my divorce from Leila has retired. He recommends a friend in his old firm, Fred Haas. The back and forth begins. I need to find a place to nourish me while I fight and to live pleasantly in afterward. I find a tiny two-and-a-half room penthouse I can afford on East 40th Street. At that time, the main room had a gorgeous view south down the East River toward Wall Street. The view vanishes two years later as a large apartment building rises on the south side of East 40th.

I rent a station wagon and Adam Kennedy, along with a childhood friend, Bill Graham, the TV director, help me move. I do this almost immediately, before positions can further harden. By this fast move I secure, in addition to clothes and shoes, both of my Munch oils, *Vampire* and *Girl Nude by a Red Bed*, and most of my books. Also, to my surprise, some beat up copper kitchen pots and pans are in a box labeled for me. When Jane first sees these she remarks, "Mary really hated you, when she gave you those."

I am aided in my divorce battle by a secret trump card. During one of the Sunday visits I am allowed with my children, Kate and I sit and talk on the stairs that lead from the living room to the bedroom floors. Kate tells me that seated on these same stairs she heard Mr. Randolph say he wanted to marry Mom if I kept giving trouble. And that Mom said that would be nice. I thank Kate and promise not to tell anyone. To understand Kate's giving me this card, I have to pull way back to Kate's birth in 1950.

I sit in Mary's private room in New York Hospital overlooking the East River. It's the hospital where I was born, and from which Grandmother Hadley phoned Dr. Peabody. I wait for Mary's return from the O.R. A short while ago, our obstetrician called me to report all is well, and I am now the father of a fine baby girl. I am delighted. I already have a son by the Army bride and have wanted a girl. I hear someone being wheeled down the hall. It's Mary. I hear her screaming: "It's a Goddamn girl. It's a Goddamn girl. Take her back! Take her back!"

The kindly nurse wheeling Mary into the bedroom tries to comfort me.

"It's the anesthetic. She really doesn't mean that."

"Oh, yes she does," I reply.

Choice

Then and there I promise that girl, the soon-to-be Kate, that there will be no sex discrimination in my family. I will make certain — be both father and mother if necessary — that she grows up to know her worth equals that of any man.

I live this *Choice*. When we lay out the mammoth electric train tracks in the 74th Street attic, Kate builds it with Nick and George. I want her to know she can build just as well as boys. I do not throw a ball with Kate. Kate does not like to throw a ball. But in Washington I spend as much time playing poo sticks with Kate in Dumbarton Park as I do throwing a ball with either of the boys. When I realize she is learning words from the stories I am reading to her outloud by reading the words upside down, I send her to be tested. When an extraordinary report on her IQ comes back, I use the report and push to get her into nursery school a year early. In Washington, when I teach her to ride her bicycle, I explain first that her mother rides as well as I and she will too. But learning to ride a bicycle is easier if you have someone to run fast and push you. And I can run faster than her mother.

I know all is not perfect, because several times when I have promised to do something for her — to wake her up to see the Fourth of July fire works or come up to her bedroom after I have finished my martini to listen for mice — she is surprised that the promise has been kept. Mice had indeed gotten into her bedroom soffit. The next day, we find the hole in the basement wall where the mice enter. Once her cat, Stripey, sees that gap, the mouse problem disappears. Kate and I celebrate.

About a year before she deals me the divorce trump card, I come home to find Mary and Kate crying together on the living room balcony couch. "What," I ask, "is the matter?"

Through her boo-hoos Mary sobs: "Now your daughter can get pregnant."

I realize Kate has started to menstruate. I chose to overlook the fact that I had always believed Kate to be *our* daughter.

"Kate, congratulations. You are now a woman. Let's go out and buy a present to celebrate."

We go to a nearby low-price jewelry store and Kate picks out a sparkling ring. The only other ring I ever buy with such delight is Jane's engagement ring.

In 1994 Kate breaks the glass ceiling against women's promotions with a bang. She becomes the first female scientist elected president of the International Society of Petroleum Engineers.

After some nine months of strained negotiation, I leave for a dude ranch outside Reno. I have to spend two full months there because, at Mary's insistence, I must obtain what is legally known as a "contested divorce." I go West with no joy. I face, at best, an unsettled future. About halfway through my Nevada time, I receive a telegram from Mary. Her wire states that, in addition to the house in Edgartown and the house New York, plus the lump sum, the alimony, and children's' education, all of which she receives in our signed separation agreement, she now also wants the 320 acres in West Tisbury on Martha's Vineyard. Unless she gets the West Tisbury land she will declare the separation agreement invalid.

I telegraph back that we have negotiated back and forth for a long time. She has never mentioned the Vineyard land. I will not change our agreement. I am in no rush to divorce. I assume she is not. I will return to New York and we can abide by the terms of the separation agreement and live apart. Two days later, Fred Haas telegraphs that he has a notarized letter that Mary has dropped her request for the Vineyard land and will let the agreement stand. Kate's card trumps.

In the destabilized and unhappy period of separation, negotiation battles, the unfamiliar singles life, and finally divorce, the ability to cook shines out as a life-preserving skill. I take pride in being a better than adequate, though by no means an epicurean cook. Now and then I disguise my limits with delicious party dishes prepared at my club, which I then bring to my two-bedroom penthouse home with its sleeve of a kitchen, and serve out of my own casserole pot. Jane will remark, years later, that she can almost always predict which of her divorced or divorcing male patients will remarry well. Those men who can cook, sew on buttons, and shop will take their time and remarry for their own complex but correct reasons. Those who cannot handle such chores will search in desperation for a wife/housekeeper and rush into a new marriage to be fed warm food.

Luck

Lawrence "Larry" Hughes, whom I first met when we were four and members of my mother's Long Island play group, has seen *The Hollow Crown*, a play that tells in their own words how certain kings of England felt about their vast powers. I, too, have seen the play and, like Larry, enjoyed it. Larry feels that a book telling in their own words how U.S. presidents felt about and used power would be even more interesting and sell well. His publishing firm, Morrow, would like to publish such a book. Later it might be turned into a play. He asks me if I would I like to tackle such a book. I find the idea fascinating and say yes. I am payed an advance, hire a skilled researcher, Constance Cornish, and obtain a cubicle in the Alan Room, a wonderful space in the New York Public Library where authors can work and keep reference books at their desks. Instead of boredom and a desperate hunt for work, a fascinating project occupies me. The book, *Power's Human Face,* does reasonably well. The play I adapt from the book is optioned twice but never makes the stage.

Robert Heilbroner, the economist and author, introduces me to Jane Danish. Being a successful economist and therefore unfamiliar with actual life, he inadvertently gives me a fantastic build up. "Jane," he says, "I'm going to introduce you to Arthur Hadley. He is good for dinner and the theater, but nothing else. Strictly nothing else." He has no idea what that says to a wise, beautiful, and female woman: "Ah, but he has not met me yet"

At the Heilbroners' small dinner, there begins between Jane and myself *"The Luck that Keeps on Lucking."* I give this peculiar *Luck* that name because it takes its own foot-dragging time, fifteen years and many zigzags, not to mention zagzigs, to work its way. In a reporter's phrase "The Luck that Keeps on Lucking has long legs." At its surprise conclusion, Jane and I marry and enter twenty-five years of passionate happiness: Blake's "ligaments of gratified desire" all reinforced by a knowledge of lost time.

Jane Byington Danish is a Ph.D. candidate in psychology at Columbia University. Jane is thirty-seven years old, four years younger than myself. She had led her class at Music and Art, a New York public high school that, like Bronx Science, required entrance examinations. On her graduation, both the University of Virginia and Smith College grant her a full scholarship. Virginia's offer is more generous. Jane, whose strained circumstances in childhood made her an expert at "squeezing the nickel," chooses Virginia. She graduates in 1949, a junior Phi Beta Kappa and summa cum laude. She also receives the graduation rings of five Naval Academy seniors. To help support herself she models with success, joining a leading agency, and becoming "Miss Chesterfield."

Fifteen years later heads do not merely turn as she walks, they swivel. Her laugh, known to a select few as "the second-dirtiest laugh in New York," lights up a room. She marries a TV executive almost immediately after graduation from college. Now, with that marriage in trouble, she has begun her plan to become independent as a psychoanalyst.

But in those years between our meeting and our marriage occur a series of events that, were they not true — which they are — would be too incredible for belief. Twice we come close to marriage. The second time, as we part in 1969, we vow never again to talk or write to each other. Powerfully drawn together, in the end we cause each other pain. We live up to our vow for ten years. We both keep our promises. Then, *"The Luck that Keeps on Lucking"* takes an extraordinary twist to shatter our silence. No wonder the friendly judge who finally marries us first reads us our Miranda Rights.

Jane does not wish to be escorted home across town that night. I call her in the morning. We begin to date. After our second date comes a slight pause. I have told Jane that I do not like to go out on Saturdays. I find restaurants and theaters overcrowded that day. She tells me Saturdays are her favorite days. On the next two days I suggest for dates, she says she is busy, but adds she is free on Saturday. I get the message. I offer Saturday.

Our dates start up again. We find and explore unexpected shared pleasures. She likes my favorite restaurant, the Café des Sports. We both like to cook. Jane is a superb cook. I throw two small dinner parties so she can meet my friends. We are basketball fans, we find we have used the same ticket agent. We cheer on the Knicks over beer and hot dogs from good seats at Madison Square Garden. We take the train to Philadelphia, rent a car, and visit the Barnes Collection. Our tastes in Expressionist art and artists mesh. On another weekend, we visit the Longwood Gardens and the Dupont Museum. Jane shows expert knowledge of flowers and garden plantings. Next day at the Dupont Museum her expertise on export china so impresses our guide that we are invited us back after lunch for a private showing of trophy items not on display. Everywhere we go we find unexpected, mutual delights.

Jane sits on my bed smoking pot for, she says, the first time. One of the pipes I used to smoke is now loaded with grass. As she puffs away she keeps saying, "It's not affecting me at all." About the fourth time she affirms this, the pipe falls from her mouth and lands on the bedsheets. She does not notice the pipe's absence but repeats, "It's not affecting me at all." She sees me pick up the pipe and put out the ashes and giggles. Some months later I have a birthday and Jane gives me two perfect presents. I have separated the living room of my apartment from my dining area by a seven-foot potted Asian palm with tight serrated leaves. Jane finds an extremely large birthday card that shows a monkey in a tree. The card says, "Have a Swinging Birthday." She hangs it in my palm. It's perfect. The other gift is an etching of four Khmer heads. It, too, is perfect. It hangs just left of my computer screen today.

Our sex is exciting, varied, loving, and tender. Our major problem is finding the time. Jane has two young daughters, a maid, and a separated-from husband. I have three children — two boys and a girl approaching their teens — and a separated-from wife. I am allowed to see my children every other weekend. Jane once tells her five-year-old daughter, Elisabeth, who has climbed into bed with her in the middle of the night, "It's time to go home now, Arthur. The children will be climbing into my bed soon." Fortunately Elisabeth is too asleep to hear. One weekend, when I do not have the children, Jane and I hide out at Montauk Point on the eastern tip of Long Island. Ten-year-old Nick develops acute appendicitis while playing baseball. Mary tries to find me to get joint permission to operate, part of our separation agreement that, fortunately, can be waived.

No ordinary time with Jane exists. e. e. cummings describes our together hours.

> true lovers in each happening of their hearts
> live longer than all why or any how.
> Yea, and if time should ask into his was all now
> their eyes would never miss a yes.

Jane and I write back and forth during the two months I am in

Nevada. On my return in the late fall of 1963, we come inches close to announcing our engagement. I lay out my financial worth for Jane. I meet her mother and take part in Jane's life with her children. The two girls, Elisabeth, five, and Caroline, three, are thoughtful, well behaved, and mischievous. Elisabeth, the most adventurous, offers me the choice of Scotch, scrambled eggs, or a Rorschach test when I enter Jane's apartment. When I help bathe them, Elisabeth squirts me with her rubber duck while Caroline, more thoughtful and withdrawn, watches warily from a crouched position. Jane's family is so different from the one into which I was born. She treats her children the way I try to bring up mine. I would like to be part of such a family. We neither of us get much help from those whom we married.

Fate and Luck

Fourteen years later, entwined in bliss inside our marriage, we wonder why we who now fit so perfectly, twice flew apart, once in 1963 and once in 1968. We conclude *"The Luck that Keeps on Lucking"* arrives at an unfortunate time. We are both impaired by wounds in our self-confidence from the failure of unpleasant marriages. Neither of us then realized the deep power of *Luck*. As others we believed *Luck* a minor player, even a trickster. In battle I knew I lived in *Luck*'s Kingdom. Did the bullet hit him or me? But back in the peacetime world, supposedly a more real place, I forgot that we all live in *Luck*'s Kingdom all the time. I heard phrases as "a man made his Luck" and "Bad Luck is no excuse" and believed them.

Luck gave Jane and me a great *Choice*. At this difficult, decisive moment, we can risk a joint future and grab it with both hands, or avoid that future. Our *Fates* had filled us with warnings about hasty marriage, especially after a divorce. We presently live in worthless marriages that give us emotional and intellectual pittance. We are wary, even frightened, of another mistake. I was brought up to see a third marriage as playboy doom. Jane is in analysis to help control fears that her *Fate* means she will again be drawn to a man who will desert her, as did her father and now her husband. Her studies reveal that many men change after divorce. Will I? Should she become my third wife? Neither of us posses the self-regard to lay our fears before the other. We distrust our *Luck*. Our *Choice* is to avoid *Choice*. Neither of us flips the coin. I start to cry as I write this now.

On my part I am not thinking of a real marriage, but a romantic one on the Greek island of Samos where "out, out, out" will become a reality. I will live with a family and write fiction. A major part of me knows this will not happen, but I need a dream and so talk a lot about Samos. Then I misread Jane's clothes. Incorrectly, I believe the colorful patterns she favors indicate her desire for a suburban Greenwich lifestyle. In my battle against my *Fate*, I need encouragement. Jane misses that need. Recently fired, with no job, the arms control book still not out, embroiled in a fighting relationship with my parents, concerned about the next book, I am not secure enough to tell Jane of my need. She hears my talk, sees the maps of Greece that decorate my apartment, and believes they are my reality rather than my reminder that I want out.

Jane visits the Heilbroners on the Vineyard that summer, during the month I have my children. She comes over to Edgartown several times to visit us all. I handle those days badly. I am more eager to get Jane into the bushes than to present my family.

I love Jane. I miss Jane. But overly involved with my own struggle to escape, I am partially blind to the real Jane: the Jane that grew up church-mouse poor. The Jane who desperately seeks the independence a career as a psychoanalyst will bring. The Jane who bears two wonderful appendages, Elisabeth and Caroline, and who wants reassurance they will be loved and cared for. Involved with my concerns, I overlook her needs.

In the middle of all this, I make a sweeping decision. I will build a house on my land in West Tisbury overlooking the ocean. I will keep my apartment for visits, but quit New York City to live on the Vineyard and write. I have a friend who is an architect, Hugh Hardy, who has just formed his own firm: Hardy, Holtzman and Pifer. Friends at *Progressive Architecture Magazine* and others laud their potential. I and the three partners spend several months talking over needs, and costs and studying plans. We work well together. The process proves exciting. My house is the first the firm will build. One of the members flies to the island every week to inspect the work and deal with any problems. I live on the island that winter in the houses of various friends.

The house is ahead of its time, though the type has since grown more familiar, all big windows, peaks, angles, and towers. *Progressive Architecture* makes it one of its "Houses of the Year." I am on Martha's Vineyard that whole winter and spring while my house is built and seldom see Jane. In early summer back in New York, I ask Jane to fly up with me to see the house, now finished. She refuses to fly with me in my small plane and takes the commercial flight from New York to the Vineyard and back. I fly up to meet her at the airport.

Jane does not like the house. She finds the site wonderful, the views extraordinary, but the house itself depressing, with its bare wood walls that are merely stained. The only painted parts of the interior are the heating pipes: the pipes carrying the hot air are painted red; the cold air returns painted blue. I explain I got the idea from those on submarines. The pipes are round and exposed to increase the air flow. And also because I believe that machined parts can be among America's most beautiful artifacts. "Paint everything white," she says. I cannot believe she sees the house that way.

Fate

Only years later do I realize that, in my struggle to escape my *Fate*, I have built totally the wrong house for our marriage. I never consulted Jane over the plans. There is no place for her children to live and play. She can neither get her psychology degree nor do her internship and practice on this island. This house, built by three men for a fourth, is a man's house, definitely not a livable home for one as deeply feminine as Jane. The house lacks soft private spaces, places to be alone. Everywhere sharp angles define the corners. In my struggle to get "out, out, out," I have built a house to protect myself. I want to marry Jane. But the reality of my house says otherwise. Its structure does not connected with the reality of a real marriage to the actual Jane. With her instinctive, human insight, Jane sees what I have built. My new home, which I hoped would draw us together, reinforces her doubts.

We do not fight. The passion remains. But we start to see other people. A feeling develops that perhaps we are not right for each other.

On Martha's Vineyard, alone in my new house, I set to work on a newly started novel. The book, *A Life in Order*, is well plotted, with some interesting characters, but as I write I realize again I do not see human emotions clearly enough to write them well. Stereotypes creep none too stealthy through my work.

My new home works as a place to live and work. Mornings at five the alarm wakes me. I have two clocks should the power fail, one battery driven, the other electric with radio. I lie in bed briefly, smell the sea and listen to the waves a half-mile away. I can make a good guess at what the day will be like from their smell and sound. A heavy sound that seems close and the ocean smell definite mean the day will be hot and muggy or cold and foggy, depending on the season. The reason, the more the air is saturated with water, the more efficiently it carries both the ocean sounds and odors.

By design my bedroom is the one room on the second floor. The only peculiarity I have left over from the war is that I do not sleep well in a ground-floor room. Twice when I did so bullets and tracers came through the gap where the window had been and ricochetted about the room. Not just *Luck* but extreme *Luck* prevented me from being hit. The first night I spent in a ground-floor motel room after the war, I finally pulled the mattress and covers off the bed and slept fitfully on the floor.

After washing up in the bathroom next my bedroom, I walk downstairs to the kitchen, which faces both my pond and the ocean. I use the electric squeezer to make myself a large glass of orange juice. I walk halfway back upstairs to my small, rectangular office located between my bedroom and the ground floor. The office walls are plywood, substituted at the last moment of building to save money. A workbench runs along the outer wall. On it sit my ancient typewriter, along with notebooks and writing pads. The other two walls have shelves and photographs of myself with rucksack in Norway, scenes from my two plays, and my children, also of Jane as a child and now with her children. The office has one window so I will not be distracted by what's outside. That window is on my right as I work and also above my line of sight. It faces the front door as planned. If someone comes to the front door, I stand up to peek to see if I want to meet that person.

I write from five-thirty to ten, my best hours. Then I go down and make myself a big breakfast with eggs and bacon or sausages, doughnuts or toast and jam. By one-thirty or two I am through work for the day. I make myself lunch and care for the house. Then, depending on the season, I swim in the pond, walk on the beach, canoe, ice skate, or tramp through the woods by myself or with my friend Stan Murphy, an artist of great imagination and talent who lives in West Tisbury year round. He supports himself by the pictures he sells, and his work ethic, lifestyle, and schedule parallel my own. I learn a lot from him not just about woods, birds, and mushrooms but about art, talent, and work. He says I do the same for him about books, politics, and people.

If the weather is such that my TV can pick up a signal, I listen to the six o'clock news. My house is in what the TV trade calls "double-stacked yaggi land." Which means two special gizmos, called yaggis, are needed on top of my regular antenna to give me hope of a signal. I pour three ounces of scotch or gin into a measuring cup to make myself a drink and afterward use my cooking skills to make dinner. I try to use whatever is the best on Martha's Vineyard. In winter that's not much, not even fresh fish. I say modestly that, as a result, I can do wonders with salt cod. Today my brandade is often requested, though my "Martha's Vineyard Turkey," fried salt cod with fried diced salt pork, is seldom called for. By eight o'clock, nine at the latest, I have read a bit in bed and am asleep.

At various times of the year I go duck hunting or clamming or oystering, often with Murphy or John Mayhew, a member of an old island family who teaches in the high school. Once a week I shop. In the summer I shop on a beautiful sunny beach day. Then the stores are at their emptiest. There are good restaurants and many people in summer and now and then I invite up friends. In the winter I make good friends on the island: Milton Mazer the psychiatrist and his wife, Virginia; the island doctor Robert Nevin and his wife, Barbara, the publishers of the two island newspapers; and Everet Whiting and his wife, Jane. Many of the West Tisbury wives like Jane Whiting, Polly Murphy, or a nonwife, Louise Tate King, are marvelous cooks. Everett Whiting, the sheep farmer and the man who runs West Tisbury, gets tired of the endless summer question: "Mr Whiting, what do you do in the winter?"

In his slow island drawl he replies, "Well, m'am, in the summer we fish and we farm and we fuck. But in the winter it is too cold for fishin' and farmin'."

I visit New York over Christmas to see my children. Jane and I meet; nothing happens. Jane is trying to get back together with her husband. Pat invites me to the ritual late Christmas dinner where the stage designer, Will Steven Armstrong, cooks a goose for others, who like himself, myself, and Pat, have no family on Christmas. I spend the first part of January in New York and upgrade my flying skills with an instrument-flight license so I can fly in all types of weather. Then back to the Vineyard and the book, *A Life in Order*. I am sad a great deal of the time. A few short affairs lead nowhere. I try to blanket my sadness with work to escape the chills.

Chance and Luck

I plod along this way convinced that I am finally "out, out, out," and believing I am enjoying myself a great deal. Then *Luck* and *Luck*'s big brother *Chance* strike. This *Chance* is unfortunately a war, just like the first *Chance* that gave me an escape route into the Army. America fights a controversial and growing war in Vietnam. The *Luck*: Jim and Jean Gavin are visiting me to see the new house. Jim is one of the first generals to come out against the war. My agent and friend of many years, Sterling Lord and his wife, Cindy, are staying on the island and we are all having lunch. Jim is now head of Arthur D. Little, a company that invents needed items and provides solutions for problems. Jim wants to write a book explaining his stand against Vietnam. The book will also examine new ways to explore and start to solve some domestic problems such as poor schools. I agree to help him write his book. Ever the alert agent, Sterling is horrified at how little advance Jim has been offered. He gets on the phone to its publisher, Random House. The executives there keep saying, but the general has already agreed to X dollars.

Sterling keeps replying but with Arthur Hadley aboard this is a now a new book and suggests five X as a fair advance. Random House replies with a lower figure. In the end, Sterling gets us three times the original offer.

The *Chance* that America fights the Vietnam War, and the *Luck* that Jim plans to do a book and the further *Luck* that he, Sterling, and I all lunch at my house on the same day means that I rent a small apartment in Boston and am given an office near Jim's at Arthur D. Little. Jim and I collaborate well and the book gets off to a fine start. Then life gets complicated. Jim accepts a draft from antiwar groups to run for president. At the same time, in a shrewd move to box him in, President Johnson offers him a trip to Vietnam so he can view the war for himself. I move from "book writer" to "book writer," plus campaign manager and adviser to a presidential hopeful. A few evenings later with our full campaign organization, Jim and myself, inside Jim's Beetle, hear the authoritarian voice of Walter Cronkite intone: "And in Boston, antiwar candidate General James Gavin is putting together a vast staff for a run at the presidency." Jim, shaking with laughter, almost puts the Volkswagen in the Charles River.

Totally out of my depth, I try to inveigle some of my politically astute friends, such as Ken BeLieu, to come aboard as campaign manager. They decline. But they all give me a great deal of detailed and experienced advice that can be summed up as "watch your ass." With the help of the Boston/Harvard/MIT world we recruit a young, bright, and enthusiastic advance team for the New Hampshire primary. To make sure no hidden forces are at work, I fly down to see Robert Lovett, then part of a small, secret committee advising President Johnson on Vietnam. He assures me no hidden agenda exists and volunteers some truly excellent advice. I do recruit a former paratroop officer and congressman, Stuyvesant Wainwright, to go to Vietnam with Jim. I pound into his head that Gavin must never be alone in Vietnam with a group where he can be misquoted or quoted out of context without a friend there to correct the record. I would like to go with Jim myself, but I have a book to finish.

Politically, it is a tumultuous spring. Senator Eugene McCarthy enters the presidential race as an antiwar candidate and files in New Hampshire. Faced with such fire power, Jim wisely quits the race. McCarthy wins over President Johnson in New Hampshire by a large margin. President Johnson, burdened by the Vietnam War and seeing his future presidential defeat, in the size of McCarthy's victory, drops out. Then Senator Robert Kennedy enters the race, also as an antiwar candidate, against McCarthy. Vice President Hubert Humphry is also in the race as the candidate of the regular Democratic organization. Senator Kennedy defeats both candidates in the crucial California primary, but is shot later that night by Sirhan Sirhan. The Democratic race descends into farce and chaos.

Meanwhile Nelson Rockefeller, governor of New York, has entered the Republican primaries as an antiwar candidate and would like General Gavin's support. With Kennedy's death, Jim believes Rockefeller the strongest antiwar candidate. The former Gavin campaign has a problem about which Jim dies without ever learning, though I tell Jean. The campaign is $200,000 in debt. I contact a friend in the Rockefeller camp. A few weeks later I rent a car to drive to Chatham on Cape Cod. At six-fifteen the following morning I park on the right-hand town pier. At six-thirty another car driven by one man pulls alongside me. In the cold spring fog we get out of our cars, greet each other by first names, and shake hands. A briefcase passes between us. The Gavin campaign now has no debt.

In addition to the political campaign and Gavin's book, *Crisis Now*, the *Luck* of that lunch brings me further adventures. I come to realize I have made an imperfect choice to sit on the Vineyard and write novels. I love my life on the Vineyard and plan to keep both house and land. But I do not write fiction that well and therefore make no money. As importantly, I miss the action and excitement of reporting from Washington. I must restart my reporting career and when I write books they should be nonfiction. These choices lead to three months in Vietnam and, it appears, the permanent loss of Jane.

I know I am a fairly good reporter; one of my few certainties.

Further, because of my background and friendships, I do excellent military reporting. The obvious way to restart my career is to report from Vietnam. I search for a sponsor. My friend Bob Manning, then editor of the *Atlantic Monthly*, grubstakes me to press credentials, provided I sign a paper agreeing to pay my way back to America if wounded or killed. I don't blame him; his budget is tight. A press card is a press card is a press card. I got press VIP treatment covering the 1967 Montreal World's Fair for the *Vineyard Gazette*. The *Atlantic Monthly*'s card will work in Vietnam

As I start to change my life, I realize how badly I want to see Jane. We make a date. All seems to be going well, though it's delicate. Jane is back with her husband, trying to make the marriage work. I tell her about the vast staff of the Gavin campaign and the novel I have just finished on which she once helped. We laugh, make love, agree about the Vietnam War. Then not just the roof falls in, but the enormous water tank on top of the roof follows. When I mention that I am going to Vietnam to report, she becomes upset and cold. I do not know what I have done. Now we make our lasting bargain. We both love each other, share many of the same ideas and ideals. We physically delight in each other. But in the end we cause each other pain. Will I please neither write to her nor call her again? She promises to do the same. I say the words, "I promise." She leaves my room.

Fate

Years later I discover why the *"Luck that Keeps on Lucking"* sprinted from us at that moment. Like my Martha's Vineyard house, I had said one thing but presented another. Jane, torn over whether to try again with me or make her marriage work, suddenly faces a man who has been unstable before and now says I want to marry you, but first I am on my merry way to Vietnam. Please wait for me. She finds this macho and irresponsible. In college several Naval cadets at Annapolis had asked her to remain faithful while they went to Korea. This appears to be the same nonsense.

Neither my plays nor my novel had gained me true success. Wrapped in the feelings *Fate* presses on me, I start again to partially believe I am the "profound disgrace." I will be up against the records of major-league reporters in Vietnam: Homer Bigart, Neil Sheehan, David Halberstam, Ward Just. Can I compete with them? Will I make a comeback? This was my moment to flip the dime. To take the risk and tell Jane my fears, my reasons, and my hopes. I didn't. By the time I explain all this, I am inside the serene excitement of our marriage. Jane has read my Vietnam piece.

"If you'd only told me why, I'd have hugged you. I'd live in a garret with the man you are. The man who wrote that article." Nine wasted years.

I finish my new novel, *A Life in Order*, and send it to Sterling Lord. I start to canvas friends, reporters, and officers who have been in Vietnam. Neil Sheehan, David Halberstam, and Ward Just offer names of civilians or officers serving in Vietnam either in the Army, the CIA, or the embassy who can be trusted to tell, or at least hint, at the truth. A friend in the Pentagon gives me a list of all West Point graduates who will be "in country" when I am. The list also names their outfits and location. Several names on the list I knew as cadets at West Point or are people I served with in WW II, now promoted to colonel or even general. Other stateside officers write letters to friends in Vietnam. Bob Sorley, just back, not only writes letters, but being roughly my size lends me his jungle fatigues, asking me please to bring them back without blood all over them. I run in the sand of the ocean beach in front of my house with boots on to get in shape. I am well set.

As a final piece of *Luck*, when I arrive in Vietnam in early September of 1970, the *Newsweek* bureau chief is Kevin Buckley, a friend from *Herald Tribune* days. He treats me not just as a friend but as still a member of the Newsweek-Washington Post organization. He leads me through the ins and outs of Saigon, introduces me to Gerald Hickey, a saintly anthropologist who speaks fluent Vietnamese and who has been trying to mitigate the caustic effects of the war on the primitive highland tribes. Buckley's bureau Vietnamese staff also save me hours of battle with the Vietnamese bureaucracy.

During the three-plus months I am in Vietnam, I develop the

following rough schedule. I will spend five days in Saigon gossiping with friends, reporters, State Department staff, CIA agents, and military officers. Great dinner parties thrown by anthropologist Gerry Hickey were an obligatory event to understand high level "facts on the ground." I would type up my notes in duplicate, keep a copy, and mail the other to Stanley Murphy on the Vineyard. I would write my four children and to Susan, a young woman I met just before coming to Vietnam. I also send an occasional word of encouragement to Manning at the *Atlantic Monthly*. Then using my old-boy network, I would locate and, if possible, contact the next unit I want to visit and learn how the hell to get there. Then take off for two weeks in the field to go on patrol with foot soldiers — the grunts — in a unit in actual contact with the Viet Cong. I will spend nights in the mountains or jungles with the patrol. I will go where they go and do everything they do, except I will not go on night ambushes, known as "night bushes." I am too old at forty-six for that.

I learn what every wise reporter or officer or CIA agent soon learns in Vietnam. The country is a magic mirror perfectly reflecting back to the viewer his own beliefs. To find the real Vietnam requires self-knowledge as well as knowledge of how to look. I have an advantage here. I know the signals. Look for the units with clean weapons, where the grunts walk with good spaces between so one machine-gun burst or booby trap explosion wounds or kills only a few. Also where the men talk and joke together both black and white. Beware of the sullen, silent unit with dirty weapons. I try to visit all types, question and compare their answers, and study their actions.

On one jungle patrol I spend three days and nights with an outfit as good as any I knew in World War II. The men's packs are all checked for extra weight. No one can carry soda water in them. The pish of a bottle being opened can alert the V.C. In the three days and two nights I was there, no one spoke much above a whisper. No one blew up their air mattresses or cut down palm branches, noise again. Most of their communication was by hand signals. The men, "grunts," tell me what a great captain they have. "He's cool to the max, man." And what a fantastic soldier and shot they have as their "point man." Walking point is a thankless job. You are the in-front guy. Everything before you is hostile. Each minute seems to stretch till it tears with an audible sound. The job should rotate, but often the best soldier in the unit does it day after day after day.

Another patrol that I spend a day with had the night before staged a fake mortar attack on themselves to watch the helicopters fire and maybe pick up some medals. They show me the holes the exploding mortar rounds have made. I've seen a great many mortar holes and these holes look to me like ones made by hand grenades. From beneath the ponchos covering some of their foxholes comes the odor of pot. The magic mirror shows you any face you want.

Luck and Luck alone

The Blind/Dead Kid once lived happily with his family in this valley, part of the area of operations (A.O.) of the patrol I now walk with. The Viet Cong tried to recruit the boy's parents, and when they refused, they killed his mother and father and burnt out his eyes. He became the Blind Kid and his shell of a home became in the patrol's list of addresses: the Blind Kid's Hooch, along with Hotel Hooch, the One-legged Man's Hooch, the Daffy Duck Hooch, and others. The Blind Kid starved most of the time and the patrol members fed him when they came by. They tried once to get him on a helicopter to take him to a hospital, but the boy kicked and screamed so they let him stay. One day while no one watched, the boy picked up some composition C explosive and ate it. That killed him. In the mock military nomenclature of the patrol his hooch became the Blind Slash Dead Kid's Hooch.

We are walking through rice paddies heading for his hooch now. The men move well spaced, weapons clean. In addition to the captain and his radio operator, an artillery lieutenant and his radio operator walk with us. Once again I have the feeling I am frozen in some ancient stone carving of a ritual long dead. We head for this hooch, which is on a slight rise, because there is a monsoon forecast and headquarters has ordered everyone to higher ground. When we get there, I find the front wall of the hooch mostly gone. The end walls and some of the back wall still stand and support the damaged roof. At one side of the long earthen room is the frame of a double bed. Machine guns are set up and the men cut palm branches to make the poncho tents slightly monsoon-proof. The artillery lieutenant, walking with us to adjust artillery fire if needed, rigs up a hammock beneath one solid part of roof. Boards are put across the bed frame and after dark the captain and I lie down on them. I blow up my air mattress, the captain does not have one, and after some talk about the war and his future — he wants to be a doctor — we fall asleep. I have taken off my boots and socks — they are wet and cold — and massage my feet to keep from getting jungle rot. I have a brief debate with myself, whether to leave my boots off or put them back on. I leave them off, put on dry socks, placing the wet ones against my chest to dry. I would have put my boots back on in WW II.

Suddenly explosions blow me out of sleep.

"Incoming! Incoming!" That cry has not changed. I am off my mattress stretched out on the mud beneath my bed, my hands clasped over my head. Pieces of steel splatter over our heads like heavy drops of rain. I cower in the dirt. The radio operator is partially on top of me. The captain beside him whispering in his ear. The captain does not think the situation serious enough yet for gun ships. *Why am I here? Why am I here?* And without my boots. Another round splatters us. There are cries of "Medic." "Medic."

I have my boots with my flashlight inside them in my hands, my helmet on, and am crawling to one of the standing walls. I hear the artillery lieutenant, also flat on the ground, talking into his microphone pleading for artillery. I pick up an M-16 from one of the wounded lying on the floor. It is three-ten. I figure they may try to overrun us in the dark and get away before daylight.

"Where's a flashlight? Where's a flashlight? This guy is dying. I need a flashlight." The soldier's voice rises in panic. All the flashlights are in use dressing other wounded. Flashlights are hard to find in Vietnam. Mine is infinitely precious to me. In another moment it may save my life. I have moved my flashlight from my boot into the safety of the lower left pocket of my fatigues. I reach in there. "Here's a flashlight."

The artillery begins to fire flares and by their light I see the platoon sergeant going from wounded to wounded and telling them; "You'll be all right, man. You'll be all right. You'll be all right." Once someone above me in the dark spoke those words to me. The face of war does not change. Young men lie bent on the ground while others try to pour energy into them.

No more mortar rounds slam down. Placing the wounded on ponchos we wind down a jungle trail to debouch like hornets from a nest into a rice paddy where the medevac helicopter can land. We squat down at the paddy's edge, hunched over like beetles. Two gunships protecting the Red Cross bird rake the jungle with cannon fire and the double crack-bang of rockets. Out of the black, hanging backward in the air, the red cross just visible on the bulge of its front, the medevac chopper lands. The wounded walk to it or are ferried aboard. We who have survived the night walk back to the Blind/Dead Kid's Hooch to wait for daylight.

When light arrives, I see blood everywhere: on the floor, on the radios, on the leaves around the hooch, on my Sorley's fatigues. My air mattress is rent, the artillery lieutenant's hammock full of holes. We have one dead and four seriously wounded, one of whom will later die. I am alive. Alive by *Luck* and *Luck* alone. A reformed line of Yeats flows into my head:

> This is no country for old men,
> The young at one another's throats.

The rear, too, can show you your own face of Vietnam or America. On my weeks in Saigon, I have now and then eaten with friends who are generals at the generals' mess outside the city. A senior general orders that stopped. "He is the press. He is part of the enemy." I would liked to have asked that general if he knew what the Bible says befell the house divided against itself.

Another time, I am eating in a Chinese restaurant in the heart of the Chinese district of Saigon. The three of us are the only Yankees in the midsize dining room, with some twenty-four tables. We are in the middle of an extraordinary multicourse meal, when suddenly, in a crouching, stumbling run, a Vietnamese with a knife in his back staggers through the restaurant door. As he lurches across the restaurant floor, he is desperately plucking at the knife, trying to pull it out. But the knife has been so cleverly inserted into his back that he cannot reach it. He disappears into the kitchen. Several members of the restaurant staff rush out to slam down steel shutters. No one in the restaurant misses a bite. Violence has taken over a society.

Fate and Luck and Chance

Out in the field again with another patrol. This time I watch *Fate* and *Luck* at play in the lives of others. The point man and the three soldiers behind him, plus myself, have been in a brief firefight near a swamp. Most of the enemy escaped quickly into a swamp, but the patrol has captured one Viet Cong soldier, badly wounded in his left leg. While being questioned by the patrol's Vietnamese scout the prisoner *chou-hoys*. He gives the location, numbers, and weapons of his fellow Viet Cong soldiers. By the book this makes him a defector, entitled to the same medical treatment as a U.S. soldier. The "Doc" with our patrol, a sergeant, young and intense, a recent high-school graduate from East Texas, with a small gold cross around his neck, wants to call in a medevac helicopter to take the prisoner to a hospital before he bleeds to death.

The doc pleads and argues with the radio operator to call in the ambulance chopper.

"No, Doc, I ain't goin' to make the call. Let the son of a bitch bleed to death."

Some five or six grunts of the patrol gather in a circle around the doc and the radio operator. The two officers along with the other men have drifted away. "He's chou-hoyd," pleads the doc, with intensity close to tears. The circle around the two is divided, most side with the radio operator. The bandage about the prisoner's leg turns red. The doc places his chest against the operator's chest and lifts the microphone from its attachment at the operator's shoulder. Before the doc's determination, the operator relents and orders the chopper: "Dusty Lobster this is Husky 56." The medevac operation has begun.

The Doc comes over and sits beside me. He wants to make certain I understand why the men behaved as they did.

"They got a lot of friends blown away last week. They're up-tight about the V.C. That's why they acted as they did. You can't blame them."

"I don't, Doc. In another hour or some day next week they may react completely different. Besides, they count on you being here."

The Doc pulls his jungle hat, with sergeant's stripes pinned on, down against the sun. "It's so unfair. It's so unfair. It's the hard chargers who are dying. The guy's who've got it all together. They'll be the ones who chase after the V.C.; the others will hang back. And all those back in the world. It's the best are getting killed, sir. The best."

"If I learned anything from my war, Doc, I learned just that. Welcome to the club."

I know a problem about which he does not ask. *Chance* has made this war so unpopular that to fill the ranks of the Army and Marines the draft has become completely corrupt. There should be more here to share the risk of those whom their *Fate* has made hard chargers. In my entire time in Vietnam, I met only three soldiers from the elite Eastern or Western universities. After the war, when I called the Harvard press office to find how many Harvard graduates have died in Vietnam, I am told: "We do not keep unimportant statistics like that." The poor are drafted out of proportion to their numbers. But, not unsurprisingly, they lack the inner discipline, the psychic power, or, if you will, the Freudian superego to stand up to the strains of combat. The middle classes make up the majority of those in the front lines.

As I sit in the hot sand and watch a patrol of hard chargers go into the swamp, I remember a line Keith Douglas, the British war poet, wrote shortly before his death: "How can I live among this gentle obsolescent breed of heroes and not weep?"

The gentle, obsolescent heroes here are bound for 360 days before their "home bird" takes them "back in the world." Or they get wounded or killed. I have only ninety days and can leave when I want. No reporter, not even one who has served in combat, can, even with good intentions and great imagination, impose that burden on himself. I can understand the Vietnam War but never fully experience "the grunts' war."

As my own "home bird" flies me to "back in the world," I have one major memory and three emotions. The memory: A senior general, one I have known since he was a young lieutenant colonel, remarking, "Vietnam is a poison in our blood. Will we learn from it or let it fester?"

The three emotions: The first is rage against the unfair draft that lets the rich escape and sends the middle class to serve and die. The second and third are sympathy and even love for those most intimately involved, perhaps some corporal walking point in the 90-degree heat with over ninety days left.

On my return from Vietnam, what appears to be really poor *Luck* turns out to be a bonanza. Bob Manning at the *Atlantic* does not take the piece. Sterling Lord thinks it one of the best reports from Vietnam yet written. He says to get to work on my next book (there is no next book just then) and he will sell the piece. He does that immediately to *Playboy* at four times what the *Atlantic* had offered. Appearing in *Playboy*, my piece is seen and talked about widely. Stewart Alsop bases a *Newsweek* column on the piece. The *Washington Post* devotes its entire Sunday magazine to it; cancels everything else, and runs just my piece alone. I go on TV and radio talk shows. I am back in the big leagues, not exactly on the Yankees or Red Sox yet, but maybe a bonus player. There are dissenters.

"*Playboy*," sniffs my mother. "How could you?"

"Just what I expected," intones my father. I think of quoting Dr. Samuel Johnson to them: "We that live to please must please to live." But realize that gets me nowhere.

Luck and Fate

I am walking across town in New York City somewhere in the Fifties, when I see coming towards me George Hersh. He used to be one of the editors of *New York Magazine*, which I helped create and for which I sometimes write. We pause and chat. He congratulates me on the Vietnam piece. I ask what he is doing.

He says he is starting a new, irreverent news magazine, *New Times,* for younger readers who find *Newsweek* and *Time* dull. I make sympathetic clucking noises, admiring any man about to risk his and his friend's money.

I ask about the Washington bureau. They don't have money for a Washington bureau.

I probe further, "How about a Washington correspondent. A presence in the capital?"

They do not have money for that yet either.

"How about money for a tiny office space, and an address in the National Press Building?"

"What would we do with that?"

"Find a one-man bureau whose chief could work for nothing provided you didn't mind him writing for other publications and maybe doing a book or two."

"Could you bring that off? And how much would it cost?"

We make a lunch date. *Fate* has provided me with the money to work for *New Times* for nothing, provided I can write and sell outside articles and books. At the end of lunch, *New Times* has a Washington bureau, and an office in the National Press Building, and I a job. When I apply for Pentagon and White House passes, they still have my files from the *Newsweek* days. Many have read my Vietnam piece in *Playboy* or the *Washington Post* and welcome me back. A press card is a press card is a press card.

Fate and Luck

I have hit a dead spell in my personal life. My *Fate* is powerfully at work to convince me I should remarry. I know now *Fate*'s work must have been silent, because if I had heard the hokum my *Fate* now suggests, I'd have made it shut up. I have been married twice and have been raised to believe that I am already well down the road to dissipation. A road, I must admit, of which I do not always completely disapprove. I need help to stand against my *Fate*, and I am alone. To lose Jane depresses and upsets me. I love her and I do not understand what in me makes me fail at a lasting connection. The one-night stands or one- and two-month affairs leave me lonely and dissatisfied. Patricia, now summering in the Vineyard close by, has a new boyfriend.

With all these conflicts in my head, plus the recent experience in Vietnam, I come to believe I must get married. Since I never seem to bring this off with women my age who interest me, I convince myself some younger woman would probably be best for me. I could explain my life and help her understand the world and we would both be happy. My commonsense filter should have picked up the sound of absolute bull in this unreasoned nonsense, plus the dangers of marriage on the rebound, in recommending this *Choice*. Why it did not, I do not know. I thought I knew enough about my *Fate* to be wary and ask questions. I did not, and my filter failed.

Now *Luck* takes over to augment my nonsense. Before I went to Vietnam, an old flame, a *Vogue* editor, introduces me to Susan Bryant, a former *Vogue* worker, during a Connecticut weekend. Before going to Vietnam, I begin a one-month courtship of Susan. She is four years out of Bennington College, has worked on *Vogue,* and is now job hunting in New York City. Susan fit the mumbo-jumbo matrix I have let my *Fate* elaborately construct. After returning from Vietnam, I take up the pursuit again. At a candlelight service at an old inn outside of Framingham, Massachusetts, I marry Susan Bryant.

I will follow my former rule with my first two wives to say as little as possible about a marriage that ends in divorce. Particularly in this marriage where I am the instigator. Seven years later when, at my request, we divorce she understands, is pleasant and understanding. This is my third marriage. I can't just leap out. I would land in nowheresville. I have not that much courage.

I buy a house for Susan and myself in Northwest Washington, near the Naval Observatory, where the vice president now lives. It's a pleasant house on a quiet street with a swimming pool, but like all houses it needs work. I realize the education of Susan is going to take time. She hires an expensive decorator who puts up bookcases with out checking if the wall can support them. The wall crumbles down. Susan finds Washington terribly competitive and the social life a mysterious challenge. After a year, she decides she would be happier staying in the Vineyard. She leaves for the island and her Morgan horse. We see each other about every other weekend, depending on the time of year, and for longer periods when I am in that stage of my writing. She says she is quite happy. I hope so. Outside of my work I am miserable.

I find keeping two houses an impossible and unrewarding burden. I sell the Washington house and move into the apartment, part of the Watergate complex. I buy a three-room penthouse, with a slim kitchen, and large living room where I put a dining table at the far end with a view of the Potomac. There are two bedrooms, one for myself and the other for the occasional visits of my children. The penthouse has roof access to my own private space with a gas grill, where I have some pleasant, interesting parties. I am a long way from the elegant Georgetown house of the *Newsweek*-and-Mary period and much lower in the press pecking order. Personally, I am unhappy. Yet I would rather be here than where I was back then. I have worked part way free of my *Fate*. The mistakes I make now are more my own.

Washington has stories bursting out all over. Nixon is fighting for his political life. Politics has grown nastier than ever. Senators and congressmen need to spend more and more time each year raising money. One result: record numbers of congressmen are retiring. Over and over I hear the same words I heard from officers and old-time sergeants on Vietnam, "I'm getting out Hadley. It's no fun anymore." Defense Secretary Robert McNamara's legacy has left the Pentagon demoralized, with an organization that does not work and weapons that do not function. In Europe, troops are setting fire to their helicopters. The little press group I founded in the fifties has added some fine new members and still reels in inside information over lunch and dinner. They welcome me back without too many snide remarks about *New Times*.

After one such dinner at Stewart Alsop's, Robert McNamara invites me to ride back to the city center in his car. Now president of the World Bank, he tells me he has solved the population problem in India. He has spent some research money and scientists have devised a wire that can be buried in the ground and when a man walks over this wire he becomes sterile. "Now all I have to do," says McNamarra, "is devise a method to persuade Indian men to cross the wire. And I am a great expert in motivation and rewards." The idea of getting Indian men to step over a wire while getting their balls zapped is so extraordinary that I realize I can't report it. I'll never be believed. But I certainly learn more about McNamara. The one-on-one interview once again produces fascinating information but not news.

As usual when miserable, I bury myself in work. *New Times* only occasionally takes my pieces. I realize the editor, much younger than myself, has his own stable of writers he trusts and who think his way. For example, my piece on Congressman Morris Udall builds around his effect on the Democratic presidential primary fight if he, a Western liberal, enters the race. The piece they take from another writer is how Mo Udall managed to play professional basketball with only one eye. No matter, both the *Washington Post* and the *Boston Herald* are running my military pieces with some regularity.

I start asking questions, meeting people, reading reports and academic journals, looking for a subject on which to write a book. So soon after Vietnam a military book is not going to sell. A history of the World Bank is another nonstarter. In Washington, politics is hot but that is being thoroughly covered by press and television. There has just been a presidential election with Nixon defeating McGovern, which means the next primaries are three years away. Conventional wisdom has it that presidential politics truly begins with the first primaries. Writing about the presidential primaries and campaigns is Theodore "Teddy" White's territory and he already has several seasoned competitors. David Broder of the *Washington Post*, a justly famed expert on politics, had written: "Nothing that happens before the first presidential primary has any relevance at all."

Luck

I lunch several times with Mark Seigal, a political planner for Robert Strauss, chairman of the Democratic National Committee. This follows my general rule that the Number One in an organization is usually so busy flummoxing other Number Ones and being flummoxed by them, that to find out what really goes on you talk to the Number

Two or Three. The negligible amount of clout given me as *New Times*'s bureau chief now reinforces that rule. Mark sends me several academic papers about the changing political process. Buried in one of them the following nugget flashes. Since 1936, when scientific polling began, the active candidate most popular with his own party in the Gallup Poll taken one month before the New Hampshire primary starts has won his party's nomination 85 percent of the time. In other words, since 1936, in seventeen out of twenty presidential contests the race was over before it supposedly began. *WHAT?* Before reporters and TV crew pull on their galoshes to head for New Hampshire, the race is already over? Forget the conventional wisdom. How and when does the race truly begin? As a result of this flash of *Luck*, buried in a paper I never would have read had Mark not sent it to me, I spend a fascinating three years reporting on and writing *The Invisible Primary*.

The Invisible Primary begins three years before the first actual primary in New Hampshire. Uncovering what happens in that time, I discover six tracks on which to judge the probable success of presidential candidates. These six tracks are: 1. The Psychological Track, 2. The Staff Track, 3. The Strategy Track, 4. The Money Track, 5. The Media Track, and 6. The Constituency Track. Working out the six tracks is intellectually exciting. Following the candidates to test and refine the tracks becomes a reporting challenge. I am on the edge of a new idea that upsets perceived political wisdom. Since not so many reporters, if any, are following the candidates at this stage, I often have the candidates and their early staffers almost to myself.

Track 1. The Psychological Track differs from the others because it lies outside politics. This track can be the most difficult to report with impartiality. Also, it takes time to learn the small but vital physical and psychological details that can aid or hurt a candidate. This track reveals how badly a man (and in the near future, I hope, a woman) wants to be president. How much will he give up of his family, friends, time, and other joys of life to handle the stress and strains of a long campaign? For example, Senator Edward Kennedy found the presidency not worth opening the Chappaquiddick wound. Senator Walter Mondale found himself a candidate because Democratic powerhouse Senator Hubert Humphry enthusiastically pushed him into the race. Mondale himself was not sure about the race and soon dropped out. I talk with his wife, Joan, in their Washington living room two years before the New Hampshire primary. My notes quote Joan as saying, "I don't think that he (Mondale) ever did make the decision to run. Hubert said those nice things about him on television and the invitations started to come in."

Small traits can become important. In 1973–74, for example, Senator Edmund Muskie of Maine is plagued by the need for nine hour's sleep a night, Governor Ronald Reagan needs an afternoon nap, Senator Henry "Scoop" Jackson develops a post nasal drip when tired that hampers his none-too-effective speaking ability. In the other years, Clinton's and Eisenhower's ability to project, and relate, to groups of people give them an advantage

How a candidate handles truth reveals a great deal. I continually hear future President Jimmy Carter tell *Invisible Primary* audiences: "I will never lie to you, because I am not a lawyer. I am a peanut farmer and a nuclear engineer." The only part of that opening that is true is that he is not a lawyer. He was not a peanut farmer. He was a peanut middleman, warehousing farmers' peanuts and selling them. He was not a nuclear engineer. He served on a nuclear submarine. He was relieved from duty before he ever commanded a nuclear submarine.

I have trouble following Carter to report on him because, though he gives me his schedule for the next day, I can never find him. Finally I get the *Time* reporter to ask Carter where he will be the next day shortly after I ask him. That *Time* reporter gets a completely different itinerary from the one that Carter has just given me. I check with a Carter staff member with whom I have become friendly. She tells me Carter does not want to be followed by any book writers, "particularly that nosy Hadley." I am not surprised by Carter's White House lies and failures.

In August I hear candidate Birch Bayh, senator from Indiana, tell a group of Young Democrats that he will never be for unconditional amnesty. In September I hear him say to a liberal Democratic audience in Springfield, Massachusetts, "I am for unconditional amnesty." This says more about the man than that he lacks a program. Other reporters in those days not covering *The Invisible Primary* miss some basic facts about the candidates. That has changed. Since the book, reporters start much earlier to cover the potential candidates and their staffs.

Even being there you can miss one. I usually take down the tail numbers of the planes in which candidates fly, then I check with the FAA to find out who owns the plane. I never take down the tail numbers on the plane in which Jimmy Carter travels. So I miss the fact that he is being flown for free by a wealthy Georgia banker, Burt Lance, whom he will later make his Treasury secretary.

Track 2. With the increasing complexity and expense of today's politics, plus new media outlets on the Internet, the Staff Track grows in importance. The two major political parties are no longer strong enough to furnish staff to the candidates. This leads to the rise of a large group of paid political gunslingers whose ranks boast specialists in everything from TV advertising, the Internet, cultivating the media, fund-raising, polling, and old-fashioned direct mail. In 1974, the decisive factor in persuading Senator Charles Percy of Illinois to run is that a top Republican political-management firm, Bailey Deardouroff, volunteered to manage his campaign for $5,500 a month. How well a man chooses and handles his staff predicts his future strengths and weakness running the government. Here senators enjoy an advantage over congressmen. Senators and governors posses large staffs and are used to running them. These staffs can be put to campaign uses.

Track 3. The Strategy Track is a function of the Constituency and Staff Tracks. Politics would be more pleasant if the Strategy Track was about the future of America. Unfortunately, it is more about where to go for the money and how much time to spend in which state, say, two days in Wisconsin against three in Florida. A liberal from Massachusetts is going to campaign for different lengths of time and in different states than a conservative from Mississippi. But within such easy cases are nuances. Staffs spend a great deal of time debating where and when they should go and what to say when they get there. A candidate's strategic decisions indicate not only what he and his staff think is important to their constituency, but also whom they believe makes up their constituency. Had Senator Gore spent more time in either his home state of Tennessee or in President Clinton's Arkansas, he would most probably have carried one of those states. That would have made a Florida victory unnecessary.

Track 4. To describe the Money Track is simple. It stinks. From Watergate to Clinton's pardons, it stinks. Those bright young staffers sitting before TV screens in the White House, the Senate, and the House are not studying legislative programs. They are looking up the names of callers on their TV screens to learn how much the caller gave and so decide to whom the caller talks. Look yourself in the mirror and say slowly: "I truly believe money does not make a difference in politics." If you can do that without breaking up, you have superb control over your facial muscles.

I sit with Senator Jackson and Howard Hughes and a lawyer in Howard Hughes's inner office in a Las Vegas casino. Hughes is very much pro-Jackson, but knows there are limits to how much he can give outright. Hughes and his lawyer explain to Jackson a deal, which I can't understand. It involves a tanker of Indonesian crude against which Jackson can borrow and later use the oil to pay off the borrowing. Jackson turns it down flat. "Even if it is legal, I won't do that." You do not hear that often in politics these days. The Money Track must be reformed, but to balance fairness against political pressures requires wisdom at least the equal of the Founding Fathers.

Track 5. Rule one of the Press Track: If a candidate is getting five times as much publicity as all his opponents combined, he will still feel discriminated against. Choice and Luck in the old-fashioned sense can greatly help with the press. A candidate who picks an issue that suddenly becomes hot, say the price of gasoline, just before prices start to rise, or has spoken against a war before casualty rates increase, will automatically find himself news. Luck also works in the assignment of reporters who cover a candidate. Some reporters are better than others at grabbing air time for their TV report or landing their stories on the front page. The candidates covered by these reporters often find themselves basking in what they are certain is well-deserved glory.

The best in the press continually watch themselves to make sure they do not slant the news to favor a candidate they find sympathetic. Writing *The Invisible Primary* I watch this with Mo Udall. Both of us are ex-basketball players and pilots of small, single-engine planes. We hold much the same political values and became good friends. I occasionally fly him to Martha's Vineyard on weekends to relax. When I cover him or his rivals, I review my copy with extra care. In the main, reporters tend to be wiseguys who like their work and find it fun. A candidate who himself and his staff play life that way, will tend to have good press coverage.

Track 6. With the Constituency Track, it's all about who is for you and how committed they are. Do members of your group have money? Big Money? Are they with you on only one particular issue — antiwar, low farm prices? Or are they a group who know a great deal about you and your past history and agree with you on a number of issues? Are they of an ethnic mix and age that tends to vote? Do your followers have the time, energy, and ability to do volunteer work, such as door-to-door canvasing and mailings? How do you energize them to do this work? This all leads into strategy. How much time do you spend where and what do you say while there?

The amount of time you have to spend is crucial. And your total time is limited particularly if you have another job like senator, governor, or active businessman. In 1974, during the invisible primary I spend three days alone in the back seat of his car with Ronald Reagan and his long-time staff member and confidant, Mike Deaver. A driver and bodyguard sit up front. I am surprised at Reagan's openness in talking about everything from politics to family problems. Among my underlined notes I find Reagan saying, "I never could have run this hard when I was governor."

Do you have the full support of your constituency or is there another candidate they also favor? In 1974 Scoop Jackson, through his long support of Israel, held the Jewish vote. Jimmy Carter had the religious vote. However Mo Udall's liberal constituency was split between himself and ex-senator Fred Harris on the far liberal left. Four years before, Fred Harris had run as the candidate of Big Oil. This drove the Udall supporters wild, and indeed may have cost Udall the candidacy, but the ultra-liberal left welcomed Harris as a lost sheep.

The last Gallup Poll before the '76 election gave scant evidence as to whom would win. The two most popular candidates in the poll, Senator Ted Kennedy and Hubert Humphry, are not on the ballot, having dropped out of the race. Scoop Jackson leads those still in the race by a whisker's whisker. Finally, Governor Jimmy Carter clinches the nomination by beating Mo Udall in Wisconsin. Carter carries the rural Republican parts of the state. Wisconsin is the only state where Republicans are able to vote in the Democratic primary. The numberless debates, caucuses, and deals that brought this about would take a book in itself. By the date of the primary vote in Wisconsin, President Gerry Ford has won the Republican nomination. Post-election polls in the state later discover that Republicans, with no reason to vote in their primary, crossed over and entered the Democratic primary in large numbers. They voted for Carter, the man they thought Ford could most easily beat. Jimmy Carter is elected president by Wisconsin Republicans.

After the campaign is over, I have breakfast at a Harvard conference with Carter's press secretary, Jody Powell. "You know," I say, "your candidate is the luckiest man alive."

"I know that," replies Powell, "and you know that. But the candidate does not believe that."

The Invisible Primary had a good commercial success and, more importantly, an impact on future reporting. Three years later, friends would drop me a note about the number of people reading the book on this or that campaign plane. Mark Shields, a reporter I do not know but whose political and cultural insights I admire, became a "great mentioner" for the book on public television.

The Invisible Primary leads directly to my next book. While covering endless banquets, rallies, conventions, candidates, and constant caucuses, I strike up a warm friendship with Robert Teeter, the talented Republican pollster. We are both interested in political trends. We hold some different opinions but neither of us is opinionated. We discover we are both concerned over the rapidly escalating number of non-voters, those people eligible to vote but who do not. What effect will these dropouts have on future elections, and, finally, on our country? First we have to know who are these nonvoters, these political abstainers? There is general agreement on some untested "truths," but no research. We agree to produce a book together to find out more about these voter dropouts. His company will poll, I will write, and we will split whatever advance and profits we get from the book, *The Empty Polling Both*. What we find are, to quote Lincoln on the Civil War: "Results fundamental and astounding."

Nonvoting, as you would expect, remains highest in the poor, rural areas of the South and the impoverished slum areas of the great northern cities. But when you look at trends everything changes. While not voting remains high in these areas, voting is growing fastest in the same places. Voting is actually rising there, in the poorest areas of America. Not voting now grows most rapidly in the affluent suburbs of America. People have a hard time grasping these numbers. They keep repeating the conventional wisdom that not voting is highest in the poorest areas of America. That is true. But that is not the reason not voting is on the rise in America. That rise is caused by nonvoting in the suburbs.

Desperate to get this point across, a point that goes against the grain of perceived political wisdom, I develop the following metaphor to use on TV talk shows and in meetings. If I tell you that the rate of tuberculosis is highest in the poorest areas of America, you would yawn and say we know that. But if I tell you that the rate of tuberculosis while high is falling fastest in those areas, and where it is rising most rapidly is in the affluent suburbs, you would say, "That is astounding. Run that by me again." That is what is happening with nonvoting. The drives to get the poor to vote are working. It is the wealthy who now cause the rise in not voting.

Both the press and our readers find our facts in *The Empty Polling Both* hard to believe. Another book comes out shortly afterward that misinterprets its data to stress the old popular belief. Another of our surprise discoveries is that a dividing factor that separates voters from nonvoters is the measure of control they believe they have over their lives. A high school dropout, working in a garage who feels he has choices, is more likely to vote than a successful Ph.D. who feels he or she must go with the flow. The *Washington Post* and PBS do understand the book and give it good notices. The *Post* leading its Sunday magazine with: "The Affluent, Happy, Content Non-voter."

With my two nonfiction books, articles, and another novel that never sees a publisher's warehouse, I find the only lengths of time Susan and I get to spend together are summer vacations. I also celebrate Christmas in West Tisbury and two weeks' skiing in Lech, Austria, with Susan and her German friends, Dirk and Marlene Ippen. Marlene lived in Framingham with Susan and her family as an exchange high school student. I enjoy these times. With my damaged left leg I can't do downhill skiing. I have little ankle motion and doctors have told me that if I ever break my leg again I will most likely lose my foot. However, I enjoy cross-country skiing and each year the number of cross-country trails around Lech rises. Also I enjoy the Ippens. Dirk edits and publishes a liberal newspaper in Munich and owns papers in some small towns throughout Germany. He quotes both Goethe and Shakespeare with equal aptness and delight. His insights into European politics are original and astute. He and Marlene both have a nice, wry sense of humor.

Susan and I come back to Martha's Vineyard in early December of 1977. I will be at the Vineyard until after Christmas working on *The Empty Polling Booth*. I drive my jeep down to the general store and post office for some supplies and the mail.

Luck

One of the letters I take from our box has my six-year-old address on it, 305 East 40th St., and no return address. On the back of the envelope is written. "Postman no longer has your address Mr Hadley. This from my book. Hope you get it. Mike." Mike is the head doorman at 305. We became friends when I lived there. The handwriting on the envelope's front is Jane's.

Jane's letter begins with apologies for breaking the promised silence. The reason she does so now is that Caroline very much wants to go to college and Yale is her first choice. The other seniors in her Hotchkiss class who want to go to Yale all have family or other connections with the university. Jane has none. Would I write a letter for Caroline? I look at the date by which the letter must be in. Tomorrow. I will write the letter today and bring it back to the post office early tomorrow morning. It will be postmarked on time.

I shut the door to my office in the Vineyard house and write for Caroline. Having read many letters from friends who are reporters, I believe most reporters, myself among them, usually write supurb letters. Letters that conform reasonably close to truth. I mention that I have known Caroline since she was three, leaving out the fact that I have not seen her since then, and always found her bright, humorous, and original. However, since Yale's selection and interview process is so excellent, rather than talk about Caroline, I'll tell them something about the mother. I start with harsh early circumstances, move on to music and art, the full scholarship to Virginia, junior Phi Bata Kappa and summa cum laude. (With a brief aside about putting this Yale mere Phi Bate and magna cum in his place. The subtext of that sentence being: "We scholars should stick together; admit Caroline.) I close with Jane's graduate degree in psychology, her internship, and her success as a psychoanalyst.

I also drop Jane a letter at the old address I have for her, explaining why Caroline's recommendation has just gone out, but that it is in time. I add I have not lived in 305 for six years but now have an office in Washington at the National Press Building, covering politics and strategic affairs and writing books. I try, unsuccessfully, to force myself to not think about Jane.

Chance and Luck

Professionally my life brightens. Martin Peretz, the editor of the *New Republic*, has recently been to Israel. During his interview with Prime Minister Golda Meir, she berates him for risking the security of Israel. Why does he have nothing in his magazine but negative references about the U.S. armed forces? The excellence of these forces alone, she tells him, guarantees the survival of Israel.

Martin returns determined to mend his coverage. His problem, he tells his staff, is that he finds most military reporters limited and unpleasant people. Unbeknownst to me, I have some fans of the *New Republic* staff. They exonerate me of these faults, point out that I wrote a popular book on arms control, and arrange for an interview with Martin.

We hit it off immediately. A close friend of mine, General John Ralph, commanded the initial fighter squadron that, with aerial refueling, made it from the Nebraska to Israel in seven hours to help stop the Egyptian tanks. I give Martin some inside information.

It turns out we both courted women from Music and Art. I tell him how in a last moment switch of votes, Jane was beaten out for most beautiful girl in the school by Dianne Caroll. Martin is the first person I have met, other than Jane, who understands how and why and says it. "Of course the Jews would rather have their candidate lose to a schwartz than a shiksa."

I have a new outlet for my military reporting. I write a *New Republic* cover story, "Why Johnny Can't Fight." This so impresses the *New Times* editors that they start running my pieces. One of these, on Congress's flubbing of the energy crisis, gets anthologized. A military revolution, truly a revolution, has begun with the advent of "smart weapons" that can accurately locate their targets. Many newspapers are interested in articles about this revolution. On Thursday, April 13, 1978, my youngest son Nick's birthday, I have to sign my income tax forms that afternoon in New York. I have reserved a bedroom at the Yale Club for that night. The next day, Friday, I fly to Boston and from there on to London with Susan. I am going to Scotland to fish with my son George. She is going to visit friends in London. On Wednesday afternoon, the day before the income tax signing, I plan to go back to my Watergate apartment and pack for fishing. I literally have my hand on the office door, when the phone rings. All reporters must answer ringing phones. They know this is the call that leads to fame, fortune, and perhaps even a Pulitzer Prize.

Luck and Choice

It is Jane.

Jane apologizes for the call. But she says she has some good news and wants to thank me. Caroline has been admitted by Yale.

"The next time you are in New York I will buy you a drink."

Ever the perfect WASP gentleman, I reply, "A drink is chicken shit. I will buy you a dinner to celebrate Yale's good fortune. It so happens I go to New York tomorrow to sign my income tax. I'll take you to dinner tomorrow.."

"I can't do dinner tomorrow."

"Why not?

"I work late at the clinic."

"How late?

"Till eight."

"Where's the clinic?"

"Six East Sixty-first Street."

"Isn't there a hotel on that street?"

"The Pierre on Fifth Avenue."

"I'll meet you in the bar of the Pierre between eight and eight-thirty and find a place near that serves until nine."

"All right."

I do not know it yet, but the world is about to change

I have been sitting in the bar of the Pierre for about fifteen minutes, hugging a martini on the rocks, when Jane, white blouse, black jacket, and skirt, pushes through the revolving door. Her effect is instantaneous. She does not have to walk toward me, she just has to come through the door. When I did not marry this alive, striking woman I made the mistake of my life. What happens next happens very fast. Jane says later that I look so sad she was gripped. We sit in a booth and have one drink together. When we get up to leave we are not just holding hands; to get through the revolving door we have to untangle. We tangle up again as we walk down five blocks to the restaurant. La Côte Basque is a favorite of both of us. I remember nothing that we ate. We sit in a banquet in our own world.

We leave the restaurant and I disregard the warnings of numberless sages to go slow in courting, including the advice of one of my heroes, William Blake, "Never seek to tell thy love, love that never told can be." I finally flip the coin. Banal, and soupy, I say, "Jane I want to take you home and make love to you. I love you. I want to marry you. I will pursue you and pursue you. I don't want to mess it up again."

Jane's reply is pure Jane. She looks at me and cracks a smile to melt the Arctic ice pack. Then looks ahead toward Fifth Avenue. At the corner, a cab has stopped for a red light, its empty sign lit. She says, "There's a taxi." *The Luck that Keeps on Lucking* now even does empty taxis.

Riding back to Jane's apartment, I am tense. What happens next is so important. We undress apart and come together naked. The night becomes easy, warm, exciting. We wake completely tangled again. Untangled and eating breakfast, we talk about marriage. We finally begin what Jane will laughingly name our BLT life. We are both great fans of BLTs — bacon, lettuce and tomato sandwiches. Our BLT marriage will be built on Brains, Lust, and Trust. Our marriage bed as deeply rooted to the earth as that of Ulysses.

At the start there is one small problem. We are both married to someone else. A day later, Susan and I are flying to London, there to go our separate ways. Sitting together on the jet is no place to tell her. After a week's fishing with George, I fish for a week with my close friend and lawyer, Walter Skallerup, the wise man who advised me to lie low when I wanted to challenge McCarthy. Like all good lawyers, Walter sees a dark future. But he agrees to help me when we get back to Washington with an outline of the procedure and some points to negotiate with Susan. After meeting Jane, Walter's wife, Nancy, becomes an enthusiastic supporter of our freedom to marry. A few weeks later, I call up Susan, then working in New York, and explain the problem. She is extremely reasonable. She even wants to give back the two Agon Schiele etchings I gave her as a present. She does not like them and just took them to please me. I tell her to keep them; even hidden in a closet they will be more valuable some day. The marriage was upside down like that from the beginning. Susan signs the divorce agreement and we get it notarized. Jane is not so fortunate. Now that she really wants a divorce, Roy negotiates month after month. When July comes with still no compromise, Jane and I decide on a pre-honeymoon.

I think I have rooms in a great hotel in the resort of Positano, on the Amalifi coast, but the friend who claimed he would arrange this flunks out. In the guidebooks I find a small hotel an hour south of Salerno recommended in both the Red Michelin and Fodor, an unusual cross check. An Italian reporter from the *Il Corriere della Sera* office in the Press Building checks out the hotel and reserves us a room with balcony overlooking the Mediterranean. Jane and I take a first-class flight to Rome with a connection to Naples, where we will pick up a car.

At Naples, omens portend a possible change in our world. Our luggage makes it. Once out of the airport I start to drive in the wrong direction, but have studied the map enough to realize this and turn around. Jane is impressed. In the hot sun on the road we get thirsty and the knowledge floats up from somewhere that Campari and soda is the drink called for. Some of the country along the Mediterranean south of Salerno looks pretty grim. But San Maria di Castellabate appears pleasant, and beyond it, on a hill, a small-white painted hotel sits in the woods. The entrance to the hotel is inviting. The assistant manager, who speaks some English, takes our bags and leads us to our room. The room is quite small. Jane's shocked look of dismay reflects the thought of spending a week and a half here.

The manager opens the shuttered doors at the end of the room. There is a private balcony, tree shaded, with a clear view of the Mediterranean. A large yacht moves gracefully past. The balcony contains a round table and two cushioned chairs. On the table is a container of what must be ice. Jane's dismay changes into a smile and a hug. The world has changed since April 13, and we are beginning to realize that nothing happens as before. That night we sit on the balcony after dinner with a Scotch, while the Perseid meteor shower, hundreds of shooting stars, explodes in streaking glory over the sea.

"Arthur," she says, "you have done it." The world is changed.

We swim, find a tiny fish restaurant in one of the narrow alleys near the beach, do the sights: Herculanium, Pompeii, Paestum twice to see the serene, radiant blue mosaic of "The Diver," a young man who dies and dives beneath the sea to be greeted by friends already there. We eat the wonderful food, dance, sit on the balcony, and, of course, live up to the L part of the BLT. We missed fourteen years. "Though we cannot make our sun standstill; yet we will make him run."

Our only problem is finding peanuts to munch with our Scotch. The word is not in any of our guidebooks or pocket dictionaries. No one in the hotel or the stores understands the word or our miming of eating nuts and drinking. Then Jane suggests the British phrase "ground nuts" and bags of *nicolonees*, a word neither of us ever forgets, emerge from their shelves.

On return to the real world, our premarriage time becomes hectic. We live and work in two places, meet each other's friends and attend parties in New York and Washington. We solve future life questions. Jane volunteers to move to Washington. I say that is ridiculous. It is much easier for me to move a typewriter than Jane a practice. I get a tiny cubicle in Washington with a small desk and a phone with call forwarding. In New York I rent an office just abandoned by a dentist in a run-down building on 42 Street near Third Avenue.

"No, I can't make lunch today at the Capitol. But how about breakfast tomorrow at the Willard?" That does not quite say I am in Washington. But it doesn't say I'm looking out my office window at 42nd Street, either. Jane and I live in both the Watergate and her apartment on Riverside Drive, while we both hunt for a New York apartment. My appointment book shows a mass of shuttle flights mixed in with an occasional flight in my single-engine Cessna 210.

Jane's pressure on Roy continues along with that of our friend and lawyer Stanley Pleasant. Stanley and I are bound by a *Choice* that many regard as a rash act of crazy youth. We both enlisted in the Army the week of our eighteenth birthday. Stanley had a tough war, emerging as a decorated infantry captain in the 36th "Texas" Division, one of the best. Finally, on Friday, January 19, Roy signs the agreement that permits Jane to divorce. Stanley suspects that Roy has signed to impress a girl he's taking to the Las Vegas TV convention that weekend. Stanley arranges for Jane to get a divorce in the Dominican Republic on Saturday morning.

I expect to get one at the same time. Unfortunately I can't. My father died on Wednesday and the funeral is Saturday. Jane goes by herself on Friday afternoon. I meet her when she comes back Saturday evening, shaken but free to marry. On Monday, Roy returns and says he has changed his mind and is canceling his permission. Stanley says he can do that, but there is a problem. Jane is already divorced. I follow two weeks later. I am sure that the roosters on the court house steps that crowed as I walked out were the same wiseass birds she saw and heard as she walked out.

A month and a week later, Jane and I are married in the apartment of Justin and Janet Feldman, two old friends of Jane. Only our children are present, and Walter and Nancy Skallerup. The room contains a share of jokers. Judge Wallach, also a friend, reads us our Miranda Rights before he starts the ceremony. Later, at the phrase "if anyone knows any reason," George and Nick race to the apartment door to make sure it is locked. At the wedding's end, I ask Walter if now he thinks I am married. He replies: "Arthur, I'm sure you're married. I just don't know to whom." In group wedding pictures, Elisabeth is reacting in shock to the size of Jane's engagement ring, while Caroline wipes tears and boasts proudly of her new title, "Carrie the Cause of It All."

Choice, Chance, and Luck

The next day, because of a complex jumble of *Choice*, *Chance*, and *Luck*, a recently married couple called Hadley board the morning Concorde flight for Paris. Stuffed in this wonderful jumble are *Chance*: that Yale had such a fine reputation that Caroline decided to go there. Then a *Choice*, Jane's first to break silence and write me and then to call me, then *Luck* that Mike had my address in his book, and my *Luck* that I am still at my office when the call comes. And then my *Choice*, to invite Jane to dinner, and Jane's *Choice* to agree. Finally two ultimate *Choices*, mine and Jane's. Mine, to drop safety and risk all I have with my marriage offer. And Jane's *Choice* to become my fourth wife. (Now there's a flip of the coin.) And at the end that the *Luck that Keeps on Lucking* supplies an empty taxi.

That Jane insists on splitting the cost of the honeymoon week is not part of the jumble. That is part of Jane. I pay for the Concorde; she pays for the hotel room.

How to describe our BLT marriage of believable joy? Anthologists lament there is little poetry, let alone great poetry or great moments of fiction, dedicated to marriage. Even Trollope can stumble. What wise, feminine woman does not know she could have done better for "Panty," Plantagenet Palliser, later the Duke of Omnium, than the highborn, beautiful but slightly ditsy Lady Glencora.

Love gets much celebrated, but marriage? Shakespeare's 116th Sonnet comes close:

> Let me not to the marriage of true minds
> Admit impediments. Love is not love
> Which alters when it alteration finds
> Or bends with the remover to remove.

All true; but there is no happiness in these lines. Rupert Brooke's poem that ends:

> We wonder bathed in joy complete,
> How love so brief could seem so sweet.

This is probably about marriage, but neglects to say so.

I once risked doggerel to solve this problem. But I'm afraid I too have failed.

> The poet yet does not exist,
> Who wrote his verse while being kissed.
> When she lies close, he lacks the time
> To spend himself on making rime
> But when she goes, quite the reverse
> Then gloom and doom and lots of verse.

Ours was a marriage, take it for all. Few will look upon its like again.

After the poetry, I fall back on reporting. First, some of what others said about our marriage. Second, some of what we ourselves, inside the BLT, thought, acted, and said. And last, some of what we did together.

First, how others saw us.

Don Page, an old friend and architect, a partner of I. M. Pei, toasting us at our tenth anniversary party: "I know a lot of people. Or at least I am meant to know a lot of people. And Jane and Arthur are the happiest couple that I know."

Stanley Pleasant: "Jane loves to flirt. She does it so you know it doesn't mean anything. But she is so beautiful and sexy you began to hope, *maybe this time*. And then you remember reality. This is the tightest couple in New York."

Friends of our daughter Caroline: "Please don't bring your parents to dinner again. They are so completely happy, we wonder why our marriage is not like that."

Another of Caroline friends: "I am walking up Fifth Avenue and I see this couple ahead of me holding hands. I think: They look so happy. I get closer. It's Jane and Arthur."

The first-grade class of our seven-year-old granddaughter Ali is asked to write about their grandparents. Ali wrote: "Traveling. Reading, Talking. They love to love."

Some of the compliments are a bit backhanded. A divorced woman, a friend of my ex-wife Mary, nicknamed Blondy: "I don't see how any couple so evil as you two can look so happy."

Dr. Milton Viederman, the senior psychiatrist who helped Jane through her last months, writing to me: "I thought you would like to know that in my many years of practice I have never found another couple with such tenderness and passion and so little tension."

Second, some ways we talked and treated each other.

In the twenty-six years together in the same bed, we sleep apart only three times, other than with the rare bad cold. The first two: In the night, I come to Jane, who has taken the extra pull-out bed in the library. I ask her to please come back and hold out my hand. She does. The third time, we are still separate at breakfast. We look at each other and agree. This is ridiculous. We have this wonderful BLT marriage. This must never happen again. It never does.

Every night, unless we go out or one of us is sick, we cook our evening meal together, helping each other as we recount our day. Mornings Jane is a slow starter. As I rise wide awake, I make our breakfast.

Lying in bed together in the morning, touching and talking, we marvel at our fortune. We realize we are finally "Out. Out. Out." Both of us had known that a somewhere must exist that combined both work and marriage, a somewhere we could be happy. Neither of us had been able to find that place. Doubt had begun, even despair, that we ever would. One time I say, "Jane, you had the most difficult job to escape. You had no money."

"No, Arthur, you had the more difficult part, your life was so seductive."

"I still believe yours the more difficult."

Jane always calls me "Arthur."

"You are 'Arthur.' Not 'Hadley.' Do not let them do that to you! Don't call yourself 'Hadley, you stupid idiot again.'"

Once in bed I say, "I never believed love could be so easy. So complete without strain."

"Tension, Arthur, my love, tension. We don't play 'who is on top.'"

When she calls me Arthur and smiles, I admit my heart leaps.

I call her "Moonbeam." In some adventure book set in a foreign land, I read of a hero who called his wife: "Light of my life and daughter of the Moon." I liked that, and put it in my memory bank. But at a cocktail party you cannot say: "Light of my life and daughter of the Moon, it is time we left to go to dinner." I shortened it to Moonbeam.

When we talk, a three-word subtext often lies beneath what we are saying.

"Did I leave that light on?"

"Maybe I did."

"I don't know who did."

"Does it matter?"

"No."

(Sub text: "I love you.")

"You make the best blueberry pancakes."

"Not as good as yours."

"Yes they are."

"No."

"Shall we fight?"

(Subtext: "I love you.")

"Shall we go to the movies Sunday?"

"I'll find the schedules."

"If it's good weather."

"Or we could just stay here."

"Where's here?"

"Yes."

(Subtext: "Let's stay in bed.")

Third, some actions together.

Jane takes over the Martha's Vineyard house. She apologizes for at one time suggesting the interiors should be painted white. But the house built by three bachelors needs living space. Jane, who reads architecture magazines religiously, has a room plan all ready. When Hugh Hardy realizes he faces a united front on Jane's plan, he folds and agrees to follow her room design. She creates a wonderful new space with bookcases and a freestanding fireplace, in back of which are indoor trees that stand before picture windows that light them. A sliding door opens on a low deck with a central cut-out, in which to plant flowers, supposedly out of reach of even adventurous deers. The sliding door also faces a view of another arm of our pond. In addition to the magnificent living room, the house also acquires another upstairs bedroom, and a separate guesthouse. I am enthusiastic. Jane has not merely changed my house; she has transformed it into a warm and inviting structure full of comfort, ease, and life.

Luck

Eleven years later the house burns to the ground. Some workers, sanding the floors, put a floor plug back incorrectly. We realize that this will either be a disaster that defeats us and makes us smaller, or an opportunity. Martha's Vineyard has changed to become another crowded Hamptons as our taxes rise precipitously. Our insurance policy contains a clause that for two years while we look to buy a new house, we can rent a house comparable to the one we lost. I convince the insurance company that it is cheaper to rent in France than on the Vineyard. Quite literally the truth.

Adam and Susan Kennedy, experts at squeezing the nickel while renting abroad, tip us off to look in the Princeton University magazine. We do. By *Luck* we find a thoughtfully remolded sixteenth-century manor house in the northwest corner of the Dordogne, with a swimming pool, four bedrooms, a large kitchen with modern equipment, and a superb, fourteen-foot-long antique, applewood dining table. We like the town and our house so much that after our two free years are up, we rent for another four, bringing over family and friends to stay. A photograph of us at the kitchen dining table holding out our arms to each other and laughing, shouts how we felt and lived. I hope, from the number of bottles on the table, that the photograph was not taken at breakfast.

All this time we look for a summer place, one that we can afford, that will be near a few friends, and not too far from New York City. A place that both invites and excites. Finally we find a house — Jane calls it a "Palladian prison" — made out of cinder block impregnated under pressure with a new substance plastocrete that makes the cinder blocks both waterproof and to resemble ancient stone. (The watrerproof part turns out untrue.) The house, on nineteen acres in Spencertown, New York, has a small pond and a magnificent view west over the Hudson Valley to the Catskills and Hildeburges beyond. Don Page is sure he can take care of its problems. Jane does not like the house at all. Not at all.

"Jane," I say, " I will make you a promise, a shake-hands promise. I like this house immensely and want to live here. I think you will like it too. Let me buy it. If at the end of two years, not one year, two, you still do not like it, I will sell it and we will look some more. That's a promise."

We shake hands. That is our marriage. We live in a small room in a disconnected part of the house on and off one winter and half a summer, while the builders change and lengthen. Jane squeezes the nickel and finds Chinese ancestor paintings and Khmer stone friezes. At the end of half a year Jane says, "Arthur, you have done it again. I love this house." There is a two-acre pond in front of and below the house. On my seventieth birthday, Jane gives me a fountain that throws a great eighteen-foot-high jet of water into the air. Our marriage is so secure she names the fountain, "Arthur's Last Squirt."

Fate and Luck

Now *Fate*, not the Greek Fate as in "Fated to be," but modern *Fate*, our genetic make-up and the experiences of early childhood, gives our years a passionate prodigality. Though we come from widely different backgrounds — "The Pearl of the Bronx and the Caviar Kid," as we nickname ourselves — we share an uncanny similarity of childhood. That we both heard the whistles blow, "Out. Out. Out," results from environment, not coincidence.

Both of us were physically and psychologically abandoned. Jane's father walked out on her, her brother, and her mother when she was three. Her mother was distant and competitive. Jane had run away from home three times before she was ten. My parents went to Japan for over a year when I was two and were also physically and emotionally remote. We both learned the joy of physical contact only from a favorite grandparent, who let us crawl upon them. Did this build in us the hope that there must be a better someplace where we could love and be loved? Does our mutual Fate cause us to begin and continue our "Quest" for such a life and place? To look, to look, and to look? That possibility, while not certain, is not improbable.

For the B (Brains) in our BLT marriage. Our Fates gifted us with intelligence, Jane's summa cum laude and my magna cum laude. Thought and ideas remain important to us. When we come to put our libraries together, we have several hundred books apiece; over a third of our books are the same. We like the same artists: Goya, Picasso, Milton Avery, Munch, and Max Beckmann, though Jane is more sensitive to abstract art than myself. Not to slight the L (Lust) in BLT, the energy and sex drives of both of us are high. We are attractive and have watched our bodies. As for the T (Trust), you only lie to either of us once. And that includes the lie of silence. A lie both Jane and I suffered from in childhood. Neither of us ever lied to the other.

I never picked up anywhere near Jane's ability to squeeze the nickel. I tell friends I have no fear of divorce. If Jane ever throws me out, all I have to do is walk back and forth in front of our apartment building carrying a sign that says REDUCED and I will immediately be taken back.

No ordinary days with Jane exist. The typical hour with her contains more excitement than a secret weekend Paris rendezvous with the usual suspects.

I am finally happy. Writing has become easier and more precise. I no longer need to drown myself in work. On her own, with a varied and expanding private practice, Jane can take more time off. We start to spend several months a year just playing. Our fourteen lost years remind us that Time's winged chariot is at our back.

We had married in February. April finds us in northern Scotland on the Oykel, a small, isolated salmon river in the mountains. I go a week early and Jane follows. Jane is met at Inverness Airport by Raymond Blacklaw, another Scots friend who manages the hotel where we stay. As Raymond drives her up the Oykel, I happen to be on one of the few stretches of the river visible from the road. I am standing in midriver there with a large salmon on my line. I have been fighting to land this fish for about twenty minutes. My gaff, the four-foot instrument by which I intend to spear this fish, is held between my teeth. I learn later than Raymond pauses the car and points me out as I stand alone in the river, rod in both hands, gaff in my teeth. "Jane, have you ever seen the true nature of your husband before?"

Within three days Jane masters salmon fishing. She catches fish while gillies (guides), cows, sheep, deer, and husbands gape at a woman who manages to be alluring in chest waders, sweater, and Barber rain jacket. The necessary skills she picks up quickly, including the delicacy of a long cast in still water. The intense concentration and necessary energy to make a great fisher she brings with her. Within two days she knows she loves to fish.

The Oykel flows through an area where I have many friends, who all take to Jane. We return and return for friendship and fishing for twenty-three years, sometimes with children, and toward the end, with grandchildren. A three-by-four-inch photograph of Jane holding both rod and her first salmon stands on her desk along with our children, our grandchildren, and a husband. We do move our fishing from April to May, both good months. Jane complains, fairly, that the snow and ice storms of April, which freeze together her eyelashes, spoils her fun.

One Christmas six years into the marriage, I am baffled by what to give Jane. I think, after Jane, what is the most precious item I have? My children. I can't give them to Jane. One of my paintings? That is a cop out. The Oykel! I write my lawyer in Edinburgh. He responds with total understanding. He creates a beribbonned deed of transfer that begins, "For Love. For Affection. And Certain Other Considerations, I hereby deed my section of the Oykel River." I put the rolled up deed, red ribbons and all, inside a whiskey bottle-cardboard case, wrap the case in Christmas paper, and hang the result on our Christmas tree. I do not know who has the happiest Christmas, the surprised receiver or the giver.

On February 24, 1998, we make a wonderful change in our lives. After being fully investigated by the state of New York, that I have no evil designs on young girls, and with the enthusiastic support of Elisabeth and Caroline, I adopt them both. A strong emotional unit now becomes a legal entity. During Jane's illness and its aftermath, this family unit gives strength and shares tears.

For six years, at the end of summer, we and our close friends, the theatrical lawyer Robert Montgomery and his wife, Henri, charter a thirty-plus-foot sail boat with a crew of three, and explore the small harbors and little-visited ruins of the eastern Mediterranean, along the then still unexploited coast of Turkey, once part of ancient Greece. With the aid of Bean's four-volume guide to the coast, and Pausinias again, we do such things as tie up in one hidden harbor to the identical stone bollard that the young Julius Caesar used in his war against the island pirates.

Jane has not told me how much she fears sailing. The first day, between Samos and Kushadisi to the north, is rather choppy. Jane tells me later she huddled in the cockpit, thinking. *I am never going to be able to get off this boat, perhaps not even able to go to the bathroom for ten days.* When the boat ties up to a pier in Kushadisi, she begins to smile.

"Is it going to be like this every night? We're not going to anchor out there in the middle."

"No, Moonbeam, we'll be in some sort of port every night. Never out there in the middle"

Her smile deepens and deepened further at dinner. We have an excellent cook as part of the crew that year.

Two days later, after exploring Ephesus and Pirene, with its treasure of an isolated Greek temple, I am concerned about the beach at Didima, the next stop I have planned. Our captain has not been in there. How rough will the waves be off the beach? And how will we handle the four of five miles from the beach to the ruins?

The yacht's dingy approaches the waves along the beach. A Pan rises out of the water, grabs the bow of our dingy, and says, "You want car, Didima?" I relax; Jane starts to beam. To be helped ashore in Turkey by the God himself. Jane is the first to suggest another sail next year to explore farther south down the coast

Another moment in our six sailing years. We go ashore in a tiny port not mentioned in any guide, but Bean reports that about half an hour's walk through the jungle stands a virtually undiscovered Lycean village. The four of us go ashore, I with Bean and a Turkish phrase book in hand. I take Bean's picture of the Lycean ruins to several men at the waterfront and ask if they know where this is. They shake their heads. Some children standing by ask to see the book. One of the boys, eight or ten years old, points to the Lycean tombs, which are built with boats on top, and nods.

I find the phrase, "Do you know the way?" He nods violently and pulls me by the hand. The other couple begs off. Jane and I follow the boy into the jungle. After about fifteen minutes' walk on the narrow jungle trail I become concerned. Does this boy really know where he is going? Suddenly before us in the jungle looms a Roman arch. The numerals date the arch from the time of the Emperor Hadrian. Reassured, we walk on. The jungle ends at a steep grass hill. We follow the boy and climb. At the top we gasp. Cortez sighting the Pacific. In the valley before in the grass stands a complete Lycian village, house ruins, the remains of streets, and thirty-plus boat-topped tombs. The scene strikes us as some mythic village, an Atlantis, which rises every hundred years not from the sea, but here from beneath the earth. Wild boars root among the ruins. We decide it wiser not to go down. Just stand and stare.

Christmas is a bad time of year to be a psychoanalyst. Troubled people feel more left out and depressed in the midst of others' joy. The first four years of our marriage, we spend two Christmas Eves either at a hospital or on the phone with attempted suicides. Jane gets tired, even sick between Christmas and New Year's. I have read about a newly opened hotel on Phuket, a still relatively undiscovered island in south Thailand on the Adaman Sea. We begin going there in 1983, returning year after year for twenty years to stay at a wonderful, isolated midsize hotel called the Yacht Club, built in the middle of a nature preserve and facing the Adaman Sea. We loll on the uncrowded beach, read, walk, eat the fresh fish, and Thai greens, and with Jane's magic abilities make island friends.

For the other part of our vacations in Thailand we hire a car and driver and explore. We seek out "The Palaces of the Gods," the enclaves of temples throughout the country, some well known, some scarcely visited. Many of these areas contain palaces and temple buildings as mighty, though not as vast and complex, as those in Angkor Wat, or Luang Prabang. We do miss a few temples along the Cambodian and Burmese borders because of nearby gunfire, as rebel groups skirmish to control the opium trade.

In 2003, while at the Yacht Club, Jane has trouble climbing the stairs up to our cliffside rooms. Four rears older than she, being out of breath is usually my problem. Curious about the cause, Jane goes to our doctor when we return to New York. In my tiny, breast-pocket-size appointment book for Wednesday, January 29, my handwriting, suddenly turned childlike, scrawls uneven and wiggly across the page, "Cancer found."

Fate and Luck

The part played by *Luck* is obvious. The lucky many do not get lung cancer, even though some of them have been heavy smokers. The Unlucky few do. The part of *Fate* requires closer observation. Jane's genes had made her brilliant and strikingly beautiful. The lifestyle in which she grew up, while not impoverished, was strained. To provide walking-around money on top of her college scholarships, she modeled. With the focused intensity of her childhood, she reached the top of that profession, becoming Miss Chesterfield. To support that image she took up heavy smoking. When I met her in 1964, she was going through two packs a day. Three years later, with the help of her young children, she quit cold turkey. The damage had been done.

Now our life changes. Work stops, playtime shrinks; only Jane's fight surrounds us. In her battle, I provide two opposites. I must do nothing to dampen Jane's spirit or her belief that she will win. At the same time, I must never tell a lie. Not even with the best of intentions. She must have someone who she knows will tell her the truth always and always and always. My mantra becomes, "Jane, the statistics are not good. But you and I believe strongly in the mind-body connection. If anybody can beat the odds, and many do, you can do it. We can do it." This paints a bright face on the truth, but is the truth.

First, we scramble to find the best turf on which to fight Jane's battle. Fortunately we have several doctor friends, including John O'Lichney, our GP. There is close to complete agreement that we should end up with Dr. Mark Kris at Sloan-Kettering. We see several cancer specialists and chose Mark Kris. Never in the nightmare hours of hopelessness and pain do we doubt our choice. Compassion, patience, and excellence of care combine to build a place of hope.

We begin in an experimental U.S. government program, taking by intravenous drip a drug called Gleevac. The drug has worked well with colon cancer in Japan. Jane also takes intravenously the regular anticancer treatment drug, sisplatten. Every other Tuesday she sits for three to four hours in a reclining hospital chair while the poisons drip slowly into her right arm one week and into her left the next. The sisplatten is so powerful that a very robust vein must be found. Should the vein rupture and the drug leak into her arm the results would be a disaster of incredible pain. Eventually Jane gets a "port," a long tube, its mouth an opening through the flesh above her left breast, and whose inner end drips poison directly into a large vein leading to Jane's heart.

Like a skilled torturer, cancer teases Jane with periods of ease, comfort, and hope, followed by periods of pain and despair. On the Friday of the week before she gets the drip of deadly drugs Jane gets X-rays and a blood test. She gets so weak she cannot get in and out of her bathtub, even with my help. Larry Cavagnaro, our friendly builder in Spencertown, rapidly converts a closet into a shower room so Jane can shower if she makes it into the summer. One day I find her sprawled on the kitchen floor, unable to stand. She has fallen and hurt a leg while trying to lift a pot. I have been doing the cooking, but she had wanted to help. Kris stops the Gleevac. "It's doing more damage to the patient than the cancer." However, the sisplatten shows signs of shrinking the mass in the lung, though her liver shows little improvement. Still, we occasionally go out to lunch, even to dinner with close friends. Children and grandchildren come down from Massachusetts to visit. We make what grabs we can at normal life as Jane fights on.

We stay for two weeks at a hotel across the street while our apartment kitchen is redone. I had argued against so much work and making a temporary move right now. Then I realize redoing the kitchen is Jane's way of telling herself, "I am going to make it." I gladly help move her oxygen bottles, oxygen-producing machine, medicines, and clothes across the street.

In the midst of all her pain and fear, Jane turns to me with a smile and says, "If I don't make it, you are going to have trouble getting over me."

"Yes, should that happen, I will. But I will get help. Just like you're getting help."

"I've found someone for you. Dr. Kevin Kelly; he's the chief psychiatrist for the fire department."

"Thank you, Moonbeam. He must have seen a great deal of grief and survivors guilt since 9/11."

That's Jane, pure Jane. In the crisis of her fear and pain, she takes time out to care for me, children, and grandchildren.

Jane makes it into the summer of 2003. We must drive from Spencertown to New York City every other week for chemo. In Spencertown, one set of grandchildren live close by; the others visit from outside of Boston. On hot days Jane makes it into the swimming pool, though she has to place a protective cover over her port. Kris's staff have discovered both cancer doctor and also a physiotherapist in Great Barrington, less than a half hour away. They take over some of Jane's treatment load. Against the odds, I allow myself some questionable hope.

> Hope lies to mortals
> And most believe
> But man's deceiver
> Was never mine.

I never quite accept Hope's lies, but I come tearfully close.

Winter comes and we return to the city and the routine of chemo. Now cancer the torturer increases its well-practiced, clever work. Sometimes we are in the emergency room, sometimes we spend one, even two nights in the hospital. We also plan to go to Jamaica to build up Jane's strength. She does not grow strong enough to make that trip. However, she recovers enough to spend a week in the country at Spencertown. In the city we go out for dinner several times in the non-chemo weeks and even on the Monday of a chemo week that begins on Tuesday.

In the first week of December, we go to the musical *Wonderful Town* and also to the emergency room. We take two weeks in the country over Christmas and spend time with children and grandchildren. Jane gives me a Christmas card. On the outside of the card is printed JOY in large red letters. On the card's inside she has written: "In the midst of this frightful time you have shown me there are no limits to love. Thank you my darling."

Our bumpy schedule continues through February, when we visit the emergency room and also separately buy valentines for each other. Jane goes shopping with friends. In early January, Jane goes permanently on oxygen. She has a backpack bottle, six bottles on wheels, and an oxygen-making machine runs constantly in our room at night. All this time, like some mythic hero, Jane's spirit for her battle neither flags nor falters. In the first week of March she tells her friend Penny Levy, "After I get this damn oxygen mask off, we'll have lunch."

Saturday, March 13, finds us sitting up in bed together, searching the motion picture schedules to choose a picture to see Sunday. Instead, Sunday finds us racing to the emergency room with Jane in unusual pain. She is a month plus a week away from her seventy-fifth birthday. The emergency room takes X-rays and draws blood. The doctor on duty tells us something is definitely wrong and we should spend at least the night in the hospital until Dr. Kris can see Jane Monday. I get Jane in a private room, help her into bed, and spend some time with her. I go home to gather Jane's necessary items for a hospital stay and for myself to spend the night. I call the children. During the night the staff put Jane back on oxygen with a mask.

Monday morning Dr. Kris arrives and removes the oxygen mask. He tells Jane nothing more can be done in the way of cure. Her liver has been too destroyed by the cancer to handle more chemicals. He will start the morphine drip to remove her pain and help her to her end. "Something we do well here."

In the room, after having her oxygen mask removed and seeing the morphine bags wheeled in, Jane asks, "Arthur, is this the end?"

"Yes. The cancer has all but destroyed to your liver. Kris is going to start the morphine so you feel no more pain." Hard to say. But no time for the first lie.

"I want to see my grandchildren."

"Elisabeth, Caroline, and the children are on the way. "You'll see them. I'll be here."

I go outside to weep and tell the floor nurses about the grandchildren. They will adjust the morphine drip so she will not be in pain, but be conscious enough to talk. I go back in, sit by her bed, and take her right hand. Caroline arrives and takes her left. Jane smiles at us both and talks a bit, already semiconscious. Elisabeth too arrives and Jane is able to talk with her. The two daughters say they will spend the night with her and I must go home and get some sleep.

Tuesday, Jane drifts more and more into a private world. The three of us keep her company with time out to weep in the corridor. Wednesday, both sets of grandchildren arrive with their fathers. Jane rallies and talks to them and looks at the drawings they have done on the way down. She speaks with difficulty and can move but little. They kiss her and squeeze her hands. Husbands and grandchildren go off to spend the night with one of Jane's great friends. Caroline starts to tell her Mom how much she loves her. Jane says: "Please, we will have time for that later." Caroline and Elisabeth say they will spend the night again so I can go home and get something to eat and more rest.

At three in the morning they phone me. I had better come now. I grab a taxi and race through the empty streets. Jane is deeply unconscious. When the Thursday morning nurses' shift takes over, the head nurse presses the morphine button three times to increase the drip rate. My son Nick arrives. (Kate and George are out of the country.) After a while, the nurse again presses the morphine tube button. Again I take Jane's right hand, Caroline her left. Elisabeth sits at bedside, Nick at the bed's foot. Jane battles on, unconscious. I watch the quivering blankets show her heart rate increase, as her body refuses to die. "Break, Heart. I prithee Break." She does not hear us as from time to time we hold each other and weep. Finally, the horrible blue-gray color begins to creep into her face. Then comes the gurgle. "That's the death rattle," I tell the others. "It's just a few minutes now." She dies. A remarkable woman surrounded by love.

All lovers make love against the clock. Our clock had raced ahead fourteen years while we failed to *Choose* and learn that *Luck* had willed us a "bounty as boundless as the sea, a love as deep." The more we gave it to each other the more we had. If we knew when we married that we had only twenty-seven years until the caustic indifference of cancer devours Jane, we might have cried sometimes. We could not have loved more.

Luck and *Luck* alone dealt me three enormous gifts. I was born; that unique lottery won by all here. I lived through the war. I met Jane. Birth, survival, and Jane's love, *Luck's* three great gifts. And the last and greatest of these begins its tidal flood as Jane looks up 55th Street and says, "There's a taxi."